TABLE OF CONTENTS

FOREWORD

Ted Turner, owner of the largest cable network in the nation, told me, "Television is the most powerful force in this country; it is even more powerful than the government! It elects the government!"

More powerful than our elected leaders? In a country that has prided itself on being "of the people"? Who are these unelected dictators of our once-free media? Obviously, they aren't Christians or they would not attack Christian leaders and Christian values.

Jesus Christ said, *"By their fruits ye shall know them."* By the *anti*-moral, *anti*-Christian, *anti*-free enterprise, and *anti*-human life message that consistently comes over the airwaves and through the printed press, we know those who are hostile to Christianity and the Christian moral values which made this nation successful.

We are now in a struggle for survival in this country. The humanists say they will make America a humanist nation by the year 2000. That means Sodom and Gomorrah if they succeed. Who is there to stop this moral slide into national perversion? The church of Jesus Christ! The Church is the one army large enough to awaken this country to the loss of its moral foundation and call her to return to moral sanity. But who will awaken the sleeping church, many of whose members are not even registered to vote? The preachers!

Jimmy Swaggart is one such preacher. He is using his enormous influence as America's most watched television minister to confront the Church with her responsibility to be *"salt"* and *"light."* He has spoken out courageously on every moral issue of our time and has incurred the wrath of the liberal media establishment in the process. But he is undaunted.

This new book is his latest attempt to stir Christians to action, for he knows that if enough of God's people will take up the call, we can yet rid our government of those elected and appointed individuals who do not share America's traditional moral values.

Reading this book will enable you to be a part of the cure of America's ills and help you to preserve the future for our children.

Tim LaHaye,
Author, Minister,
Educator

CHILDHOOD LOST

Utter the word "childhood" and any number of images might flood your mind — depending on the type of childhood you had. Even to the person burdened by a less-than-perfect one, the word may still elicit a sense of nostalgia and the warm glow a person associates with an idealized picture of those early years. Unfortunately, there are few persons (or perhaps none) who are lucky enough to experience a *perfect* childhood.

Like most of life's experiences, growing up becomes a series of compromises and accommodations as circumstances intrude in a more or less haphazard way. Generally, however, childhood has been, for the last several generations, a pleasant and profitable experience, more often than not fitting the young person to reach legal age prepared to meet the responsibilities of adult life. (This isn't necessarily the situation today, however, and it hasn't always *been* the situation.)

Living as we do in the middle of the twentieth century, we tend to think that childhood has always been what it is now — a period set aside for growth and development, a time when the child is insulated from the stresses and pressures of the real world. Childhood over the centuries has varied considerably, however, differing greatly from one historic period to another. In some societies childhood has been enriched, in others degraded, and in still others, more or less ignored.

In America today, childhood is rapidly disappearing. A shocking statement? Shocking perhaps, but true. The long-lamented "generation gap" has finally begun to close, and with its closing, childhood has been squeezed almost out of existence.

Where have our children gone? My heart was recently burdened with the realization that the minds of our precious little ones, perhaps our nation's richest treasure, are literally being *raped*. Rape imposes someone's will on an unconsenting victim, and that's exactly what's happening to our youngsters today. You don't have to be a psychologist or sociologist to recognize it. It's obvious to anyone who has any degree of contact with the young people of our society.

THE HISTORICAL PERSPECTIVE

The majority of children being reared today, especially in middle-class America, are being cheated of childhood. Adult secrets, pressures, and demands assault the blissful ignorance, the blessed wonder, and the sense of innocence that *used* to characterize the younger years. Now, children are being physically *ejected* from the womb and thrust directly into the path of stresses and pressures that cause even adults to stumble. Our present society robs children of their childhood by pressing them into the mold of miniature adults, and it is evil beyond imagination!

Of course, viewing children as miniature adults is not a new concept. During the Middle Ages, childhood didn't exist! If you were to search the historical records, you would find that children of that period were offered no special status from that of adults. Neither were they offered protection from the problems of adult life. They were simply viewed as "small adults." In fact, the concept of childhood as a unique condition or period of life didn't come about until the late 1800s and early 1900s. It was during that period that childhood began to realize a special status and importance in America.

For the first time ever, efforts were made to get *all* children into schools, out of the factories, and into their own clothing, furniture, literature, games, and social patterns. Hundreds of laws were passed to preserve and protect the rights of children. Even during this progressive period, however, Satan plotted to rape the minds of children, and he chose one of his brighter students — Charles Darwin — to clear the path. Darwin presented the notion that "individual development relives species development." He proposed that evolution could best be understood by studying the individual development of children.[1] In this way, broad conclusions could be drawn that would apply to society as a whole. Children thus began to be considered as a "scientifically valuable" commodity.

And lest we look too innocently at the efforts to increase the educational levels of children, it should be realized that it was originally a thinly veiled effort to train children for more effective factory work. The educational movement was pushed along by one John Dewey, now known as "the father of modern education." He was, incidentally, a socialist interested in promoting the advancement of socialism.[2]

John Dewey constructed the framework that resulted in the surrender of our educational system to the philosophy of secular humanism.[3] Dewey can thus be remembered as the messenger who brought Satan's diabolical scheme of liberal mind-control to our American system of public education.

Interestingly, his philosophy is the undergirth of an ever-diminishing concern for human life and is the same philosophy that was imported to Rome (through Greek "scholars") and which led to Rome's decline and eventual collapse. With the introduction of Greek humanism, such moral evils as abortion, infanticide, pedophilia, and child abuse became widespread throughout Rome. We shouldn't be surprised, therefore, to see an appalling rise in these same sordid practices in our land today.

It seems obvious that this is not a haphazard series of incidental occurrences. It was a regressive accumulation of events in Rome that led to its demise, and current events in our nation closely parallel them. Rome fell. We are in grave peril of following Rome down the same path to destruction.

THE RIGHT TO LIFE

In ancient times, the right to life wasn't an automatic consequence of birth; it was "ritually bestowed." In other words, at some traditional age a ritual was performed — at which time the recipient became a "person" within the society and received all the conventional rights of personhood.[4] Until then? Children had *no rights,* being as valueless (and as helpless) as unwanted puppies or kittens are in our society. If you didn't have any use for them, and if you couldn't sell them, you could easily dispose of them.

During such periods, unwanted children were routinely drowned. Infanticide was sometimes *compulsory* in order to spare society the problem of caring for the weak, the premature, or the deformed.[5] Girls especially were in jeopardy of being killed, sold, or abandoned. The mentally retarded (considered to be possessed by Satan) were almost universally disposed of. Many young boys were even castrated to produce eunuchs for harems or to retain their soprano voices for church choirs.[6]

Other barbaric practices included "hardening." Hardening was the practice of plunging newborn babies into an icy stream or of leaving them in the snow for some period of time to test their hardiness. Abortion, abandonment, and wet nursing (during which 50 percent of infants died), the sealing of children into the cornerstones of buildings, and the use of children as "playthings" in sporting events were other common practices during these barbaric times.[7]

Historically, sexual offenses against children were common.[8] Supposedly enlightened, civilized human beings gave vent to their depraved and sinful natures by practicing the vilest of sexual acts on children. In many cultures, wives and daughters were supplied to guests as an act of hospitality. Since children were considered more commodities than human beings, they were also frequently hired out as sexual partners. Brothels housed large numbers of 10- and 12-year-old prostitutes.

Pederasty (sex with young boys) was stylish and almost openly practiced in Rome and Greece and other early cultures.[9] Nurses quieted irritable or unruly children by stroking their genitals.[10] Rape, incest, and flagellation (sexual stimulation through physical abuse such as beatings) were also common. Sex torturers (sadists), using secret codes known to fellow perverts, placed ads to obtain children for their sordid practices. Even colonial newspapers in this country carried regular ads for runaway children.[11] Adults addicted to sexual experimentation with children exploited children mercilessly.

Society, considering children as an economic drain, refused to concern itself with their welfare.[12] If they were not to be disposed of, they could certainly be put to work. Child labor cast children into the direst of straits and the most deplorable of conditions. The excesses were so extreme that there began to be a reaction around the middle of the nineteenth century.[13] Until that time, children of six or seven labored as beasts of burden, dragging coal buckets down narrow mine shafts. The wet shafts, coupled with temperatures of 40 to 50 degrees and 16- to 18-hour workdays, created a high mortality rate among child workers. As such conditions began to receive publicity, the public responded by supporting laws to restrict the conditions of child workers — *under the age of eight!*

In the United States, the first child abuse literature was published in 1871.[14] Among the incidents described was that of a child found chained to a bed from which she was regularly beaten for no reason. The problem in such cases was that there were laws to protect animals but not children. In order to bring justice to bear in such cases, it was necessary to have the child declared a member of the animal kingdom.

Child abuse and child neglect are almost an American tradition, or as one public service organization expresses it: "Child abuse is as American as cherry pie." While an eye-catcher, the slogan does little to focus on the fact that child abuse is a tragedy so hideous and complex that it staggers the imagination. It is, nevertheless, part of the warp and woof of our American culture.

Child abuse is a nightmare that is only beginning to be exposed. The depth and breadth of the problem goes beyond anything imagined by the average person. Literally thousands, perhaps millions, of American children will be scarred for life as a result of early exposure to the pain and frustration of abuse and neglect. Whether the scarring is from physical, emotional, or sexual abuse, the consequences are far-reaching and may manifest themselves as they did in the cases of Lee Harvey Oswald, Jack Ruby, or Charles Manson. It is frightening to think that we now have similar personalities being formed in the witch's cauldron of child abuse.

This very day young lives are being molded into distorted personalities, alcoholics, drug addicts, prostitutes, criminals, and mental retardates (through brain damage from physical abuse). These same individuals will, in the not-too-distant future, become parents themselves and be responsible for shaping the future of *their* offspring. Tragically, the majority of abused children later inflict the same type of indignities on their children. Hence, we're constantly building a reservoir of warped individuals to reinfect our society. They perpetuate the tradition and tragedy of child abuse to the detriment of an entire society.

If we were *truly* concerned about today's social ills and the moral and spiritual decay of our nation, perhaps we could persuade ourselves to take a few moments to look at today's child. While we're shocked at the heathenistic practices common to earlier civilizations, we tend to ignore the tidal wave of promiscuity, violence, and selfish concern for personal gratification that dominates *our* civilization. It should prove more than a little discomforting to realize that some future generations may look at us with the same disapproval and shock with which we view former permissive societies.

THE MOBILE SOCIETY

The eruption of the industrial revolution of the mid-eighteenth century produced a force that shattered all previous concepts and institutions. It allowed parents, for the first time in history, to live out their dreams through the lives of their children. For the first time, enough goods were available at all levels of society; therefore, parents held aspirations of "something better" for their children than they had had. Their "American dream" persisted throughout the succeeding generations — up until now. Now, we are beginning to see the children moving down from the levels attained by parents.

Why is this happening? For one thing, it's a conscious choice on the part of many young people. While some are still driven by the will to succeed and to improve their status, many have become disillusioned with the complexities and pressures that society imposes as the price of success. Many, having seen how their parents have reacted to success (and seeing the actual degree of life-style enhancement *delivered* by success), have chosen to drop out.

In the 1960s young people began to follow this path, with the tradition of doing better than their parents taking a back seat to the new philosophy of doing their own thing. They often rejected eventual rewards for early labor, opting for the immediate (albeit smaller) reward of the easier life now. While something can be said for the more realistic perspective of some young people today, their attitude does little to improve the general quality of society.

During the post-World War II years, society was preoccupied with (perhaps *obsessed* with) the needs, wants, psychological development, and constant gratification of its children. Its attitude was largely fostered by statements of child psychologists and social planners who drummed into parents' ears (and hearts) the insidious message that if you don't instantly and constantly gratify your children, they won't love you. Well, they did gratify them — and their children don't love them. Score another one for the great god of modern science.

As a result, we are now seeing a withdrawal from the concept of the child as the center of the parents' universe. Women who once found fulfillment in the rearing of the young now often pursue jobs or careers, thereby diminishing their traditional need to channel all of their energies into motherhood. We can only guess what tomorrow's child will face.

What we really need is *balance*. Children shouldn't be placed on pedestals as though they possessed the wisdom of the ages and the beauty of gods. They should, however, be treated as human beings and given room and opportunity to grow and develop into mature, useful adults.

We've created many excesses over the last few years, and these excesses have no doubt contributed to the irresponsibility of many of today's young adults. One of these continuing problems is the matter of extended adolescence. While the concept of childhood — as a separate and special segment of life — is vanishing, the socioeconomic demands of our day have extended the period of "adolescence" far beyond what God intended for the growth period.

Our societal structure locks young people into a role they are no longer physically suited to occupy. Adolescents, aware of the secrets and privileges of adulthood, want the freedom to enjoy them, but their imposed position of "student" or "dependent" prevents them from accepting the *responsibilities* that should accompany adult privileges. Consequently, rebellion and hostility lie barely suppressed in many of our older adolescents and younger adults.

For example, tiny children were once brutalized by child labor. Now the child receives *no* contact with productive capability. The current trend produces an unnatural state of affairs. Many factors — our national tax structure included — contribute to this condition. Unfortunately, it has produced a generation of young people who spend the first third of their lives as consumers. When they are finally forced to become producers, many fall apart emotionally.

The emphasis on consumption by our younger citizens isn't accidental. The forces running our society impose attitudes on our youngsters that stay with them throughout their lives. They've generated an "I deserve . . ."

attitude in our youth. The latest clothes, records, books, movies, cars, and everything else that's "in" are *musts* in today's society. It's no longer a matter of wanting; it's a matter of wanting *now*. Being deprived used to mean doing without. Today deprivation means having to wait a few days for satisfaction.

Are our young people really deprived? I think they are. They've been deprived — as a result of a complexity of causes — of knowing the satisfaction of a job well-done, of seeing something they've produced, of starting something and seeing it through to the finish. If there is one common lack in our young people today, it lies in the almost universal feeling of deserving everything while doing nothing.

WHO'S RESPONSIBLE?

Who's responsible for this? We'll try to assign some specific causes as we progress in our discussion, but one area should be pointed out right here, and it is the failure of today's parents. *We* as parents have followed the Pied Piper of child psychology and sociological expertise to the point where our own good common sense has been permanently impaired. There are definitely thought-formers and social planners promoting unsavory developments in our society, but we as parents are supposed to serve as a buttress between our children and these forces. In general, we've done a poor job. As a group, we've delivered our kids into the hands of the very people who are bent on their destruction. In truth, the forces aligned against the individual parent present an awesome force. With God's help, however, we could have done a much better job than we've done.

Is there no hope then? There isn't much if we look to those around us, but we must begin somewhere, and it might as well be here and now. If we serve as an example of what *can* be done — by returning to God's good order and by resisting the forces of Satan with prayer and good old-fashioned horse sense — we may be surprised at how many would follow our example.

We must accept our responsibility toward our children. "But isn't that what we've *been* doing?" No, it isn't. We've been catering to our children and buying their affection, but we've failed to spend the time necessary to positively affect their lives. Childhood is so short, and the time we have with our children so brief, that it's a tragedy when many parents choose not to invest in that time.

FAMILY INFLUENCE

Infants don't suddenly *bloom* into adults. They don't become kind, decent grown-ups by happenstance or by heredity. The qualities of decency, honesty, and kindness are not incidental personality traits; they are qualities developed through long years of nurturing. When a seed sprouts and pushes up through the ground, it is at its most vulnerable stage. Children, like young seedlings, must be cultivated during their tender years. Later it will be too late to encourage desirable qualities in them. Every succeeding year, the potential for instilling moral direction in the child becomes less. Parents who wait until such and such a time to begin training their children will completely *miss* the opportunity.

In essence, we are speaking of the prolonged, loving care needed by each and every child. This is the only factor guaranteed to produce desired results when properly applied — and guaranteed to serve as an antidote to undesirable influences when applied early enough. The home and the family are the *earliest* influences on a life and the longest lasting. Many factors intrude in the course of a lifetime, but attitudes generated by home influences will still remain when all others disappear.

I'm reminded of a story I once heard. A father, finding his son with nothing to do, tore a map of the world out of a magazine. By cutting it up, he managed to produce a jigsaw puzzle that he hoped might help to teach his son geography. He was surprised when his son returned a few minutes later with the map completed.

"Why, Son," he said. "I didn't think you were that good at geography. How did you put it together so fast?"

The boy hesitated and then confessed. There had been a picture of a boy on the back of the map. By turning it over, he had quickly managed the simpler task of reconstructing the boy's face. "And you know, Dad," he said, "I figured, if I could get the boy to turn out okay, the world would come out all right, too."

There's much truth in what that boy said. If we don't have some boys (and girls) turning out okay, world conditions could become even worse than they are in our present state of decay. We need young people growing up with the responsibility and courage to restore some order to the badly flawed world in which we live.

CHANGING PATTERNS

We offer no easy solution. A vast multitude of social and cultural changes over the last several decades have seriously weakened the potential of the home for instilling values in children. The sexual revolution of the 1960s, a skyrocketing divorce rate, changes in women's economic and social status, modern child-rearing methods, and legislation which interferes in parent-child relationships all contribute to the altered nature of childhood.

There is even today at least one organization promoting the child-free life — a condition that is becoming more and more acceptable in today's society.[15]

There is also an ever-increasing number of adult-centered homes — as opposed to the traditional child-centered home.[16] At one time, almost *all* homes were child-oriented. At the turn of the century, there were very few singles in society, and the majority of parents didn't survive long after their youngest child left home. This is no longer the case.

What has been called "the graying of America" is a result of medical advancements and longer life spans. Hence, the population of the elderly is increasing, and political power (and thus social power) is rapidly shifting from the young to the middle-aged — and even to the elderly.[17] While it is right and necessary that our older citizens receive attention, the focus away from children can produce unfortunate results. It's always the weakest political group that ends up neglected within a nation, and children are rapidly becoming one of our smallest population segments.

The rapidly disappearing division between childhood and adulthood breaks down the traditional generation boundaries. While there are those who delight at the thought of youngsters addressing their elders by their first names, generation boundaries are essential to an effective family structure. When these are distorted or lost, aggression, hostility, insecurity, and frustrations usually develop among the youth. In some cases, overt mental illness can result.

TELEVISION

Although we tend to blame vanishing social institutions for the disappearance of childhood, God still holds *parents* responsible for the protection, training, and well-being of their offspring. All too often, parents obsessed with personal fulfillment, or social or business success, inadvertently surrender their children to exploitation. While some unfortunate incidents have arisen through situations involving human baby-sitters, many more arise when the baby-sitter is an electronic one — the ever-present television set.

A subsequent chapter is devoted entirely to an analysis of television's role in today's society, but certain points should be included here. Television, more than any other single factor, provides children with information that was traditionally reserved for adults. Television is a compelling force which serves not only as a training school for initiation into the adult world, but also as a broadcaster of gloom which emphasizes the stress of living in a world teetering on the brink of destruction. Certainly our world, because of technological advances, is not the stable planet it once was. But tiny minds were never intended to be bombarded with the potential problem of survival in a nuclear war.

Then there is the matter of using young children as pawns in national marketing schemes that reach into the billions of dollars. Children who are habitual (and unregulated) viewers are exposed to *hours* of commercials directed at adult viewers. While the immediate effects of such commercials may not seem important, the subtle, long-range effects can be far more revealing than one may think.

Television doesn't just sell products, it sells attitudes. Unfortunately, many of the attitudes promoted on television are not healthy, or even realistic. TV promises to satisfy the child's (and the adult's) needs and wants — but seldom delivers in an effective way. It can lead to early disillusionment and a lifelong attitude of suspicion and cynicism. Commericals also use people's insecurities as a lever to induce unnecessary spending. Such steady manipulation of a person's weak points can eventually lead to mental problems.

If we are truly concerned about our children's welfare and development, we will make ourselves aware of the *hidden* messages constantly beamed to the child's subconscious. Such messages aren't accidental; they are boasted about by admen and TV promoters and are known as "subliminal" suggestions. They deliberately set out to instill attitudes and values in our younger generation that are *not* those which parents desire for their children.

Most commercial messages aren't lost on young minds. When a commercial declares that "gentlemen prefer Hanes," no little girl is going to rush out to buy panty hose — but it can leave the lifelong impression that women must dress to please men, that the attention of men is a competitive market, and that if one is to compete successfully in this market, one must use *all* the weapons at one's disposal.[18] Once the youngster reaches adolescence, this apparently innocuous subliminal message could be a factor in inducing promiscuity.

The day-in, day-out repetition of suggestive messages can't help having an influence on the attitudes of children. Though mom and dad may speak out against something, the kids see all the sophisticated people on television doing it, so who suffers by comparison? Stuffy old mom and dad, of course. No one can question the social and economic success of those serving as role models on TV, so why pay any attention to what the old fogeys think?

Television, for example, exalts the use of alcohol, intimating that alcohol consumption is glamorous, or macho. Television shows and commercials lead youngsters to believe that drinking is not only desirable, but necessary, for social acceptance. Although alcoholism was long considered an exclusively adult problem, it is now becoming one of the major problems associated with growing up. We find full-blown alcoholics in their early teens, and they are not isolated cases. Teenage alcoholism is epidemic, and its consequences (auto accidents, injuries, permanent paralysis, et cetera) are among the major tragedies of teenage living today. Statistics also show that the youth of our nation consume as much marijuana, cocaine, and heroin as do adults.[19]

SEX MISEDUCATION

Both the drug and alcohol industries are divided into two groups: the abusers and the users. The pornography industry also caters to two distinct groups: the demented porno addict and the curious. Unfortunately, our children are all too often the curious, and they don't have much trouble finding material to satisfy their curiosity. Not only are printed materials readily available, but also hour after hour of frankly prurient visual materials which are beamed into our homes every day. Who watches this filth? You're right, the babies we are trying to "raise unto righteousness."

Television promotes and glorifies promiscuous and perverted sex. Television's preoccupation with sex, and the transference of its preoccupation to our young people, is unquestionably a factor in the rise of venereal disease, illegitimate births, abortion, sex crimes, and the breakdown of the family. The consequences of pushing children into adult sex situations mushrooms in all directions as a frightening aspect of our "modern" society.

Television's view of sex actually makes the perverse seem glamorous. Young, prepubescent girls are regularly presented in commercials and printed ads as sex objects. They are presented as worldly and sexually attractive potential partners. There is no question of the role they represent — they're "Lolitas." They know what it's all about, and they aren't opposed to anything. It wasn't so long ago that even suggesting sexual activities with minors was an offense that could land you in prison for a long time. Today, TV executives and admen do it routinely and society passively accepts it.

Within a civilized society, it is generally accepted that sexual impulses must be rigidly controlled. Pressure is constantly placed upon adults to "cool it in public." Sexually suggestive actions just aren't acceptable around children. A barrier of secrecy is considered the proper shield to protect children from information that can be disturbing or harmful.

But what does television do? It throws open the gates and immerses the youngest and most innocent of children in a labyrinth of responsibilities and concerns that cause many adults problems. When this occurs, it tears down a major boundary separating childhood from adulthood.

Today's children are hard to distinguish from adults. They dress like adults, demand inclusion in adult conversations, and participate in adult recreations. In short, they are just small adults functioning in an adult world.

Unfortunately, most do not have the mental and emotional resources to cope with an adult environment. Their collection of wisdom and experiences fall woefully short of equipping them for grown-up responsibilities. As children openly indulge in sex, drugs, and alcohol (not to mention crime and perversions), it becomes painfully evident that we are paying an awesome price for television and its values. Suicides, drug overdoses, violent deaths, alcoholism — they're all part of the price our youngsters pay for the *privilege* of wandering unprepared into an adult world. Does this sound a little like conditions in the Middle Ages?

Of course, history *does* repeat itself. As a wise man once said, those who don't learn from it are doomed to live through it again. Civilizations come and civilizations go. History recounts the manner in which the events of one age are repeated again (sometimes over and over) in succeeding ages. It records man's efforts to elevate himself above the bondage that often seems to be his lot in life.

But bondage isn't man's lot as intended by God. Bondage is always imposed by some other man, or group of men. Today, there are clearly men who feel that Christian virtues and traits are unnecessary or unacceptable and so must be excised from our society. These are the men who principally control our media today. They are consciously striving to root out every vestige of Christianity and replace it with anarchy, vileness, pornography, and atheism.

Thus far, they've done a mammoth job. It would seem that they're about three-quarters of the way down the road toward reaching their goal. And to be painfully frank, as long as Christians blindly support them by watching television, buying movie tickets, and subscribing to (or even peeking at) the girlie magazines, it won't take long to *finish* the job.

I think it's apparent that we're nearing the end of our age. The disciples asked Jesus (in Matthew 24 and Luke 21) what the signs would be to indicate the time. He gave a number of signs, and Paul and other Bible writers gave additional signs in a number of places throughout the Old and New Testaments. Among these was the list of traits pointed out by Paul in II Timothy 3:2-4, which he said would characterize the general state of humanity in "the last days":

> *"For men shall be lovers of their own selves, covetous, boasters, proud, blasphemers, disobedient to parents, unthankful, unholy, Without natural affection, trucebreakers, false accusers, incontinent, fierce, despisers of those that are good, Traitors, heady, highminded, lovers of pleasures more than lovers of God."*

Perhaps — unknowingly — we are responsible for creating such a people, especially among the younger group.

God has given us the resources to protect our children and to insulate our homes against the forces of evil. It is our *grave* responsibility to prolong the innocence of childhood while we train our children to be mighty in spirit, not wise in the ways of the world.

In the Old Testament, the family with children was presented as the key unit of society. David, God's great psalmist, wrote in Psalm 127, verses 3 and 5: *"Children are an heritage of the Lord . . . . Happy is the man that hath his quiver full of them."*

Proverbs 22:6 speaks with regard to child-rearing, saying it is our responsibility to *"Train up a child in the way he should go: and when he is old, he will not depart from it."*

Judeo-Christian ethics maintain a high regard for children, placing the highest of priorities on the welfare and education of the child. Children are commanded to honor their fathers and their mothers, while parents are cautioned to diligently teach the commandments of the Lord unto their children.

In the *New* Testament, children are esteemed as a gift from God. Jesus Himself reinforced Old Testament teachings when He invited the little children to be brought unto Him. Wherever Christians have been found throughout history, this ethic profoundly influenced society. Within the Christian point of view, children were seen as much more than chattels. They had an intrinsic worth and value within themselves because of their potential as God-fearing adults. Each was considered a divine creature possessing the dignity of human life and the precious commodity of an eternal soul.

Neither did early Christians shrug their shoulders at the heathen practices of infanticide, pedophilia, and abortion commonly practiced about them. Instead, they challenged the pagan Mediterranean world. They were also the operators of the first orphanages for unwanted or abused children.[20]

OUR EDUCATIONAL SYSTEM

Although society as a whole accepts the Christian concept that children are valuable as individuals and that their education is the responsibility of society, the general moral decay of our time eats away at the foundations of the educational system charged with that responsibility. As a matter of fact, if the average Christian parent would take the time to read the books supplied to our youngsters, he might be shocked by the amount of freethinking, liberal, humanistic propaganda that infiltrates today's schoolbooks.

Then there's the matter of "sex education." Liberal "educators" have determined that it is the responsibility of the school system, not the parent, to explain sex to youngsters. The manner in which they handle their new responsibility is a major factor contributing to the breakdown of the former, beneficial division between childhood and adulthood. A number of these programs have sparked intense conflict between parents and school administrators; but after prolonged battles, the liberal courts almost inevitably rule that the responsibility for establishing sexual attitudes among the young belongs to the *school boards*.

Theoretically, school board members represent the parents. In actuality, however, these boards turn to experts in the field for guidance without even consulting the parents. Who are these experts? They are generally "specialists" within the field of psychology who are known as "sex therapists" or "sex counselors."

It would seem that some sex therapists spend their every waking hour thinking about sex, fretting about sex, and wondering how they can make sex even more acceptable and open. According to the sex therapists, "abnormal" sex doesn't exist; hence a new breed even favors incest as a "healthy expression of affection between parent and child."

Even those who don't go to this extreme feel that such things as lesbianism and homosexuality are nothing more than "just another view of sex" and that everyone should have the right of choice in sexual matters.

Somehow, the poor, misguided sex educators think they know what's best for our children. Without consulting or even informing parents, they spring fully formed sex education programs on them. That in itself is cause for alarm.

Considering our society in general, there is a need for some sex education among youngsters. Because of the number of perverts roaming our streets and preying on the young, children should be taught to recognize (and avoid) any advances of a sexual nature. From this standpoint, sex education is both necessary and valuable. The whole objective of sex education should be to protect the child both physically and morally.

The point to be stressed, however, is that sex and morality mustn't be separated. Every sexual relationship should possess a major component of morality, and to exclude it from any discussion of sexuality is to place reproduction (and all associated acts) on the barnyard level. Sex involves right and wrong, and until general moral values are clearly defined in a child's mind, the rights and wrongs of all aspects of sex must be a part of any discussion on the subject.

Unfortunately, the sex education courses commonly offered in our schools do not include morality in their sex discussions. As a matter of fact, they specifically *exclude* morality. The widely promulgated liberal position insists that morality is an individual matter and cannot be legislated or taught. Public sex education courses must therefore be "value-free." In other words, they teach the *mechanics* of sex with morality deliberately excluded. And if the parents happen to be concerned? Then they can *try* to impose a thin layer of morality over the dank pool of physical sex established by the "professionals."

Many parents, on learning what is being imposed on their children under the name of sex education, react with disbelief and anger. The contents of a proposed text for a sex education course in California included such topics as homosexuality, lesbianism, premarital intercourse, prostitution, incest, sodomy, bestiality, masturbation, abortion, and drugs.

Advocates of one sex education program wanted to waste no time in rearing their students to an adult level of sexual knowledge. They suggested that preschool and kindergarten children be taken to the rest rooms in *mixed* groups, followed by a description of the male and female genital organs. The program would also provide instruction in human sexual intercourse for these children — aged three to five years![21]

Their proposals continue: At nine the child begins the study of menstruation, conception, ejaculation, and nocturnal emissions. Children are encouraged to read two Planned Parenthood pamphlets that state that "masturbation is a perfectly acceptable, useful, and comfortable thing to do with sexual feelings."[22] One of the executives of this organization boasted on a national TV show of her rapport with the group of young boys to whom she had been giving sex instructions. When asked how much masturbation was *too* much, she proudly replied, "Until your arm gets too tired." She and the host had a wonderful time chuckling over how much the boys had appreciated her remark.

Twelve-year-olds are taken on a field trip to the drug store to receive firsthand information on the availability of contraceptive devices. They are also given instructions on the law regarding emancipation of minors who are making their own decisions. It is stressed that pregnancy-prevention services are available to young people *without parental consent*. They are further given the opportunity to role-play the part of a boy or girl asking the doctor for birth control information. Finally, they are given information on available procedures if contraception should fail, resulting in an unplanned pregnancy.[23]

Sex education courses of that type are far removed from delivering a basic understanding of the body's role in sexual development, pregnancy, and childbirth. Sex education is a subject that should ideally be taught by informed, concerned parents. Instead, some sex education courses in our schools offer explicit information — not only on human sexual intercourse, but also on alternative life-styles; life-styles which show such aberrations as promiscuity, pornography, and homosexuality in a favorable light.

Subjects that once would have been dealt with in shame are now openly brought out as subjects of public discussion. Many acts and matters that shouldn't even be discussed have been thrown into the public view, and in the process they have lost their furtive and shameful character and thus are "documented" as socially acceptable.

A sense of shame is a desirable and necessary quality in a civilized society. Natural sexual impulses and drives must be restrained to allow for the character development of the individual and for the smooth functioning of society. Despite this need for restraint, certain practices in public sex education courses approach actual perversion.

One course spends a session (apparently meant to desensitize the pupils to any normal reaction to sex) by requiring that children write every dirty word they know on the blackboard.[24] They are then led in a discussion of just what the words mean and their implications. It used to be said that if children weren't taught sex properly, they would pick it up in the gutter. The gutter has apparently moved full circle and now resides in the classroom.

Such crude practices are diametrically opposed to civilized sexual practices, and they act to desensitize children to the intimacy and affection that should be a part of sex. In short, they reduce sex to the animal level. The God-given sexual appetite is a powerful force that is crucial to the growth and maintenance of the normal person's civilization. It must, however, be channeled and controlled.

The spiritual and moral elements of sex must not be separated from the physical aspects. To do so is to desecrate the intimate, affectionate, and monogamous nature of human sexuality — reducing it to a physical function with no more sensibility involved than in the evacuation of the bowels or the bladder. Is it any wonder that people today bewail the fact that "romance has gone out of marriage"?

Without a conscience, the individual becomes a barbarian or a savage. Without the capacity for shame, civilization disappears. Both conscience and shame are essential to the preservation of the condition and state of "childhood." The very innocence that characterizes childhood must be protected. Many of "the secrets of life," though suitable within the privacy of the marriage bond, are *not* appropriate when scribbled on public blackboards before immature tots.

Repeated exposure to such provocative material eventually desensitizes the viewer to the point where he no longer feels a sense of shame. When this stage is reached, all moral questions are removed from the equation. It is no longer a "social problem."

The next (or ultimate) step is arrival at the liberal position that *nothing* is a social problem — that all acts and situations are *consequences* (which may *create* social problems), but that the behavior itself is blameless. This then removes all guilt and allows anyone to do whatever he chooses, with no sense of shame or responsibility.

Since some sex educators contend that there is no such thing as sexual deviance or perversion, when confronted with violent psychopathic behavior they cast the blame on family, religion, local influences, or political considerations. To them, so-called perversions are merely erroneous notions of Judeo-Christian bigots. Therefore, the individual is blameless.

Apparently, it never occurs to them that the emotional problems may stem from their perverted methods and their unwholesome interference — creating conflicts with family, church, and community. It also never occurs to them that they are blatantly raping the minds of the very youngsters they purport to teach.

LETTING IT ALL HANG OUT

From kindergarten through the twelfth grade, many sex educators commit themselves to freeing the child of "hang-ups." Hang-ups are almost exclusively, in their view, associated with physical sex. How do they eliminate hang-ups? By bringing them all out into the open, as early as possible and as often as possible. Ignorantly, they dismiss the question of responsibility for the *new* hang-ups, created by them as a result of their imposition of overkill on the subject.

The buzzword among sex educators today is that "sex is for everyone!" Everyone? Yes, no one is too young to start enjoying the fun and games of sex. In the process of instilling this new freedom in their charges, it is subtly implied that mom and dad may be a little backward on the subject, but don't let that interfere — if you've got it, enjoy it!

With mom and dad shunted out of the ball game, who does the youngster turn to when questions of propriety arise? Well, the sex instructor first, then the peer group (with all their combined wisdom in sexual matters), and then, presumably, the local adult bookstore.

The media has grasped this new package of moral freedom with joy and alacrity. They've already been packaging everything else with sex, but now they have sex itself as a commodity. Sexual precociousness is being packaged and promoted throughout our society as just another normal item. As a consequence, an ever-higher percentage of our children are becoming sexually experienced before they're even out of braces. And without an understanding of the underlying moral values and responsibilities, few can handle the emotional implications that must inevitably arise.

THE PARENT OR THE STATE

Completely interwoven into the programs promoted by AASEC (American Association of Sex Educators and Counselors) and SEICUS (Sex Education and Information Council of the United States) is the push for the "right of the child."[25] It is not only a national problem, but an international one as well, as was demonstrated in the recent "Year of the Child" sponsored worldwide by the organization UNICEF. Although a high-minded principle on the surface, the basic intent of the program is to remove parental restraints on the child who chooses to rebel against parental authority.[26]

There is, of course, a fine line here, and injustices certainly occur on both sides of the line. Several things should be kept in mind, however, before we completely reverse the traditional role of the parent and the child. One of the most important of these is that a child's judgment is immature. His rights, therefore, must be overseen by parental discretion.

Irrespective, a completely new judicial concept called "Children's Rights of Privacy" collides head-on with the traditional rights and obligations that enable a parent to act as head of the household and to raise his minor children.[27]

It has never been God's plan that the school or the state should rear children. Of course, that statement would be strongly argued in communist countries where it is the aim of the state to seize and control all minds from their earliest inception. Outside of Marxist countries, however, it has been traditional throughout the millennia that the parent holds the responsibility for rearing the child. (Once again, it is amazing how many liberal programs mirror the methods suggested by Marx.)

God uniquely ordained the family for bearing children and forming their character. Therefore, any attempt by man to substitute artificial means is contrary to God's plan. The rights of children must of necessity be subjugated to those of the parents, except in cases of gross abuse (which is not being discussed here). Such restrictions protect the child from his own immaturity, as well as from exploitation by others who have none of the responsibility for his care.

One can't help suspecting the true dedication of some who lobby most intensely for "the right of the child." One wouldn't promote the right of a toddler to play with a loaded gun in his crib, and one can't help but wonder about statutes that would legalize sexual decisions by a minor that would involve perverts. The fact is that children can be easily allowed too much latitude, and it must be restricted — especially when it endangers their physical, moral, and spiritual well-being.

Now this is not to say that children have *no* rights. Children have the right to be loved, to be nurtured, and to be protected. Adults do *not* have the right to oppress them, to exploit them, or to harm them. There can be an extremely fine line between oppression and protection, but there is a fine gray line in almost every human relationship. If such lines are approached with honesty and good intentions, most differences can be amicably and fairly dissolved.

We must recall that, within the perspective of history, it is an extremely short time since children were considered the *property* of their parents. During most of history, children were thought of as little more than slaves. No injustice could be inflicted on a child because it was impossible to inflict injustice on one's own property. It was that type of thinking that led to abortion, infanticide, and the mutilation of children to enhance their value as beggars or freaks. Today's perverted, "enlightened" thinking on abortion and genocide (which is supported by the same people who promote "children's rights") will eventually meander down the road to the same result — a point where children are again property, but this time the property of the state.

A CHILD'S POSITION IN SOCIETY

A child is the property of neither the parent nor the state. A child is *God's* property, and a human being with rights and privileges uniquely his own. God gives parents the responsibility and privilege of caring for children, but children should be reared and cared for under the leadership and guidance of God Almighty.

Whenever man seeks to live his life based solely on *his* wisdom, he is trying to draw water with a flawed bucket. In any human endeavor, the bottom line is *always* that man is imperfect. He may be well-intentioned and he may be bright, but he *is* imperfect.

Human judgments are never infallible and the best of intentions can't protect us from our quota of mistakes. In rearing a family, we will inevitably look back and see situations that we wish we had handled better. Nevertheless, turning our responsibility over to political bodies will be at least as fallible as leaving it in the hands of parents.

God, and only God, is infallible. It goes without saying that under any legalization of the child-rearing responsibility, God will be legislatively excluded from the process. He has already been drummed out of every other governmental function by our atheistic social planners, and there is no reason to think that they will suddenly have a change of heart and invite Him into *this* area.

Imperfect people have gone much too far in the matter of human rights. Some situations are almost as ludicrous as giving toddlers the right to drive or to redecorate their homes. Certainly, to exclude them from these rights infringes their "free expression." But some of their free expression could visit indelible harm on their bodies and souls. We are talking about life-long attitudes and emotional stances that cannot be erased by repealing a particularly harmful statute. How much better to think out the matter to its logical conclusion before irreparable harm is done.

We must protect our children!

NO REGARD
FOR LIFE

While the blood of more than 1.5 million aborted babies cries out to God in America each year, the Christian community remains virtually silent. The silence is horrifying! We, as Americans, and even more appallingly, as Christian Americans, would seem to have no regard for human life.

A professor at the UCLA Medical School asked his students this question: "Here is a family history. The father has syphilis, the mother has TB. They have already produced four children. The first is blind, the second has died, the third is deaf, the fourth has TB, and now the mother is pregnant again. The parents are willing to have an abortion, if *you* decide they should. What do you think?"

The majority of the students decided on the abortion.

"Congratulations," said the professor, "you have just murdered Beethoven!"

The professor's disclosure to his students is chilling. You may conclude that if Beethoven's parents had lived today, he would likely not have been born. The same could apply to literally *thousands* of other great men and women who, by living out their productive lives, have made the world a better place in which to live.

Regardless of how ignorant anyone may be to the true facts of abortion, abortion is sin. I will go even beyond that and say without qualification that abortion is *premeditated* murder — the murder of an innocent infant with a body, soul, and spirit that needs only the protection of its mother's womb to survive and mature.

For long centuries no decent person (and certainly no respected Christian) has advocated or condoned the killing of unborn children. Like any *other* act of wanton killing, it is murder. Nonabortion is the law of all civilized nations — and more importantly, it is the law of God.

Without question, abortion *is* the primary issue facing America today, and the Christian community can't hide behind a false claim of ignorance. Yet God's people slumber, offering no true resistance to this wanton slaughter of human life. And all the time, Satan feverishly inspires evil men to pursue their course of destruction.

In all honesty, the present-day slaughter seems somehow unreal; and of course, those who advocate abortion go to great lengths to direct our attention *away* from the victims themselves. In an age that boasts of enlightenment and humanity, it is ironic indeed that it promotes — and then hides — the reality of an issue of such abject corruption.

America is being weighed in the balance, and the pivotal point of that balance is the issue of abortion. Abortion actually challenges the inherent sanctity of all human life. We can recoil with good Christian horror as we recall Roman mothers clutching their babies to protect them from the terror of Hannibal. Hannibal's god was Baal, who insatiably demanded infant sacrifice. But how do we react when Baal takes up residence in *our* fair land? Baal has many names. Moloch, the god of the ancient Phoenicians (who demanded the sacrifice of children by burning) is one of them. Here in America, his name is self — and the religion of his followers is secular humanism.

Secular humanistic thinking is responsible for the millions of babies who have been deprived of life because they did not appear, as they resided in their mothers' wombs, to offer an *advantage* to their parents. They are the innocent victims of this evil, ultimately *selfish,* religion.

OUR "JUSTICE" SYSTEM

In 1973 the Supreme Court of the United States opened the door to an American holocaust by allowing abortion-on-demand. Since then, nearly 1.5 million babies a year have been murdered in their mothers' wombs — that's over 10 times the number of Americans lost in *all* of our nation's wars.

Then, in June of 1983, the Supreme Court chose to provide even greater *convenience* (and less stigma) to the pregnant female and to the medical profession as well. As a result, we should see an annual *increase* in these already appalling statistics.

The new, less-restrictive laws now basically state:

• The mother-to-be no longer has to have a 24-hour "cooling off" period before making the irreversible decision to end the life of her unborn baby.

• Abortions for women more than three months pregnant no longer have to be performed in hospitals, but can now be performed in abortion clinics — *even up to the ninth month!*

• Doctors no longer have to inform those seeking abortions about possible alternatives to preserve life, the medical and psychological risks of abortion, or even the simple fact that the "fetus" is indeed a human life.

• It is no longer necessary that aborted fetuses be disposed of in a "humane and sanitary manner."

• Pregnant, unwed girls *under 15* are no longer required to obtain the consent of either a parent or a judge before having an abortion — if the physician considers her "mature."

PLANNED UNPARENTHOOD

The confirmation of an unplanned or unwanted pregnancy can create panic, whether due to a real crisis such as rape (though rare) or illness — or as a result of teenage experimentation, a threat to the family finances, or just pure selfishness on the mother's part. However, after the initial panic and shock, the pregnant female may search for help and possible alternatives — from keeping the baby, to child care, to putting the baby up for adoption.

Although several alternatives may be available, abortion-on-demand seems to provide an easy way out, a way that is progressively easier as its social acceptance increases. It is all too convenient today for a woman to go to an abortion clinic where she pays a few dollars to have a doctor kill her unborn baby. How does she stifle the pangs of conscience? Apparently her selfishness overrides any guilt she may experience — at least temporarily.

Of course, advertisements and posters such as those put out by Planned Parenthood ("Abortion Should Be Between You and a Doctor") help to soothe her conscience and aid her in seeking a quick escape from her dilemma. In the midst of a personal crisis, a woman's mind becomes a fertile field for planting suggestions that may lead to abortion as the solution. Planned Parenthood, a world leader in arranging and promoting abortions, presents its message with great clarity and diabolical cleverness.

Such proabortion literature focuses on emotions in a situation that should involve moral and logical reasoning to reach a wise decision. In this business of making the unthinkable acceptable, emotions play a big role. Language therefore becomes critical. Could it have been a factor in the Supreme Court's decision in 1973 when the victim of abortion was referred to as a "fetus" rather than as a "human being" or "baby"? By using this term, they resorted to the common humanistic practice of employing a "euphemism." A euphemism is an inoffensive word substituted for a more commonly used, but more disturbing, word. "Fetus" is an impersonal word — one that allows the hearer to think of the unborn baby as a mere "blob" of flesh. Consequently, abortion becomes abstract and impersonal (and less murderous) — at least, it certainly seems to be that way in the thinking of those who promote and support this crime.

In September of 1948, the World Medical Association (with the United States as a founding member) adopted the Declaration of Geneva which states, "I will maintain the utmost respect for human life from the time of its conception."[1] The committee that drew up that code thus said that abortionists stood condemned, and this was reaffirmed in 1979 by the World Medical Association's Declaration of Oslo which restated the Declaration of Geneva's call for respect for life from conception.

Apparently the United States Supreme Court set aside the scientific evidence behind these opinions, and said that it couldn't decide just when human life begins. It thus opted for abortion-on-demand during the earlier stages of pregnancy. In June of 1983, however, it set aside all restraints and made it clear that it holds no regard for human life.

President Reagan cast aside all smoke screens when he made the statement, "The real question today is not when human life begins, but what is the value of human life?"[2]

IS THE UNBORN CHILD A HUMAN BEING?

I believe the unborn child (the "fetus") is a human being, a person, or an individual from the moment of conception. Some have foolishly stated that the unborn child, up to the sixth or seventh month, is little more than a "blob of tissue." That just isn't so.

The tiny, unborn baby is not "just a part of the woman's body" as supporters of abortion like to claim, nor is it a "mass of undifferentiated tissue." It is a distinct and separate life. All of the child's traits have been charted in its genes. The sex of the child, the color of its eyes and hair, its physical features, and its special talents and gifts are determined at the moment of conception. At that point, the mother and father have contributed all they will contribute to the genetic characteristics of their offspring.

• Within three weeks of conception, the human heart of the unborn child begins to beat.

• By six or seven weeks, all vital organs are present and fingers, feet, and toes develop. The first movements of body, arms, and legs occur. Even at that early age, sex can be determined. The buds of the little milk teeth appear and brain waves can be recorded.

• By eight weeks the child is able to grasp an object and make a fist.

• By 10 weeks the hands and feet are formed. In fact, the fingerprints and footprints are already engraved on the skin. Even though in the mother's womb, the child can suck its thumb, fingers, or toes.

• At 11 or 12 weeks, the baby is very sensitive to touch, heat, sound, discomfort, and pain. (It is often at this stage that abortion is accomplished through the extremely painful injection of saline solution.) During this stage the vocal cords are forming and the baby goes through the motions of crying. His face now shows the features inherited from his parents.

• By 16 weeks, fingernails, eyebrows, and eyelashes appear to enhance the natural beauty of the tiny being. He also becomes more active as he kicks his feet and curls his toes, or rests while sucking his thumb.

Here we are presenting known medical facts. Does the "fetus" sound like a formless blob, or is it clear that life begins at conception? The tiny being needs only food and time to grow into an adult life.

THE LAW AND THE BIBLE

In a "pluralistic" society, one which tries to create a compromise of all viewpoints, we are told that individuals should not be prevented from doing whatever their religious principles allow. We are further told that a free society should not "invade the privacy of a woman's body." Furthermore, it is contended that a just society should not pass laws which create unfairness, nor should a merciful society make laws that impose handicaps on children. Finally, a wise society will not pass laws that it cannot (or perhaps does not have the will to) enforce.

Men, exalting themselves in their superior enlightenment and humanity, use these arguments to promote abortion. On the surface, these may appear to be valid assumptions for a society that professes concern about all of its members. They are, however, based on the false assumption that unborn babies are not human beings entitled to the same protection as all other members of society.

According to the Bible, man's thinking concerning abortion is contrary to God's way of thinking. The Bible says that the unborn child is a living soul. The Holy Spirit inspired David to say,

> *"Behold, I was shapen in iniquity; and in sin did my mother conceive me"* (Psalm 51:5).

When David said, "I was shapen," he clearly implied that from the moment of conception he was the same person who would later be known as David, the great king of Israel.

Again, in Psalm 139:13-14, David was inspired to write,

> *"Thou hast covered me in my mother's womb. I will praise thee; for I am fearfully and wonderfully made."*

From the moment of conception, and as the Holy Spirit purposed, David was indeed a person. It was David's body, his very substance, that resided in his mother's womb.

We find the same type of teaching concerning Jeremiah. He said:

*"Then the word of the Lord came unto me, saying, Before
I formed thee in the belly I knew thee; and before thou camest
forth out of the womb I sanctified thee, and I ordained thee a
prophet unto the nations"* (Jeremiah 1:4-5).

God knew the Prophet Jeremiah before he was born, plainly signifying that his soul and spirit were already in his maturing infant body. If this fetus had been aborted, it would have constituted murder, for more than a mass of tissue would have died — the Prophet Jeremiah would have died. His mother might not have known he was to be a mighty prophet, but God knew. His mother might not have even known his name if he hadn't survived to birth, but God knew that as well.

I am saying that in God's eyes and according to His Word a fetus is unquestionably a person. It is a living soul from the very moment of conception. It is a child — whether born or unborn.

John the Baptist was filled with the Holy Ghost *"even from his mother's womb"* (Luke 1:15). Mary, the mother of Jesus, went to greet Elisabeth . . . *"And it came to pass, that, when Elisabeth heard the salutation of Mary, the babe leaped in her womb"* (Luke 1:41). John the Baptist, yet a "fetus" in his mother's womb, may not have understood why he leaped at the sound of Mary's voice, but God knew. Even as a fetus, John responded to the presence of the Saviour, who was then within Mary's body.

It is interesting to note the words of Jesus in Mark 10:14: *"Suffer the little children to come unto me, and forbid them not; for of such is the kingdom of God."* Here He was referring specifically to the small children being brought to Him for His blessing. But the Greek word translated in Luke 1:41 as "babe" is *brephos*. And *brephos* means "an unborn child or newborn." Based on this, it seems clear that every infant — born or unborn — has an immortal soul, since Jesus said, "of such is the kingdom of God."

WHAT IS LIFE WORTH?

Jesse Helms, U. S. senator, states: "There comes a time in the history of all great civilizations when the moral foundations upon which it rests are shaken by some momentous turn of events. That time has come for America. The historical experience of Western man indicates that such upheavals can ultimately destroy a nation — the collapse of Rome being only one of many examples. Great nations die when they cease to live by the great principles which gave them the vision and strength to rise above tyranny and human degradation. Unless the abortion decision is reversed by an amendment to the Constitution, the future of America is in grave doubt, for no nation can remain free or exercise moral leadership when it has embraced the doctrine of death."[3]

The true issue behind legalized abortion (as well as the growing acceptance of infanticide and euthanasia) boils down to a judgment on the value of human life. Approval of these practices demands acceptance of the primary evolutionary premise that man is just an animal — a view diametrically opposed to the Judeo-Christian concept which affords great value to every person.

Disregard for human life and the worth of the individual is fast becoming accepted as a normal part of modern society, but an even greater danger exists. This lack of respect for life is only a symptom of a growing tendency of the state to claim total power. "The ease with which destruction of life is advocated for those considered either socially useless or socially disturbing instead of educational and ameliorative measures may be the first danger sign of loss of creative liberty in thinking which is the hallmark of a democratic society."[4]

If we don't deal effectively and quickly with these issues, we will most assuredly see the death of our country. The sanctity of human life cannot be taken lightly; it touches the very essence of man's existence.

THE WEISBERG INCIDENT

The Weisberg incident is a perfect example of innocent victims tossed about in a game of political football, a sadistic game in which human life is devalued and supposedly civilized and educated persons expose themselves as little more than brute beasts. In a well-devised strategy of rhetoric, "babies" are reduced to "abstract fetal tissue," or just so many ounces of flesh, and handled with as much emotion as one feels in purchasing a pound of ground meat!

The Weisberg incident was first reported on February 6, 1982, as a small, obscure item in the *Los Angeles Times*. One might have expected the article to be slashed across the front pages of all papers in bold black type, but that isn't the way it happened.

The newspaper reported the discovery of 500 fetuses, some weighing up to four pounds.[5] A crew of workers discovered the mangled and maimed mass of humanity — individually stored in formaldehyde-filled plastic containers — in what began as simply an assignment to repossess a 20-foot-long shipping container. Marvin Weisberg, owner of a pathology lab in Los Angeles County, had failed to pay the storage bill on the container which he used to store infants from abortion mills for pathological studies.

Workers, unloading the container behind Weisberg's posh Woodland Hills home, stared in disbelief at the evidence of mass murder while others, their senses assaulted by the odors and morbid sight, vomited in horror. One crew member later said, "I saw one fetus with legs 2½ to 3 inches long and the body and head were demolished. I was scared, frightened, and had tears in my eyes. What else can you say?"

His boss had said, "They're just fetuses, but they sure looked like little babies to me."[6]

The Los Angeles County Board of Supervisors called for a speedy determination of any illegality. Under California law, abortion of fetuses under 20 weeks of age was legal. But, since state codes required burial or cremation, improper disposal was evident. That, however, was not the first problem with disposal. In 1976, tenants who shared the same building as Weisberg's lab complained about 100 fetuses stacked in the hallway.

Four private organizations, including a Right-to-Life group, offered to pay for cremation or burial of the yet undetermined number of almost 7,000 pounds of babies whose lives were cruelly and prematurely snuffed out. It was later determined that there were actually 17,000 fetuses in the container.

President Reagan endorsed a plan to hold a memorial service for the fetuses, but the district attorney refused to release what he now considered "criminal evidence." In response, public officials and members of the California Pro-life Medical Association made a courageous attempt to initiate action and promote burial by releasing the grossly disturbing photographs of the infants.[7]

The media, of course, protected the perpetrators of this horrendous deed and echoed their perverted views. In a diabolical plot to brainwash the American public, they presented the abortion-produced carnage as a mere unemotional abstraction rather than exposing the actual magnitude of the slaughter.

How is it that a media that ordinarily specializes in the sensational and the sordid suddenly suppresses pictures of the massacred, fails to reveal the negative factors involved, and even refuses to inform the public of the medical and emotional hazards to the mother? If the truth be known, only those whose consciences have been seared into insensitivity could choose to suppress such a crime.

It seems inconceivable that a nation as great as America has been could regress to such abominable barbarism. Still, it is happening! Men as drunken savages, intoxicated with their own wisdom and power, court the god of Baal. And our nation's passive multitudes watch from the distance and do nothing!

THE MEDIA IS THE MESSAGE

Marshall McLuhan, in his book, *The Media Is the Message,* warns, "When the mechanization of death occurs on a vast scale, the minds of civilized people are numbed. Decent and well-meaning people, acting as if in corporate somnambulism, are engaged today in repeating in abortion centers the patterns of life processing which worked so well in meat packing and death camps . . . One precedent begets another by echo of remorseless logic and quantified statistical reasoning. If meat packing and death camps can resonate in a way that makes abortion centers a familiar and acceptable pattern, the abortion centers themselves constitute a further precedent for the repetition of further violence to human dignity and compassion."[8]

Marshall McLuhan foresaw that the experience with easy abortion would result in a general loss of respect for human life. Here's an example of what he was talking about: Doctor C. C. Merry, a pathologist at the Winnipeg General Hospital, found a baby boy whimpering in a garbage bag waiting to be burned in the hospital incinerator.[9] Doctor Merry said that those who perform abortions become hardened to such cases and would not try to save the life of the baby. Why? Because the whole purpose of abortion is to destroy life!

Doctor Lawrence Lawn, of Cambridge University's Department of Experimental Medicine, has been photographed experimenting on a legally aborted, but living, fetus. Doctor Lawn was quoted in the *Cambridge Evening News* as saying, "We are simply using something which is destined for the incinerator to benefit mankind."[10]

Researchers who argue that they are only making use of human fetal "garbage" in their work demonstrate the extent to which the respect and dignity afforded human life has deteriorated. Permissive abortion policies have degraded human life to the point where living, breathing babies are now considered to be "research specimens."[11]

While researchers encourage murder for the advancement of science, others do so for mere profit. In a bizarre and sordid link between European abortionists and cosmetic manufacturers, the prestigious French journal, *Gazette du Palais*, reported the use of aborted babies in beauty products![12]

Frozen bodies of aborted babies are destined for rendering in the laboratories of French cosmetic firms. Cells from the fetuses supposedly rejuvenate aging human skin by lending firmness and lustre.

THE GOVERNMENT'S VIEW

Our nation's values are misplaced. The irony of a recent event demonstrates this. Secretary of Defense Casper Weinberger, pressured by public opinion, ordered a halt to the shooting of dogs for medical experiments and training. His decision was announced in a brief, one-sentence statement following a report in the *Washington Post*.[13]

The paper reported plans of the Department of Defense to open a firing range at the nation's Military Medical School in Bethesda, Maryland. Dogs and other animals were to be put under anesthesia and then shot with high-powered weapons such as those used in combat. By using these animals, military doctors and scientists hoped to study how to treat similar wounds suffered by humans. However, as stated, Secretary Weinberger ordered a halt to the shootings.

What a paradox! Laws are passed by high public officials to stop the killing of dogs, while other high officials (the Supreme Court) pass laws to allow the increased killing of tiny human beings! In other words, it would seem clear that in today's society, dogs are more important than babies.

As a nation, we are in desperate straits. We cannot survive as a free nation under such a value system. Nazi government-approved gas chambers killed "unwanted" Jews. Now, America's government-approved abortion centers kill "unwanted" babies. How long will it be before we begin exterminating all other "unwanteds," simply because they are considered less than perfect, useless, or burdens on society?

MEDICAL ETHICS

It is especially sad when we realize the part the medical profession plays in this carnage. Historians tell us that the holocaust in Nazi Germany was accompanied by a corruption of medical ethics. Law permitted the extermination of "useless" members of society. Then those ethically committed to life and health responded by setting themselves up as gods to determine which lives were of value and which were not.

Today, a new ethic has emerged in our own nation in which a whole category of people, unloved and unborn, are senselessly slaughtered. And once again, the corruption of medical ethics is partially to blame.

For centuries, doctors have taken the Hippocratic oath as a moral standard governing their work decisions. In recent years, however, many medical schools have ceased to recite the Hippocratic oath, which specifically forbids the practice of abortion and euthanasia.[14] "I will give no deadly medicine to anyone if asked, nor suggest such counsel, and in like manner, I will not give to a woman a pessary to produce abortion."

The policy statements on abortion of the American Medical Association (made over a century ago) are quite a contrast to those set forth in the past two decades. In 1859, abortion was defined as "the slaughter of countless children; no mere misdemeanor, nor attempt upon the life of the mother, but the wanton and murderous destruction of human life." Today abortion is merely the "interruption of an unwanted pregnancy." In 1871, abortion was considered "the work of destruction; the wholesale destruction of unborn infants." Today it is a "medical procedure."

Concerning the physician abortionist, the American Medical Association, in 1871, stated that these are "men who cling to a noble profession only to dishonor it; false brethren; educated assassins; these modern Herods; these men who, with corrupt hearts and bloodstained hands, destroy what they cannot reinstate, corrupt souls, and destroy the fairest fabric that God has ever created . . . under the cloak of that medical profession; monsters of iniquity." That statement describes the modern abortionist perfectly (even though he may be considered a conscientious practitioner by some) — if he performs therapeutic abortions for reasons other than those posing a threat to the life of the mother![15]

THINK ABOUT THIS

The mother strode into the doctor's office carrying a bright and beautiful baby. Seating herself near her family physician, she said, "Doctor, I want you to help me with my problem. My baby is only one year old and I've conceived again. I don't want to have children so close together."

"Ah," he said, "and what would you have me do?"

"Oh, anything to get rid of it for me," she replied.

After thinking seriously about it for a moment, the doctor said, "I think I can suggest a better method. If you object to having two children so near to each other, the best solution would be to kill the one on your lap and to let the other one be born. It is very easy to get at the one on your lap, and it makes no difference to me which one I kill. Besides, it might be dangerous to your health if I undertook to kill the younger one."

With that, the doctor reached for a hatchet that was used to chop kindling and casually asked the mother to lay the baby on her lap and turn her head away. Not surprisingly, the woman almost fainted as she leaped from the chair and screamed, "Murderer!"

A few words of explanation from the doctor soon convinced her that his offer to commit murder was no worse than her request for him to destroy the unborn child. In either case, the act would be murder — the only difference would be in the age of the victim.

WITHIN THE WORD OF GOD

You can give it any name you want, but in God's Holy Word it is murder! All murder is wrong. In the Old Testament, even before the Mosaic law was delivered, God said, *"Whoso sheddeth man's blood, by man shall his blood be shed: for in the image of God made he man"* (Genesis 9:6).

Later, under the Mosaic law, God plainly commanded, *"He that smiteth a man, so that he die, shall be surely put to death"* (Exodus 21:12).

The death penalty for murder is also clearly implied in the New Testament. Romans 13:1-7 states that the ruler of the nation is the minister of God and he *"beareth not the sword in vain."* In the book of Revelation we are told that murderers shall never enter the heavenly Jerusalem (21:8 and 22:15).

To God, any unprovoked killing is murder, and the person guilty of murder is deserving of punishment. To Him there is no difference between the person who kills an unborn child and the person who pulls the trigger of a loaded gun.

The feminist argument that a woman has the right to do what she would like "with her own body" openly defies God's commandment concerning murder. It is certainly agreed that every individual has certain rights, but such rights never extend to the imposition of gross injustice on someone else.

Even though the unborn baby is supported and nurtured within the mother's body, it is a separate human being and must be protected — not only by the mother, but by society as well. If the mother refuses to protect the child, the medical profession must. If the medical profession refuses, laws must be established that will deliver true justice.

THE NAZI PHILOSOPHY

The butchers in Adolf Hitler's Nazi Germany, who slaughtered six million Jews in their gas ovens in Treblinka and Auschwitz and performed medical experiments on human beings, were a disgrace in the eyes of humanity.[16] But the Supreme Court and the physicians who now practice abortion in our land are no better than those Nazi butchers. One day they will answer to God.

In the future, broad-scale genetic engineering will probably be introduced in the United States.[17] Genetic engineering is the effort to "program" certain traits into a baby at conception, thereby creating a baby with desirable traits while "breeding out" undesirable ones. Naturally, the judgment of value or desirability is at the whim of individual likes or dislikes. Genetic engineering, or genetic manipulation, will be one of the most dramatic ethical issues facing our generation.[18] Scientists in the field have as their goal the ultimate control of man's biological destiny.

Cloning, which means to create a genetic duplicate of an individual organism through asexual reproduction (as by stimulating a single cell to reproduce) is one aspect of genetic engineering. Consider the clonal man: "Bill has no genetic mother. Because there was no mixing of genes from two heredities at his conception, Bill is his father's twin. He is truly a 'chip off the old block.' He not only looks like his father, in a hereditary sense he is his father with no chance of substantial variation."[19]

Sound like science fiction? Nevertheless, at this moment research is going forward on human cloning, and many scientists believe it will be achieved within the next 20 years.

In addition to genetic engineering, "sperm banks" are becoming more acceptable.[20] It is no longer necessary to find Mister Right to get the "kind" of baby you desire; all you need to do is buy his sperm from the sperm bank.

Then there are the "test-tube babies" and those born as a result of "fetal adoption," in which the human fetus of one woman is transplanted into the womb of another. We are told that this could become technologically feasible by the end of the 1980s.[21]

Strangely enough, at the same time scientists are searching for new ways to develop babies in test tubes and through fetal adoption and genetic engineering, millions of already formed babies are being murdered yearly. What type of thinking is this? What type of society can accept this type of bizarre reasoning?

Is there any difference between modern scientific experiments, wholesale abortion, and Hitler's crimes in World War II? I think not. The basic aims are identical. In each case, man attempts to play God.

In Genesis 11:5-8 we are told:

> *"And the Lord came down to see the city and the tower, which the children of men builded. And the Lord said, Behold, the people is one, and they have all one language; and this they begin to do: and now nothing will be restrained from them, which they have imagined to do. Go to, let us go down, and there confound their language . . . So the Lord scattered them abroad from thence upon the face of all the earth."*

I am concerned that men have once again reached the stage where "nothing will be restrained from them, which they have imagined to do." I also believe that God is about ready to come down and put a stop to it.

INFANTICIDE

And what about those who have been born but aren't able to function fully in society? Once murder has been fully accepted as a public problem solver, won't the sick, the feeble, the aged, and the retarded be next? Why not? They are certainly a problem and an expense to society.

When a nation strays from God, human life (which He considers sacred) loses value. Right now the life of the unborn baby lacks value because the power to attribute worth, based on relative and desirable qualities, has been delegated to the state. With this occurrence, a precedent has been set and the push for "quality control" will not stop with the fetus. (Isn't it amazing how controlled language can suppress the conscience?) By defining these precious lives as less than human, and therefore devoid of value and respect, they set the stage for another holocaust.

Isn't it enough that millions of babies have been brutally and painfully murdered? Already on the horizon, we see infanticide and euthanasia. Scores of the elderly, the handicapped, and others considered "less than human" will succumb to death at the hands of self-made gods claiming motives of mercy. One Nobel Prize-winning scientist has suggested that if a handicapped child "were not declared alive until three days after birth, then all parents could be allowed the choice that only a few are given under the present system. The doctor could allow the child to die if the parents so chose and save a lot of misery and suffering."[22]

Doctor C. Everett Koop, famous pediatric surgeon and Christian author, says, "This is infanticide. Infanticide in Great Britain usually means the killing of a newborn child by its mother, whereas infanticide in America means the killing of a born infant whether that death follows the withholding of something essential to the child's sustenance or a direct act. Infanticide is being practiced widely in Great Britain and the United States, but it is not a public issue in the sense that abortion and euthanasia are. Infanticide is carried out behind the protective facade of a hospital. The number of abnormalities, physical or mental, which seem to provide motivation for infanticide grows by the month. There seems to be a new, unwritten right developing in the minds of many — the right to a perfect child."[23]

It seems that everyone is clamoring for his rights. Some have gone so far as to promote "the right to die." Although different people use the phrase to mean different things, the bottom line is that death is not a right, but a fate we can't escape. Each of us expects to die and we can desire to die with dignity. However, promoters of the "right-to-die" philosophy actually endorse three very different concepts under the heading of "euthanasia."

"Euthanasia," strictly defined, means "mercy killing." A rhetorical smoke screen surrounds this matter, however. Today, euthanasia has been expanded to include "death with dignity" and "death selection."

DEATH SELECTION

Death with dignity essentially means allowing a terminally ill patient to die naturally rather than employing extraordinary means to preserve life. Mercy killing, on the other hand, not only allows the person to die, but actually assists him in dying by inducing painless death. Euthanasia is sometimes referred to as "the good death," assuming that contributing to a person's death is actually an "act of mercy."

In the case of death selection, babies considered hopelessly handicapped are left to die. Death selection is most commonly practiced in cases of Down's syndrome and spina bifida. Babies born with spina bifida have no skin or tissue over the spinal cord and nerves — and often the spinal cord is incomplete. Eighty percent have some degree of paralysis and urinary tract disorders. The complications are so devastating that many doctors advise against treatment.

Doctor Koop says, "To take a child who has an easily correctable lesion and to declare that his life is not worth living, and withhold food has to be called starvation. It's homicide. I suppose it's really infanticide in terms of the law."[24]

Doctor David G. McClone, neurosurgeon, has made Children's Memorial Hospital Clinic on Chicago's north side a national center for the surgery and care of spina bifida patients. He says, "Physicians by their code of ethics should not be dispensers of death. I'm appalled to hear a physician say that it may be justifiable under certain circumstances to deny a child food, water, and heat."[25]

There has recently been a heightened public concern about the adequacy of medical treatment for newborn infants with birth defects. It is becoming more common to allow infants to die than to treat their defects. The reported deaths of handicapped infants (such as those with Down's syndrome), who have been deliberately allowed to die by withholding treatment, has begun to shock the American public.

Infant homicide occurs daily in America through the willful withholding of medical-surgical care (and in some cases, by withholding food and water). One study at Yale-New Haven Medical Center showed that 14 percent of all infant deaths were related to withholding treatment.[26]

Even the most enthusiastic supporter of legalized abortion might not have pictured the quantum leap from abortion to infanticide. But then again, those who recommend abortion would probably use their same arguments to rationalize infanticide.

Consider the well-publicized case of Baby Doe. In April of 1982, an Indiana court allowed a six-day-old infant to be starved to death. The parents of the child refused surgery for their infant, a victim of Down's syndrome, to repair his deformed esophagus. It was a case of infanticide. If Mr. and Mrs. Doe had known their child would have been deformed and retarded, it presumably would have been a case of abortion instead.

The irony in the "Doe" case was that the court not only allowed the parents to evade their responsibilities, but also prevented anyone else from assuming them. At least 10 couples offered to adopt Baby Doe, but the court decreed that it was the right of the parents to let their baby die and this outweighed any rights the child might have had.[27]

John Whitehead declared, "Infanticide, once unthinkable, burst into the open and became thinkable — a reality!"[28] Our society now calls for death guidelines for Down's syndrome children, believing that saving the life of a Mongoloid idiot is imposing a supreme penalty on the family.

DEATH IN THE NURSERY

Carleton Sherwood, a Pulitzer Prize-winning journalist, produced an unsettling documentary, *Death in the Nursery,* concerning infanticide in our nation.[29] In collecting evidence for the documentary, he visited 20 different states and reviewed over 30,000 death certificates. The most controversial cases involved the deaths of children with Down's syndrome and spina bifida — and extremely premature infants where there were signs of possible mental impairment.

He reports accumulated evidence of over 100 bona fide cases of the withholding or withdrawing of medical treatment, including food and water. He further states, "We even found one chilling case of a Down's baby who died . . . not because he was starved . . . but because he was fed. He had a blockage of the bowel that the parents and doctors refused to repair. He died after 40 days of a distended abdomen and a perforated intestine."[30]

Once again, it's hard to escape the parallels between Nazi Germany and America. As in the Nazi "solution" to the Jewish problem, all humans are not given the right to life. In order to be granted the privilege of life in Nazi Germany, qualities other than "humanness" were required — and the Jews just didn't measure up. The same thing is happening to the millions of babies being "exterminated" in our nation today through abortion, infanticide, and euthanasia.

Man's philosophy dictates his practice! In some cases, we feel strongly that someone we love would be better off dead. It may seem to be an act of mercy to allow him to die, but we must examine our motives closely. Are we genuinely concerned about the loved one, or are we more concerned about the suffering *we* experience as we watch him?

We often look at handicapped people and pity them. Yet the handicapped feel normal — even if they may not *appear* that way. We tend to be discomfited by the confusion of the senile, but they are seldom aware of their own confusion. To judge whether someone's life is worth living, we need a wisdom beyond that of mere mortals. Nevertheless, there are those in positions of influence and authority who seem to claim this divine wisdom.

Sherwood and his associates point out that many physicians see little difference between aborting a handicapped child and ending that child's life after birth.[31] While, actually, this is true, it does seem that many have lost their sense of morality. Although these physicians may be excellent surgeons or excellent technicians, they can become enamored with the mechanics of their craft. They can then lose sight of what's *inside* the bodies on which they work.

Two such men are William Taeusch and Alex Haller, both leading neonatologists here in the United States. In fact, they are the head neonatologists of two of the leading medical schools in the country, Harvard and Johns Hopkins. They both argue for death injections and for the withholding of care.[32]

It may be difficult for some of us to get the full impact of what is happening in our land today as a result of the general loss of respect for life. But imagine this, as Sherwood proposes, "How would *you* like to wake up some morning after being put into a hospital, and see one of these men standing over you? Think about it. If you weren't able to verbalize, if you weren't able to tell them exactly what you wanted — what would it be like?"[33]

Amniocentesis (studying uterine fluids) and *pre*natal diagnosis are becoming common practices in medical centers. They are most commonly used to spot Down's syndrome children in order to abort them before birth or further development. Haller comments, "Now if you put it in that context, then what is the difference ethically from interrupting a Down's child in utero at 20 weeks versus deciding a Down's child born at 38 weeks shall be allowed to die?"[34]

He states it well. There *is* no difference. Both are murder! Of course, Haller would no doubt consider himself to be a humane person. In fact, he would assume that he is "doing the baby a favor." He adds that once society decides there are indications for not allowing the child to survive, "then the humane and ethical way to handle that would be to come up with some way of immediately allowing them to die. And you can make it a little bit more striking by saying 'some way to kill them.'"[35]

IN SUMMARY

Some time ago I heard a distinguished Jewish businessman commenting on the holocaust of Hitler's Germany. He stated that some of the people burned in Hitler's ovens might have held within their brains the cure for cancer or other great secrets which could have made valuable contributions to the human race. But they did not live to reveal these secrets.

I have often wondered: Of the millions of babies destroyed by a doctor's intervention or by their mother's selfishness, how many George Washingtons, Abraham Lincolns, D. L. Moodys, and Charles Finneys are being lost? Some argue that most would never rise to this stature. That's true, of course, but every one who does, makes the world a better place in which to live. We can't afford to lose even one Abraham Lincoln or Charles Finney.

Our nation must choose. We must either come *back* to God or stand condemned before Him. Our national position could conceivably become so perverted that it will cause God to turn His back upon the

United States of America. Someone said a long time ago that if God didn't judge this country, He was going to have to apologize to Sodom and Gomorrah. I am sadly convinced that the tide is indeed rolling toward our destruction.

The abortion issue concerns every one of us. Though you may recoil at the very thought of abortion, failure to speak out against it is tacit approval. Unless Bible-believing Christians arise in righteous indignation, every freedom will be stripped away, one by one, until the only freedom left will be the freedom to die.

The Christian community stands as an appalling parallel to the church in Nazi Germany. A tragic element in Nazi death camps was the denial of individual responsibility.[36] They transferred blame to the state, considering it to be an "authority ordained by God."

Christians, though used to being obedient to those in authority, must recognize that God's law supercedes man's law. When a government requires its people to bow to Baal, it is time to take a stand for righteousness and to speak out for the cause of Christ. No man, woman, or child who truly loves God would intentionally participate in the American holocaust — but it is *silence* that allows the onslaught to continue. Remember, "all that is necessary for the triumph of evil is that good men do nothing."

The truth is, the value we place upon life will be reflected by our actions — or lack of action.

A physician related the following:

"She had a number tattooed on her arm when I examined her. The origin of the tattoo was obvious and familiar — Buchenwald. I asked her if she would like to have it removed by plastic surgery, but she declined. She said she would wear it to the grave, for it was her diploma from the school of life. 'Doctor,' she said, 'I don't know where *you* learned what life is, but I know where I learned it. I don't even step on cockroaches now.'"[37]

THE VANISHING FAMILY

"The family in its old sense is disappearing from our land, and not only our free institutions are threatened but the very existence of our society is endangered."

Although that observation appeared in the *Boston Quarterly Review* in 1859, it *could* have been written yesterday.

Our children are hoisting distress signals. Their confusion, bouts of senseless destruction, fits of temper, depression, displays of sullen indifference, and lawless acts tell us they are in trouble. *They* know things aren't right, and they're pleading for us to take charge. We mustn't ignore their cries for help by passing them off as mere "stages" of growth. More significantly, they are individual symptoms that mirror parallel disorders in most of society.

In structuring society, God created three great institutions: the church, the family, and the state (the government). Each plays a vital role in order and survival as well as in individual freedom and comfort. Combined, they constitute the world's best defense against Satan's plot to take over the world.

Now one may assume that the church (the body of Christ) is God's most important institution. And, of course, the state is important because a nation must have organization to prevent anarchy and chaos. But God created the family first — in the Garden of Eden — at the time He created Adam and Eve. The family was therefore the primary institution on which God placed His divine seal of approval.

Not only is the family the *oldest institution* in society, it is also the basic element of a society. As such, it is clearly God's most important institution. It has been said, and correctly, "As the home goes, so goes the nation."

What God has ordained as the primary building block of our society, Satan attacks. He has unleashed the powers of hell, doing everything possible to destroy the family because he knows it's the very foundation and fiber of civilization. As a result, many homes are in a state of confusion and disarray.

Although Satan will not succeed in his plan to eradicate the family, steps must be taken to preserve its dignity, its unity, and its very ability to lend character to unformed young lives.

For a family to survive and function effectively, certain elements are required that are necessary for success in any type of organized group. They are organization, clearly defined responsibilities, and discipline. With these factors present and operating, the family will function most effectively. *Without* them, there will be division, lack of unity, and a condition perhaps approaching anarchy. Knowing this, Satan wages his greatest attack on the family structure in precisely these three areas.

Therefore, in most homes today, the name of the game is confusion. Everyone is dedicated only to staking out *his* rights, *his* privileges, and *his* independence. There's no head, no authority figure, no consistency in discipline and organization. The average American family today is a shambles, and this regrettably includes many *Christian* families.

AS THE INCUBATOR OF GODLY ADULTS

A family has the important job of building people and not just in training children to be Godly, disciplined individuals. The family is responsible for developing character in *all* members as they live and work together. In effect, the family is the child's introduction to marriage and all civic duties and relationships. It is an *atmosphere* where sobriety, reverence, kindness, and love should seep into his very being. It will be his training ground — for good or for evil. Ultimately it is the mold for the single brick that *could* end up the keystone of the whole local society.

In a poll of 200,000 readers conducted by *Better Homes and Gardens* in August of 1983, an astonishing 80 percent said that family life in America is in trouble. When the readers were asked about their own families, they considered their family problems common to the times rather than specific to themselves.

However, I submit that many of the problems faced by families today are nothing more than a magnification of problems within the parents. Society's ills represent a vicious cycle. Morally and spiritually, our society is a shambles. Families disintegrate at an alarming rate. Our children suffer the loss of innocence. New problems loom on the horizon every day. Our only hope for survival is a return to the basics and a rededication to Godly principles.

MARRIAGE

Marriage is one of the basics, the importance of which can't be overemphasized. It is a holy and beautiful institution, ordained and approved by God for man's good and happiness — and, incidentally, for God's glory. Nevertheless, an awesome problem confronts us today, for nearly 50 percent of all marriages find their way to the divorce court. This means that 40 percent of all children are growing up in homes where either the man is not their natural father or the woman is not their natural mother.

It is predicted that by 1990, up to 50 percent of all children will have experienced divorce and remarriage in their families.[1] If present trends continue, the next century will see the dominance of step-families. "What once was thought of as bad, distasteful, or unfortunate — the step-family — will become very normal," says child psychologist Kent Ravenscroft.[2]

Many marriages fail because they lack a key ingredient — commitment. Experts say the institution of marriage is dead because men and women don't need marriage — not for financial security, love, sex, or fulfillment. It's not even necessary in order to have children.

"Marriage is virtually universal and will remain so in our society," argues Arthur Norton of the Census Bureau. The real change, he suggests, is that "there is an awareness now that marriage doesn't have to have permanence if it isn't working out according to the desires and expectations of the people involved. It can be ended and re-entered."[3]

A high divorce rate will seemingly be a predictable part of America's future.

Scripture clearly demonstrates that marriage *is* a lifetime commitment and relationship between one man and one woman. Any person entering into marriage without commitment to the principle that marriage is for a lifetime may be heading down a path of moral degeneration and spiritual death. Such a marriage can prove to be the first chapter in a long, depressing, and sordid series of temporary, tragic relationships. And almost inevitably it is the children from such a union who suffer the greatest damage.

Senator Jeremiah Denton declares, "The family is now at a worse period of crisis than ever before in our nation's history."

"MODERN" FAMILIES

Whereas the "typical" American family has long been defined as a working husband, a housekeeping wife, and two children, today only *seven percent* of the total United States population fits this "average" mold.[4] Instead, the modern family may consist of any variety of combinations. In addition, sociologists see a growth of nonfamily households. One psychologist concludes, "The notion of the husband being the breadwinner and the wife being the homemaker will become irrelevant — a historical curiosity."[5]

The bewildering array of family forms includes homosexual marriages, communes of close friends, groups of elderly people banding together to share expenses (and sometimes sex), unmarried couples, and a growing number of single parents. These are all a result of the disintegrating family structure and of the subsequent moral decay.

Family surveys disclose many disturbing figures. The number of children living with a single parent has doubled since 1960. Estimates show that 45 percent of all children born in 1977 will live in a single-parent home at some time before reaching the age of 18.[6]

The percent of woman-headed households has almost doubled since 1970. Almost one home in five now has a woman as its head.[7] In addition, the number of persons living *alone* increased by 75 percent between 1970 and 1982.[8] More than 666,000 children were born out of wedlock in 1982, four times as many as those born out of wedlock in 1950.[9] There are 1.9 million documented "live-in" households in the U. S. now — four times the number of 1970.[10] The real figure may be closer to three million.

"One thing to be said for having a baby out of wedlock is that he'll never have to suffer through his parents' divorce," says a 32-year-old salesclerk from San Jose, California. After four miscarriages during her two failed marriages, a casual affair with a married man resulted in her present pregnancy. "We're better off just you and me," she coos at her baby. "Not you, me, and a man who will leave us."[11]

Between 1970 and 1982, the number of one-parent families headed by never-married women rose by a startling 367 percent.[12] That's alarming! If a family is to be what God expects it to be, and is to fulfill its highest purpose, there must be the marriage of one husband and one wife. Each of these partners must assume full responsibility for making the marriage work and for assuring the proper development of a functioning family.

WHERE WILL IT END?

On the other hand, Harvard University psychiatrist Alvin Poussaint asserts, "The psychological impact of serial marriage and of daycare will mean that many more people will be involved in raising a child, giving the child more options, role models, and support. It can be very positive. It will mean that people must be more communal and cooperative."[13] Do *you* believe that? It sounds a little like whistling in the graveyard to me.

Growing children require direction and balance, and that can best be given by parents who function as a team and present a united front. God, in His divinely established pattern, assigns specific responsibilities to both the husband and wife in roles which are *complementary.* Both, working together, accomplish goals which neither could attain separately. It's a partnership in which they should ideally function as one.

When children see that their parents trust each other, treat each other with respect, and consider each other's needs and wishes, they will grow up to value marriage as an institution that provides emotional satisfaction and security.

It is also necessary to distinguish between the roles of the parent and the child. In spite of those who bemoan the generation gap, a definite distinction between the roles of the parent and the child should be a normal and healthy part of their relationship. The generation gap lessens the danger of role conflict in the child and gives him room to develop free from competition with a parent.

Failure to maintain the generational boundaries is a major source of mental disturbance in children. "The sudden shift of social ground rules today, the smudging of roles, status distinctions, and lines of authority, the immersion in blip culture and, above all, the breakup of the great thought-system, industreality, have shattered the world-image most of us carry around in our skulls. In consequence, most people surveying the world around them today see only chaos. They suffer a sense of personal powerlessness and pointlessness."[14]

When a parent carries out the fundamental functions related to his respective gender-linked roles, he provides one of the most significant factors in guiding the child's development as a boy or girl. Though the functions of mothers and fathers are changing somewhat, clear-cut role reversals furnish the children images of masculinity and femininity that are culturally deviant. It is in the child's best interest that each parent adequately fill his own gender-linked function and accept and support his spouse in his or her role.

An acceptance of this truth is of the utmost importance in building self-esteem within a child. Unless each parent is comfortable in his role, the child will not feel good about himself. In addition, children *want* a parental authority figure they can look to for direction, for correction, for guidance, and for someone they can be *proud* of.

Today's confused society — generated largely by "intellectual" child psychologists with little common sense — has so blurred normal familial divisions that a great number of overt problems have developed. While the great thinkers of our society pride themselves on the "giant strides" made in "emancipating" children, a quick look around at society will demonstrate their utter failure to produce positive results.

In many cases, it is actually the parents who bridge the gap. Some parents allow normal barriers to be removed because the child can supply psychological needs the spouse doesn't: sympathy, understanding, encouragement, and so forth. Other parents (through emotional immaturity) may allow an actual rivalry to develop with their children, manifesting itself in such areas of immaturity as the father entering into athletic or physical-strength contests with sons or the mother actually acting coquettishly and challenging her daughter's relationships with boyfriends.

One of the most common threats to a healthy child-parent division is the oft-recommended (by misguided psychologists) aberration of "becoming a pal to your child." Actually, it is good for the parent to be a *friend* to the child, but any efforts to move down to his level and become one of his "pals" is instantly recognized by the child as unnatural and inevitably makes the child uncomfortable. Children *need* pals who, being as immature and lacking in experience and wisdom as they are, can identify with their problems in coping with the world. Adults should have enough wisdom and experience to be beyond this stage, however, and the pal role is therefore impossible for them to fulfill.

Finally, and regrettably, child-parent barriers are broken in cases of incest or near-incest. This sordid, tragic, and regrettable situation is simply unacceptable, and the most extreme steps must be taken to correct it where it exists.

SOMEONE TO LOOK UP TO

Children desire heroes; unfortunately, they seldom see parents as those heroes. A poll of 2,000 eighth-grade American students shows that most admire (and want to grow up to be like) entertainers and sports figures. According to the poll (by the *World Almanac and Book of Facts*), the leading role model was actor Burt Reynolds (the "macho" image). Other favorites were Alan Alda, Steve Martin, and the late John Belushi.[15]

Just recently, the headmaster of a Christian school, interested in the aforementioned poll, asked the students who their heroes were. The answers were varied, with some similar to the original poll, but one boy answered, "My mother and dad." Naturally, his answer was a source of joy and pride to his parents when they heard of it.

Many voices of this world call out to our children and bid for their attention. The example set by parents determines to a large degree which voices the child will attend to and which he will ignore or reject. If this example fails him, he is left with nothing. Morals, behavior, social control — all guidelines on these areas are lost, and he is cast adrift with no sense of direction.

In view of society's disintegration under the distorted and hamstrung remnant of traditional family life — designed and imposed by "enlightened" social planners — we would expect to witness a plea for a return to the values that built this nation. But do we? No. Instead, these social planners call for *abolition* of the family. Instead of accepting blame for their own failure, they attempt to transfer blame to God's tattered remnant of normal family life. These anarchistic social planners say that the problem lies in restraints imposed by what remains of family life and that only complete freedom will allow the "future progress" to which they look forward.

They argue that the family's attempt to establish values in the child interferes with the spontaneous, uninfluenced development of the child who, therefore, can never be truly free. Individuals who espouse this evil humanistic thinking fail to appreciate that a child *cannot* grow up uninfluenced by adults and that the undirected freedom they advocate can lead only to the child's death — or at least to a nonhuman type of existence.

With a generation already reeling under the onslaught of their early methods, will we be gullible enough to give the social planners complete license to demolish society?

Ironically, the more society falls apart under such senseless leadership, the more it looks to these mad tutors for guidance. The more the new moral code tears society apart, the more our older citizens lose confidence in the principles that *used* to work. Is this an accident? No, it is one of the basic Marxist principles that *confusion* should be generated and that the ordinary citizen should be convinced that there are *no* absolutes.

In attempting to destroy God, you must first destroy faith. Rather than going head-to-head with God, you start by destroying faith in principles, institutions, and accepted moral codes. When you've got the populace reeling under repeated onslaughts against every accepted institution, it's *easy* to transplant doubt into their fear and confusion — doubt in their faith in *God*.

A LIVING EXAMPLE

Even under the most ideal circumstances, rearing the young is a task fraught with uncertainty for both the young *and* the society that must absorb them. When you destroy the parent's confidence in his ability to do his job, everything is compounded. That's the situation we're living in today.

It is crucial that parents serve as *living examples* of the principles they want to teach, or impress. The parent who would teach morality must first *be* moral. The parent who would teach his child temperance must be temperate himself. The parent who would teach his child obedience to God must, of course, be *personally* obedient to God.

While every child possesses the *capacity* for good, his unformed potential must be nurtured and directed. The honest example the parents show serve as a lifelong example to the child. How does the parent handle disappointment, frustration, or anxiety? The child's developing personality will follow his example. Beyond this, kids need answers to questions, and they need *honest* answers. Will the parent use his own mistakes as examples, or will he try to project an impression that he was perfect as a youngster? Children will see through attempts at distortion and interpret it as hypocrisy. Children *return* love, trust, and honesty. If this isn't projected *to* them, it won't come beaming back.

Our children are tomorrow's society. Our nation's future can be only as strong as the children we build *today*. It is every parent's responsibility to train his children in a way that is pleasing to the Lord. Children, as a heritage of the Lord, can be a very special blessing *if* parents dedicate their homes as the training ground for learning moral values. With determination and commitment parents can rear morally responsible children, even in a society which shows little interest in moral responsibility — where nothing is right or wrong anymore, and *anything goes*.

The Word of God is the world's primary instrument for moral development, but children are growing up without it because our schools and colleges have rejected the Bible. As a result, most children know nothing about the Word of God. Instead, their young minds are saturated with the filth that is spewed out over television and that literally fills the pages of just about everything printed today. They are growing up in spiritual darkness. Some commit truly terrible crimes and show no sign of remorse. Millions of others resort to drugs or alcohol as their single "source of truth" — even in the preteen years.

We've seen a generation of children who have been brought up to have no respect for God, parents, country, or traditions. They have no respect for *anything*. Should it surprise us, then, when they end up in lives of crime?

What can we expect when the home fails as the source of moral qualities, principles, and habits? The home is the last bastion of decency

— and all too many homes fail in this area, too. Our nation labors under grave difficulties today because morality, spirituality, sound principles, and desirable qualities are *not* being taught and developed by the family. Children need correction and training if they are to become moral and decent adults.

THE FATHER'S ROLE

Children need guidance in developing values. They need to feel that their father makes his decisions based on moral principles. The influence the father exerts will remain long after the children leave home.

The first (and perhaps the longest lasting) influence of the father will be his attitude toward work. If he shirks or complains about work (either his job or his chores at home), the children will sense what *their* attitude should be toward work. Once established, this attitude can persist throughout life, to the good or ill of the child and of society as a whole.

Then there's the father's moral performance. It's one thing to talk about moral issues, but how does the father handle them day by day? "Do as I say but not as I do" doesn't work with kids. Fathers should leave preaching to preachers and work at being examples to their children.

And the same goes for the father's relationship with God. The father whose relationship with God lasts for an hour on Sunday shouldn't expect even that much from his offspring. A real, day-by-day, hour-by-hour relationship with God is easily passed along. Anything less can be interpreted as hypocrisy.

TODAY'S WORKPLACE

Children need to be taught to work and to expect reward for genuine effort. Many problems face our nation today because a generation has been reared to believe that work is "undignified." Work is a virtue; it is one of the basic building blocks of character.

In numerous ways, people are being taught and encouraged *not* to work — by our government and by other social forces. It is a tragedy that many of the most influential elements in our society hinder the work ethic and encourage "feather-bedding," and that they more and more pay for less and less work. These are the standard policies of just about every labor union in the country, however. Many labor groups want everything reduced to the lowest possible level of activity — which often results in a prevention of the energetic and capable individual from producing what he might.

An article in *Time* stated, "During the past 25 years, millions of students have received Federal Government loans to help defray their college expenses. But 1.5 million of them have since flunked a *morality* test: they have failed to repay their debts, leaving Uncle Sam holding the bag for $1.8 billion."[16]

It was found, through a computer search conducted by Education Department officials, that 46,000 federal employees were among the defaulters. Although 5,000 promptly paid up $2.3 million, the remaining 41,000 must either pay up within 30 days or have their wages garnished at the rate of 15 percent per paycheck.

Realizing that irresponsibility is the problem, the government is negotiating plans with credit bureaus to put added pressure on debtors. It appears that a measure may be put into effect that would place a black mark on the credit ratings of citizens who are behind in repaying government loans.

On the other hand, many of today's youngsters need help in separating those with truly successful lives from those merely "making money." Our society tends to view success as the ability to pile up money and translate it into fame, status, or power. This is usually accompanied by displays of unabashed self-indulgence in life-styles. It has produced a society which will hardly fund medical research, but which makes millionaires out of athletes and rock stars. It sends confusing signals to young people who really want their talents and lives to mean something.

The present-day pressure to adopt purely materialistic goals is so common that parents *must* help their children evaluate the current shallow perceptions about basic values.

SECURITY

A child needs a sense of security. Security doesn't refer just to protection; it means being comfortable inside yourself and being able to relate to others — at play, at school, at work, and in *all* situations.

The child's sense of security is inseparable from his relationship with his parents. No other element influences him so importantly throughout the critical development years. It is the family that must provide the child with a secure base from which to venture out into the world.

Security grows as the child recognizes that things are done harmoniously within the family, and that all is controlled with reasonable authority. Of course, the idea of authority involves discipline. The child who knows the restraint of logical rules knows the feeling of honest concern and love. Children know equally well that "freedom" often translates as parents who aren't interested enough to care.

When one is properly curbed and instructed as a child, he learns to curb himself as he grows. When a child learns to submit to authority at home, he will submit to the authority of the school, of the government, and of God. The reason thousands (and probably millions) of children will not submit to the authority of their teachers or the government is that they never learned discipline at home.

We live in a wicked and perverse generation. If the adults of our society are undisciplined and bent on nothing but pleasure, how can we expect disciplined, healthy children? Unfortunately, many homes exhibit an almost total lack of discipline.

LOVE

Many homes also exhibit an almost total lack of love. As a direct result, we live in a day when juvenile delinquency is rampant. Many teenage (and even subteen) girls and boys work as prostitutes in larger cities. Over half the babies born of teenage mothers are illegitimate. Young children smoke, drink, take drugs, and involve themselves with immoral and criminal activities. It is a cancerous growth in America!

It is a manifestation of the terrible harvest to be reaped when a nation fails to follow the ways of the Word of God. This trend has been magnified by the "enlightened" attitude of a generation of educators who have frowned on discipline of any kind. Thank God, we are beginning to get back to discipline, even if in only a small way.

A child who is *lovingly* disciplined respects and loves his parents more than the child who is *un*disciplined. There is something within the child that makes him realize that a parent who takes the trouble to administer discipline is a parent who *loves*.

Our nation will rise or fall on its children. If today's parents and homes were to return to old-fashioned, Old Testament teachings, we would have fewer juvenile delinquents, fewer pregnant girls, fewer kids on drugs, and fewer of the wrecked lives that result from these departures from God's morality. God holds the parent responsible for disciplining, controlling, and shaping the child.

Dave Wilkerson, who has worked with thousands of young people, believes that kids do not hate their parents nearly as much as they hate their parents' hypocrisy. He adds that parents can't be strict with their children if they live undisciplined lives.[17] Teenagers don't respect weak parents.

One young person expressed it this way. "As a young child in a Christian home, I didn't start out with an understanding of the word *discipline*. I simply knew that I belonged to people who loved and cared for me. That is dependence. They spoke to me and I answered. That is responsibility. They gave me things to do, and I did them. That is obedience. And it all adds up to discipline."

Some parents unfairly provoke their children to wrath! Children cheated of firm discipline, honest restrictions, and responsibilities appropriate to their age are bundles of dynamite waiting to blow up. Many lash out at parents, condemning them for their lack of morality. Even worse, some retaliate by rebelling against *all* authority, or even by hurting innocent bystanders.

Whether parents realize it or not, they stand in their children's eyes as God's authority figure on earth. As such, they are to instruct their children in the ways of the Lord. Parents must punish sin and reward righteousness. They must establish the fear of God as an integral part of the normal training process. Instruction and correction, as well as love, prayers, and tears, must be expended on the development of every child. Parents can't neglect their responsibility in preparing their children for life (and for heaven) without facing dire consequences. The state *is not* God's authority figure.

Despite concern over the crisis in the American family, many government agencies "have not only undermined the family but have endorsed programs and policies antagonistic to the traditional family unit," says John Whitehead, in *The Stealing of America*.[18] Parents, on the other hand, have assisted the state in its takeover by consciously or unconsciously surrendering their rights, along with their responsibilities. In many instances, the family has become little more than a pawn in the hands of the state.

The "Big Brother" of *1984* has become a reality. George Orwell shocked the public with his predictions that public leaders, judges, and committees would exert even greater power in decision-making. He predicted a time when people would no longer have the right to privacy or to decide what was best for themselves and their families. That time has come.

Demographer Joseph McFalls, of Temple University, explains, "Although this sounds like science fiction, it's really not so unusual for one institution, such as the family, to give up some of its functions to another, such as the government. Families used to be responsible for the education of children and the care of the aged; the government does both now."[19]

A recent article in *U. S. News and World Report* assures us that the government will become more involved with the family than ever before. The government will also control the manipulation of genetic engineering techniques that hold the potential for altering the characteristics of babies.[20]

Another recent news article entitled "Mourning the Loss of a Son" reports a case in which the state took a 16-year-old mentally handicapped son away from his parents.[21] Although there was no evidence of abandonment, abuse, or neglect, a California judge took him away from his parents and gave him (together with his assets) to another family.

The new family had petitioned the court for guardianship and persuaded the judge that they could make better choices for him than his own family. In essence, it was a case in which the government assumed the right to make decisions that would normally be made by the parents.

The Department of Health and Rehabilitative Services (HRS) puts out a brochure entitled "Child Abuse and Neglect in Florida."[22] It urges people to report any *suspected* case of child abuse. It also promises immunity from civil or criminal liability for the accuser. Further, those reporting such incidents will not have to face the parents, nor will they be identified to the parents.

Now at first glance, it may sound like a benevolent system. But consider this: Under such a system, children may be taken from parents if a disgruntled neighbor or relative accuses the parent of child abuse or if there is the *slightest* reason for the welfare worker to believe that the parent has abused the child.

It isn't just the sexual abusers or the true fiends they're after. The brochure reads, "Any punishment that involves hitting with a closed fist or an instrument represents abuse.'' Remember, the humanists of the HRS are against the loving, but firm, discipline of a Godly parent. By definition, a tiny *switch* can remove your child from your home in Florida.

In various ways, the state exploits the breakdown in traditional parent-child relationships by driving a greater wedge between the parent and child. For a generation grown up in near anarchy, they no longer know how to relate to a normal family situation.

More than ever, children are turning to their peers for relationships. Although peer relationships have always been important in the development of the young person, the move away from parental relationships makes the young person even more vulnerable to the monster of "peer pressure." Eventually the situation must end up with the blind leading the blind.

Considering the pressures that are brought to bear on our young people today and the seeming infinity of temptations open to them, parental guidance and restraint become especially necessary. Children need the benefit of a wisdom that comes only with maturity. They need a mother and father who fulfill their God-ordained functions with dedication and who are comfortable in their respective roles. Children need to receive the kind of love and nurturing that only *both* parents can provide.

DESTRUCTIVE NEW TRENDS —
THE MOM AND POP EXAMPLE

Some destructive new trends in our society appear to be producing a new breed of parents. Mothers, pressured by the demands of a career, may be too exhausted and frustrated to be anything but cold and unyielding. And fathers, feeling no longer needed as protectors and providers, become weak and ineffectual. As a result, not only do parents fail to provide for their children's deepest emotional needs, they also fail to support one another through the fulfilling of their complementary roles.

While the mother is usually the more important parent early in the child's development, her relationship requires a total family setting to be effective. The father is also important early and becomes increasingly so as the child grows older. What is very important is the mother's need for support in order to transmit love and affection. She also needs the father's support in replenishing her own needs. In most families, it is the husband who supplies such needs.

The relationship between a mother and her child is an especially important one. When it is mutually rewarding to both of them, an atmosphere develops in which the child's immediate well-being, as well as future development, is enhanced. The mother's devotion and consistent attention to the child's needs provide him with a fundamental sense of confidence and security.

As the child "blossoms" under such tender loving care, he in turn causes the mother to feel successful and competent. She feels a sense of pride in her child's growing ability to learn and adapt. Because of her love and attachment to her child, all the efforts involved seem worthwhile. Of course, the child begins to feel "special" — loved and cared for.

We simply cannot overestimate the power of positive contact or nurturing. The time a mother spends playing with her child, kissing and hugging him, praising him, and talking and singing to him, become tremendously important in creating an atmosphere in which the child can grow and learn properly.

WHERE HAVE ALL THE YOUNG MEN GONE?

Homosexuality is a tremendous problem within our nation today. According to a nationally known authority on the subject, the background of homosexuals fits a common pattern. Father is frequently absent from the home, and thus mother turns to the boy as an outlet for her emotional needs. Psychiatrists agree that they never see homosexuals who have good relationships with their fathers. In fact, Dr. Erwin Bieber, acclaimed as one of the most authoritative students of homosexuality in America, said, "Homosexuals are not born that way, they are made that way, largely by their parents."[23]

This fact suggests the solution. "The best way to stamp out homosexuality in this country is for parents to get back to the business of making parenthood their priority. Children raised in loving, well-disciplined homes — where mother and father are themselves good role models for their children — rarely become homosexuals. Unfortunately, unloved children subjected to the selfish neglect of their parents are vulnerable to a predisposition towards homosexuality."[24]

WOMEN'S LIB

The child has many needs specifically related to his father. They fall under the heading of "leadership," and the Bible always portrays the father as the leader. Although there are women who dominate in home situations, the problem is usually that of the wife taking charge by default. If the husband won't run a family, the wife *must*. We seem to have developed a whole generation of weak-sister husbands.

The dedicated parent, acting out his or her normal role of father (male) or mother (female), is the best model children can have upon which to build a comfortable and normal sex role for themselves. Today's society, where male and female roles are blurred, causes confusion and is a major factor in producing the explosion of sexual perversion today. The most *normal* children will grow up in homes where the father is a *man*, where the mother is a *woman*, and where each is comfortable and satisfied with the normal, God-given roles they are expected to fill.

THE UNISEX IMAGE

There is today a definite trend toward "androgyny," the state of being indistinguishable as male or female. The androgyny theory — also known as unisex — is considered by some to be an "ideal stage" of development. It refers to the common ground that can be found in both male and female social behavior. It promotes an ending of sex roles based on traditional patterns, claiming that these behavioral differences are based not on nature but on people's learned responses to what they feel society *expects* of them.

Androgyny supposedly presents a more flexible way of adapting to the demands of the environment. But it is uncomfortable and confusing for younger members of society.

Unless men and women understand and accept their God-given roles in the family and in society, our children will continue to suffer. Because of woman's desire to change her identity (as well as her role in society), there have been efforts to erase the old differences in the ways boys and girls are reared. Such changes can have far-reaching effects that are impossible to predict. The elimination of natural differences between the functions of men and women in society will have enormous repercussions throughout the coming years.

There are any number of social changes that are altering the very fabric of society. These include migration, industrial changes, "scientific" intrusion into child-rearing, and the tearing down of traditional moral values. These have all influenced the breakdown of the family structure, but perhaps *more* important is the revolt of our women against their traditional roles.

THE FEMINIST MOVEMENT

Radical feminism is a movement rooted in bitterness and resentment. It is an immoral blight on our nation and a threat to the Judeo-Christian tradition, cherished by so many for so long. Its perverse ideology attacks the lives of our children, our own civil liberties, and the survival of the family itself.

On August 26, 1970, thousands of women in dozens of cities celebrated the fiftieth anniversary of women's suffrage.[25] In New York they set up a child care center in City Hall Park to dramatize the need for universal day-care. In Boston they handed out cans of contraceptive foam to protest laws restricting the availability of birth control products.

In San Francisco and Los Angeles they took over radio stations (with the approval of management) and devoted the day to talks on women's liberation. In Washington, D. C., they lobbied with senators for passage of an Equal Rights Amendment (ERA) for women. And in Rochester, New York, they staged a mock tea party at the home of Susan B. Anthony — and then smashed their teacups to symbolize the end of woman's traditional role in society.

What might have begun as a sincere desire for legitimate status has turned into a movement motivated by evil selfishness and pride. The majority of women watch with embarrassment and bewilderment. If they decide to choose the traditional and necessary role of homemaker, they are lampooned — even though they, too, may be searching for personal fulfillment.

Of course, this shouldn't surprise us. NOW (the National Organization for Women) was the primary force behind the push for the passage of the ERA before it was defeated. Its goals are to promote lesbian rights, reproductive rights including abortion, and sex education in the schools.

Behind Satan's plot to destroy the family is the religion that blinds and exploits its adherents — secular humanism. Man's efforts to seize

God's instrument (the family) by using *man's* methods have failed miserably. Although the disappearance of the traditional American family presents some serious problems, it is premature to announce its death. Life is a great deal like a mirror. Nothing comes out of that mirror except what we first project *into* it. We won't find a smiling face in that mirror if we're *scowling* when we look into it.

The family is sacred, and as such can't be tossed out just because we're bored with it. It takes commitment and effort to maintain healthy, satisfying relationships within a family. But God is on our side. *He* wants each family and its members to prosper and grow.

It's true that many forces come against the family to destroy it, but we can't become discouraged. We must instead *fortify* our homes to withstand the coming assault. And, in the midst of difficult times, rejoice! If we commit ourselves to God's plan — which includes organization, discipline, and proper authority — the family will be a place to grow, a center for creativity, a place of security and safety, and the base for learning moral and spiritual values.

As long as the family reflects glory on God, He will preserve and protect it!

A STRANGE GOD

In March of 1939, a group of media representatives and a handful of casual observers witnessed a decisive moment. A signal, sent from a transmitter atop the Empire State Building, passed through the airwaves to a tiny receiver in the RCA exhibit on the site of the New York World's Fair at Flushing Meadows, Long Island. This 40-mile transmission of "pictures through the air" went almost unnoticed and was thought by many to be nothing more than a scientific curiosity.

Although the small and hazy picture was recognizable, it hardly excited observers with a potential for commercial success. A *New York Times* reporter offered the opinion that the American public would never accept "television" as an entertainment medium because it would demand mental concentration and inactivity on the part of the viewer. Americans just don't have the time for something of this type, he observed.

How wrong he was! The statistics on television viewing are absolutely *awesome* when weighed against the return — the *positive* effects — delivered to those willing to sit glued to their sets. Consider these facts:[1]

- The *average* American family watches more than 6½ hours of television (often referred to as TV) *every day.*

- *Children* watch an average of 26 hours of TV per week, or almost four hours per day.

- By the time the average child finishes high school he will have spent more hours watching TV than attending school.

- At any moment during prime time (evenings and weekends), at least 38 *million* sets are tuned in — irrespective of the quality or content of what is being broadcast.

- More American homes have television than have telephones or indoor plumbing.

- More than 98 percent of American homes have a functioning TV set.

- Almost half of American homes have *more than one TV.*

- More than half of American homes have a *color* TV.

- Of American families with an income of less than $5,000 per year, one-third have a *color* TV.

Impressive — or frightening? The single *fact* to be gleaned from the aforementioned statistics is that television has inundated and overwhelmed the Western world to a degree that would have been considered impossible at its inception.

In the early days of television, this medium was held out as a great *hope* for mankind, a means of disseminating knowledge to those unable to afford — or assimilate — knowledge delivered through conventional sources. And has it lived up to this great expectation? It has without question. The only problem lies in the *type* of knowledge being purveyed. Let's look at just what is being broadcast, who makes the decisions, and what the motives are *behind* the information being disseminated to the American public.

AN OVERWHELMING SOCIAL INFLUENCE

While historians have divided the various segments of man's development into ages (the Stone Age, the Bronze Age, the Atomic Age, et cetera), the most revealing division may well be into "pre- and post-television ages." Why this particular classification? Because, for the first time in all of history, the *entire population* (meaning *all classes of society*) has been exposed to one common and all-pervasive influence. For the first time in history, all individuals in the nation are being exposed to the same influences as all *other* individuals.

Now think about this for a moment. Down through the centuries, society has been divided into a number of categories and components. Society is made up of those with high school educations, college educations, and postgraduate degrees; it is made up of labor and management, officers and enlisted men, chiefs and Indians, and on and on. There has been an upper class, a middle class, and a lower class; suburbs and inner cities; highbrows and lowbrows. There have been the ins and the outs, the special interests, and the common people.

Now what's so important about all this? The more divergent a society, the more *balance* there is to that society as the various levels, factions, and interests *average out* their sources of information and their aspirations to arrive at a good, logical, and *balanced* level of community actions and decisions.

Of course, the removal of this wide range of inputs and influences in favor of a single, all-inclusive, and dominant influence can be good or bad — depending on the motives (and effectiveness) of that influence. If a force for morality, Godliness, and righteousness were to take over the world (as it will when the Lord returns to set up His millennial kingdom), it would be the beginning of a new age comparable to what was *lost* when Adam and Eve fell in the garden. On the other hand, if the all-pervasive force were of questionable — or overtly negative — influence, the results could be catastrophic. And where on its record does our national television industry stand? Let's look at the record.

MEDIA ATTITUDES

All media personnel are extremely sensitive to the issue of censorship. "Freedom of the press" is recognized as one of the fundamentals of American freedom and is guaranteed in the Bill of Rights. A "controlled press" is considered to be something reprehensible — a feature of totalitarian regimes, but certainly not to be found in the nation that stands as the flagship of all that is noble and progressive in the area of freedom, equality, and liberty. Unfortunately, we do *not* have freedom of the press, and we *do* have a rigidly controlled media — although by the very forces who cry out loudest whenever there is even the slightest *suggestion* of control or repression of "freedom of speech."

The truth of the matter is that all elements of the media are almost exclusively controlled by one minority segment of our populace: the liberal, secular humanists. A strong, perhaps biased, statement? Let's look at the facts and then decide.

If, from any segment of our society (representing society as a whole), we draw a representative cross section, we can predict (based on the laws of probability) that this cross section will reflect the whole society in its opinions, prejudices, and preferences. But what do we find among those who are in the unique position to influence American public opinion through their prominent positions in the thought-forming media? Let's look at a profile of the opinions of those who attempt to form our opinions. The following facts were reported by pollsters Lichter, Lichter, and Rothman, as the result of a study made among influential TV executives.[2]

• 66 percent of those polled believe that TV should be used as a major force for "social reform." ("Social reform" is an insider "code word" for almost anything from outright anarchy, to socialism, to socialistic totalitarianism.)

• The same percentage believe that TV "entertainment" programs should not be just to entertain, but to *influence* the public to accept *their* views of an ideal society!

Now, before we can be properly appalled at this cavalier attempt to conform the general public to one small segment's concept of an "ideal society," let's see exactly what their perceptions embrace. Let's look at *their* idea of what an "ideal society" may be like.

• 90 percent of media representatives do *not* attend church.

• 47 percent of media representatives have no church affiliation whatsoever.

• 75 percent of media representatives admit that they are "liberals" — a term synonymous with secular humanist, which is a term synonymous with atheist or agnostic.

- 40 percent of media representatives openly admit that they favor a socialist form of government, "socialist" being the term used by those who are in fact Marxists or Communists.

- 94 percent of media representatives favor allowing homosexuals to teach our children.

- 75 percent of media representatives believe that the United States is "an imperialist power that exploits Third World countries."

- 94 percent of media representatives favor abortion-on-demand.

- 54 percent of media representatives find nothing wrong with premarital sex or with cohabitation without marriage.

- 92 percent do not feel homosexuality is necessarily wrong.

In view of these statistics, we will leave it to the reader to decide whether those who rigidly control the content of television programming reflect commonly held American attitudes — or are, in fact, a small special-interest group dedicated to *altering* the generally held beliefs of this nation. It seems clear that this carefully guarded "elite" is *not* a force for righteousness, but rather an insidious cabal blatantly working on Satan's behalf.

BEHIND THE TV SCENE

How did this situation come about? How did a small minority, committed to the destruction of everything we cherish and hold dear, manage to take control of the greatest force for evil ever offered to mankind? Because the enemy — Satan, his demonic henchmen, and humans willing to sell their souls for momentary worldly satisfaction — works *years* ahead of the trusting (and sometimes overly innocent) body which our Lord referred to as His sheep.

The fact is that the news-gathering, news-disseminating, and entertainment industries have been systematically taken over for several generations. Journalism schools, staffed with secular humanists who make the *public* media figures look like conservatives, start the winnowing and screening process that rapidly "weeds out" anyone oriented toward morality, righteousness, or holiness. Christian young people who dream of a career in the media had better plan on either going into Christian programming or changing their field. Those who do not parrot the liberal pronouncements of their media mentors and elders will not go far (or last long) in the secular media market.

But what about the several "conservative" columnists and commentators who are allowed to speak out on the national scene? The sad, but true, fact is that these are "token conservatives" who know exactly how far they can go in discussing the failings of the majority of their media colleagues. One of the most prominent (and durable) of these "conservative" spokesmen reveals his true orientation in the occasional books he authors. These are filled with more foul, four-letter expletives than found in the average "modern" movie — language that no Christian would allow in his home.

Sad to say, the real-life situation is that the entertainment and news-disseminating industries are literally *filled* with leftist, anti-God, anti-morality types who consciously and blatantly use their privileged, high-paying positions to proselytize the general public into accepting their own perverted views.

IS THERE ANY HOPE?

To be completely honest, the answer is probably a flat-out no. There are, however, occasional mutterings, even from *within* the industry, that should serve as a warning for those in charge to rethink their brazen effrontery to public tastes and morals.

Not too long ago William A. Leonard, president of CBS News, said, "There is a tendency among us all to use freedom of the press as though it were some sign of high rank, some badge of privilege which confers special liberties upon its possessors."[3]

Obviously, if there is to be any hope for improvement in the broadcast industries, it will be *imposed* from without rather than developed from within.

WHAT CAN *WE* DO?

Obviously, the overall picture is discouraging, but perhaps not hopeless. If there were a general recoiling of the viewing audience from the product being foisted on them (to the point where ratings — and thus profits — plummeted), the powers-that-be would soon get the message. But can we *expect* a mass withdrawal of the viewing audience —

including the considerable Christian element of that audience? Let's look at the viewing habits of Americans (including *Christian* Americans) and see if we have any cause for hope.

YOUNG AMERICA'S VIEWING HABITS

In order to properly assess the impact of television as compared to every other form of thought-modifying influence, we should first look at what makes television so *different* from everything that went before.

First of all, television comes to you — you don't go to *it*. Every other form of communication requires a *positive* effort, while television keeps influencing with *negative* effort on the part of the recipient. What does this mean? Ordinary forms of communication (reading, conversation, study, et cetera) require a series of positive steps. You have to turn the page, read the assignment before class, and at least pay *attention* in order to keep a conversation moving along.

But television? Once the set is switched on, TV captures the mind of the viewer. Rapid-fire, bang-bang sequences serve to almost hypnotize the watcher.

Watch today's commercials. They're strident, almost subliminal, in the *speed* with which successive frames are transposed. Why this frantic, frenetic pace? Because it "hypes" the viewers and keeps them on the edge of their seats and at a high energy level where they're "turned on" to the message being delivered — whether directly or subliminally (we'll speak more on this a little further along).

Television, although an outgrowth of motion picture methods, has two compelling features which make it far more influential than movies. These are immediacy — and the fact that it is brought directly into *your* living room. Explosions, violent deaths, and rampaging mobs are all a part of the "now" situation, and they're part and parcel of *your life*. How can you escape it? It's here — and it's now!

So, with television's unprecedented capacity for impact, one might think that concerned Americans would use some selectivity in their *children's* viewing. But *do* they? Let's look at some facts.

In a study of preschoolers, the reported viewing times ranged from 25 to 30 hours per week.[4] And these figures persist in studies done of grammar school and high school students, as well. So we should look for a moment at just what they really mean.

The average youngster's day is largely occupied with certain productive activities. These include school, eating, homework, physical activities, social interactions, spiritual activities, and health and appearance requirements. But take four to six hours per day out of the time available between rising and going to bed, and something is obviously going to be shortchanged!

Given a choice between watching TV and almost anything else, you know what wins out. Such factors as program content, whether the show has been seen before, and whether the show's expressed opinions are contrary to *your* values doesn't matter. The kids plunk down and watch just about *anything* that happens to flow across the screen — and most of it is not what children should be seeing.

THE SECOND GOD

Tony Schwartz wrote a book called *Media: The Second God*. He observes that in all too many homes, television literally *dictates* the scheduling of family life. He makes an interesting observation, comparing the public's *former* attitude toward God with its *present* attitude toward television. The result of this comparison? In today's society, TV has become exalted to the point of becoming equal to, or even higher than, our Heavenly Father.

Some specifics? God is properly described as omniscient and omnipotent — all-knowing and all-powerful. He is a Spirit (ethereal); He is not a physical being. He exists both without and within us. He is always with us because He is everywhere at all times. We can never fully understand Him because He works in mysterious ways — ways beyond the mental abilities of the average person.

Now think about all these *heavenly* attributes, and begin to analyze the all-pervasive presence and influence of television. In doing interviews and research for his book, Mr. Schwartz heard many parallel statements used in referring to the broadcast media. "I never feel alone, because I have my radio and television." "The same programs are being seen *everywhere* as I watch them."

And what about those *other* attributes formerly held only by God? Well, TV is not a corporal body; it's transmitted through the air until it strikes the fluorescent face of your picture tube; anchormen and commentators are generally held in unrealistic esteem as purveyors of "all truth and all knowledge"; and no one will argue the omnipotence (or is it arrogance?) of the TV bigwigs when it comes to imposing their will on some social or political matter.[5] All in all, Mr. Schwartz's position is well-taken. TV *has* perhaps come to occupy a position where it *"opposeth and exalteth [itself] above all that is called God, or that is worshipped; so that [it] as God sitteth in the temple of God, shewing [itself] that [it] is God"* (II Thessalonians 2:4).

THE INFLUENCE OF TELEVISION

Historians spend a large part of their time studying the art and literature of the periods they are interested in, to gain insight into the values and attitudes of the populations of those times. While literature and art have proven, over the centuries, to be valuable tools for revealing the real interests, undercurrents, and emotional underpinnings of various societies, they can *also* (when properly analyzed) give deeper perceptions of the *stages* a society goes through as it rises to greatness — and then *collapses*. One can't help wondering, if the Lord tarries, what some future historian would conclude about *our* society if he happened onto tapes of *Dallas, Mork and Mindy,* or *General Hospital.*

Certainly it's difficult to assign specific weights and numbers to the impact of television on our times (and on our national decline), but there is little question that television not only reflects, but influences the society it permeates. While some would insist that TV is not the *cause* of certain unfortunate developments in our general moral climate (violence, sexual promiscuity, child abuse, easy divorce, abortion, et cetera), few thinking persons would deny that it influences our perception of the morality of certain acts and situations — and whether or not we decide that certain actions are "generally accepted." General acceptance, of course, lends a false sense of legitimacy to conduct that was previously illegal (and which is still contrary to *God's* laws, even if not the current laws of the land).

Someone once said, "Give me control of the money of a nation and I don't care who makes the laws." An apt paraphrase today could well be, "Give me control of the public information media, and I will control those who make the laws." The real-life situation today is that the news organizations can make or break *anyone* who opposes them by either suppressing or emphasizing happenings that assume huge proportions (or are shielded from the public) by "editorial" decisions made daily in Washington and New York. From there they are electronically transferred to the very *minds* of the American public — but always with the political "slant" previously decided upon by their "authors."

It goes without saying that those who first acquire information are in the best position to manipulate news. If only one person possesses a fact, he alone decides whether it will be disseminated as it stands — or whether it will be pummeled, shaped, and altered to fit what *he* chooses to have the world believe. A small handful of people can, of course, exercise the same control over items of information available to them — if they also control the means of information dissemination. Such is the case with American journalism as "they" arrogantly decide what will be disclosed to the American public, how it will be slanted, and what items will *not* be emphasized in their so-called "news" coverage.

This situation has made American journalism an extremely prosperous, comfortable, and *powerful* field in which to pursue a career. The opinions and philosophies of the press (almost exclusively liberal) are passed off to the public as *facts,* with no disclaimers that these are, in truth, the opinions and biases of the information-deliverers. The unique position of America's press makes it an awesomely powerful political tool, as well as an opinion-forming medium. As such, there has probably never been a comparable force in the history of the world, insofar as *general* mind control is concerned.

The American press is guilty (at best) of sloppiness and superficiality. At worst it may be suspected of actively working to subvert the noble causes for which this country has always stood. Newsmen never conduct in-depth studies of problems; they "skim off" the sensational, headline-grabbing elements and consign the rest to the wastebasket. If the final impression delivered to the general public is distorted, all the better (in their view).

While newsmen proclaim an abhorrence of censorship, they actually *practice* it daily in their editorial functions. They decide what will be emphasized and what will be minimized or totally ignored. They decide national issues and in what direction the national will should be focused. By totally ignoring questions of grave importance, they make them into *nonissues* by default.

In view of their enormous power, the members of the press owe it to themselves (and to the American people) to stand as an example of high integrity and unimpeachable honor. The powers enjoyed by the press include a grave *responsibility* to deal with issues in an unbiased and neutral manner. The power of the press can be an awesome tool for either righteousness, honor, and morality — or for national degradation.

The Sigma Delta Chi code of ethics for journalists, first adopted in 1926 and revised in 1973, states that "the *supposed* purpose of distributing the news and of expanding public awareness is to enhance the general welfare."

Obviously, media men are in a position where they should reexamine their motives and their methods. No one questions the right of reporters to hold personal political opinions, but their position demands that they suppress their personal inclinations to "preach" *their* views and deliver only a neutral version of what actually happened or is happening. Editorial opinion is also a part of news, but such editorialization should be clearly stated as being the *opinion* of those expressing it and not insinuated surreptitiously into what purports to be fact.

AMERICA'S ENTERTAINMENT INDUSTRY

The American entertainment industry has been used as a propaganda and mind-influencing medium for more than a half-century now. If one has occasion to watch almost any of the old movies made during the Depression, one can't escape the heavy ladles of communist propaganda that were being served up to the American public at that time. And have things changed? Turn on your television almost any evening, and *you* decide whether the national entertainment industry is a force for morality, righteousness, and honesty — or a *corruptive* force on our national spirit.

How do the producers of the majority of today's "entertainment" shows go about inserting their propaganda? With heavy hands and with barely disguised contempt for what has long been held as "the American ideal." A prime example of this type of blatant mockery was found on the widely acclaimed (and recently departed) *All in the Family*. The writers and producers for that show openly lampooned all the normal virtues and exalted everything that is of questionable moral value. Among the many institutions openly ridiculed were motherhood, marriage, children, the family, Christian clergymen, the Christian marriage ceremony, and the Christian moral value system. Among the institutions *lauded* were situational ethics, sex before marriage, nonreligious (and thus nonbinding) religious vows, sexual equality, and a humanistic value system in marriage. How many years did it take to cover all these subjects? It didn't take years or even one season. All these desecrations occurred within *one program!* Let's pause and examine this particular program as a typical example of the *methods* used by the secular humanists to promote their beliefs.

In the episode under discussion, a young couple is invited to Mike and Gloria's home to be married. The first bit of information delivered to the watcher is that the bride-to-be has become pregnant during the period she was "living-in" with her boyfriend — the prospective bridegroom. While this is all a normal and acceptable situation for Gloria, Mike, and the couple involved, they decide to perform some type of "marriage" to placate the bride's parents (who are obviously old-fashioned and narrow-minded).

The minister arrives — on his motorcycle — and it is made known to the audience that Mike called this particular minister after finding his name in the yellow pages, this being documentation of the fact that no card-carrying humanist would *know* a minister in the course of his normal life.

And what is this minister like? Well, as it turns out, he's a catastrophic *jerk!* His ceremony consists of a total perversion of the standard Christian marriage ceremony which has united *millions* of couples and has served as the foundation for untold lifetimes of love, dedication, and mutual commitment. The desecration of the vows and spirit of the traditional marriage ceremony is an insult to every husband and wife who have so pledged their love to each other.

The only "serious" moment in this burlesque ceremony comes when Mike reads a simpering poem about two trees growing together without either overshadowing the other (a perfect plea for equality, brotherhood, and fraternity it would appear — but hardly a prescription for a Godly marriage!). Of course, the whole show is "good clean fun" — but, unfortunately, it is fun poked at morality, marriage, sex, motherhood, and all those old-fashioned and unenlightened people who are "sexually repressed" by their "outmoded religious beliefs."

Of course, what many might consider "harmless fun" was in truth a commercial for acceptance of situational ethics — piped into every home in the United States. What is worse is the psychological gambit of debasing whatever you choose by poking *fun* at it. Now no one objects to good-natured and respectable fun. But when expensive payrolls and huge budgets are used to *ridicule* beliefs respected by a sizable segment of the population, there is something rotten in videoland.

Another program that was blatant in its intent to portray Christians — and especially ministers — as hypocrites, was the RCA/NBC miniseries *Celebrity*.[6] The leading character in this travesty was one Thomas Jeremiah Luther, a world-famous faith healer and evangelist. His name should be especially noted because it contains the names of a disciple, a prophet, and a prominent Protestant minister.

Thomas Jeremiah Luther is portrayed as a conservative political leader, a swindler, a thief, an extortionist, a rapist, and a murderer. *Celebrity's* content is vulgar from start to finish and is but a typical example of the anti-Christian stereotype which has become standard fare on NBC and other major networks.

In this case, however, RCA/NBC goes further than usual by making Luther a leader in a political movement called "The Right Side." This organization is pro-life, pro-family, pro-church, and pro-morality. The group lobbies for prayer in the schools and opposes the ERA, busing, and pornography.

Inevitably, any character on television who values individual moral choices, who respects the Ten Commandments as God's law, and who doesn't subscribe to the new morality is portrayed as some type of neurotic freak.

TELEVISION DISTORTIONS

This character distortion is one of the most common methods used to provide "impact" to television programming. In fact, the usual practice is to *so* distort the characters of those taking part in television productions that they become caricatures. In other words, TV producers seem to hold to the premise that "normal doesn't sell."

And how does this serve the purposes of those determining what will be presented? It imposes certain subliminal mind-sets on viewers (particularly *younger* viewers) who know what's *really* behind those they see as "parent," "clergyman," or "teacher." The *broader* the characterization, of course, the deeper the perception that becomes ingrained as to the character of those met in real life.

Who is caricatured on television? Almost everyone. Consumers are greedy. Fathers are stupid. Mothers are venal, unfaithful, and hypocritical. Clergymen are lechers. Bosses are ruthless and greedy. Young people are violent, "macho," and totally obsessed with sex. Is it any wonder that many of today's youth are wandering around in a semineurotic or semipsychotic state, lamenting that they "don't know who they are"?

Let's face it, there are simply no *normal* people portrayed on modern-day television. Just as normal isn't *news*, TV producers also seem convinced that normal isn't entertainment. For example, TV critic Jeff Greenfield has noted, "Marriage on television today is a cross between a bad joke, a bad dream, and a nostalgia trip. Finding a contemporarily, happily married couple on television is like finding an empty taxi in midtown Manhattan at 5 p.m. — possible, but not very likely."[7]

"Research has also revealed that the more frequently a person watches TV, the more he is likely to accept stereotyped portrayals of a group as real."[8] Thus, if a certain social or economic group is routinely portrayed in a degrading manner, habitual viewers are likely to accept the depiction as fact. They will then, of course, carry this attitude over into real life and view that segment of society as it is fallaciously portrayed on television.

What is the world like to those who routinely spend a large part of their day watching television? George Gerbner did research concerning this question and came up with some revealing findings.[9] They see the largest occupational groups in this country as policemen, lawyers, doctors, judges, and criminals. These outnumber all other occupational groups combined. There are almost no clerical workers, salespeople, artists, or engineers. In fact, the simple everyday people who actually keep the world moving along don't *exist* on television. As far as blue-collar workers (the largest single group of workers in the *real* world), they don't exist — except in beer commercials.

Television's messages undoubtedly affect what we think about others and ourselves. There is an even more insidious result, however, and this is television's ability to move us out of the real world and into a world of fantasy. Psychiatrists say that normal people dream; neurotics build dream houses; and psychotics *move into them*. Unfortunately, more than one mentally ill person has deepened his problems by moving into the fantasy world of television.

Those grinding out television programs create a fantasy/science fiction world of action, humor, sex, and adventure to satisfy their audiences who are eager to escape the frustrations and realities of the everyday world. The "charm" of escapist programming is that you are supposed to *know* that it's fantasy before you enter and therefore it doesn't threaten you (as real-life situations do). Unfortunately, some persons confuse fantasy with reality. For them, escapist programming can become a snare and a delusion.

Soap operas are particularly effective as escapist entertainment. The 13 "soaps" broadcast daily by ABC, CBS, and NBC occupy more than 55 hours of programming per week! These appallingly written and badly acted "dramas" swell the coffers of these networks by $0.75 *billion* in advertising revenues. Think about that, it amounts to over $700 *million* per year![10]

The exciting, thrill-a-minute life of the soaps requires no mental activity or exercise of the imagination. It's all *injected* into the dull, mundane life of the viewer. And, not surprisingly, the viewer's life seems to suffer by comparison. The everyday housewife can identify better with a TV doctor's mistress than she can with her own life with her hardworking (but dull) husband. The result? Dissatisfaction at home.

Instead of concentrating on *working* toward a successful marriage, all too many American wives prefer to withdraw into the fantasy world and thrill-a-minute marriages of soap opera life. Not surprisingly, that can leave a wife depressed, or even despondent, as she sees her own life as mundane and uneventful. Because TV soaps play daily to the largest, most homogenous audiences ever assembled — and because so many mistake TV's fantasy for reality — countless problems are caused because of the conflict between what people have and what they feel they *should* have.

Unfortunately, Christian mothers and their preschool children are frequently counted as members of this audience. And as they become "conditioned" to the negative moral values and ethical code of the soap opera world, it is not uncommon to find their Christian moral code distorted by the influences imposed. A tolerance for questionable attitudes and values can develop through this desensitization. While such programs are commonly referred to as "soaps," they are far from clean themselves — and there is nothing about them to make the viewer feel clean.

TELEVISION AS A TEACHING TOOL

In effect, television is the greatest single force in "teaching" the youth of this country. Its impact is actually greater than that of all the combined educational institutions which we tend to think of as our "educational system." In fact, the earliest education received by the overwhelming number of American preschoolers comes via television. Long before these unformed minds have any contact with *organized* education, they already have a great deal of information *inoculated* into their minds. Unfortunately, the information is not necessarily intended to elevate the moral consciousness of these youngsters. Despite this, parents persist in propping their toddlers before the TV set to keep them quiet.

Television is the only *unsupervised* instruction a child receives. There is no parent, teacher, or peer group involved. Very few parents can take the time to continually monitor what their children watch. With more mothers working, TV has become the great, universal, electronic baby-sitter. As such, when questions arise as to what is being presented on the screen, there is no one present to counsel or explain. More importantly, there is no one to *contradict* errant statements and viewpoints imposed on the young mind.

Although many studies have focused on two particular aspects of TV's influence on the young (the beneficial effects of educational programming and the harmful effects of TV violence), there is another element to be considered. It is the affect TV has on changing the patterns among family members. Here the TV screen serves not so much to *produce* certain actions as to *prevent* them. What specifically? Intimate talks, games, family activities, and the lively debates that *should* be engaged in, all of which serve as a large part of a youngster's learning process. Basically, this is the period when a child's whole future character is formed. Turning on the television set can turn *off* the process that transforms children into people.

Once television becomes a member of the family, it may increase the time family members spend in each other's presence (watching TV), but it decreases the time they spend *interacting*.

In truth, what we're discussing here is *robbing* children of the crucially needed interactions they *should* be experiencing with adults. It is during such interaction that emotional maturity begins to develop. This is the time when the parent begins to influence both the child's future attitudes toward honesty, kindness, and morality, and his ability to deal effectively with other people. A TV cartoon character dropping an explosive on an associate is *not* a lesson in Christian love.

A truly appalling example of the effect television can have on children surfaced in a letter to "Dear Abby" in June, 1975. This letter states, "I am divorced and the mother of a sweet, four-year-old boy named Ronnie." This mother went on to explain that she was surprised by a burglar who tied her up. Before she was gagged, she was allowed to tell her son to turn on the TV and watch the program for the 20 minutes that remained of the half-hour slot. Then he was to call the police.

"Abby," the mother wrote, "my son spent the next three *hours* watching TV while I was bound and utterly helpless. Could [he] possibly have some hostility toward me? Should I see a psychologist? Please advise."[11]

In 1975, a college professor concluded a two-year study in which he asked youngsters aged four to six, "Which do you like better, TV or Daddy?" Forty-four percent said they preferred TV.[12]

VIOLENCE ON TELEVISION

While explicit televised sex is certainly a horrendous influence on the youth of this country, many consider the matter of TV violence even more serious.

There's just no question that TV programming presents an unnatural and unrealistic environment, literally infested with violent crime. Virtually all crime and western shows (and most situation comedies) include some violence, but children's cartoons come in at the top of the violence derby by exhibiting 22 violent incidents per hour.[13] In fact, violence seems to be most prevalent when children watch the most.

By the age of 16 the average child has witnessed more than 13,000 TV murders![14] Living in such a violent atmosphere can influence a child toward more aggressive behavior as an acceptable part of normal life — and as a proper means for solving personal conflicts. Children learn, if nothing else from TV, that violence works! For the good guy or the bad guy, it gets things done!

What we actually have on television is a "finishing school" where the young, the mentally impressionable, and the criminally disposed learn a course of effective action. Criminal acts are portrayed in great detail, and innumerable incidents have been recorded where violent crimes have been repeated, within hours of their broadcast, with real — and violent — results. And even without overt criminal behavior resulting from TV portrayal, there is still a broad menu of unsavory practices for our youth to emulate. Almost without exception, today's television programs promote sex outside of marriage, homosexuality, abortion, and doing your own thing — whatever that may encompass.

SOME FACTS ON TELEVISION VIOLENCE

Three alarming conclusions are drawn from the research cited and from casual personal viewing:

• The "good" guys are as likely as the "bad" guys to resort to violence on TV.

• Violence is often *rewarded* on TV. It is the people who are violent who get what they want.

• The *consequences* of violence (pain, blood, lifelong disability) are almost never shown on TV.

What do we see as the *results* of this barrage of TV violence?

• Children (and adults) learn aggressive behavior from observing violent aggressive behavior.

• There is a definite link between violent crimes portrayed on TV and actual repetitions of such crimes.

• The effects of viewing violence are cumulative; that is, the *more* violent the programming viewed by the child, the higher the level of aggressiveness he will show.

• Some children (and adults) become fearful because of a constant stream of violence on TV.

And finally, this statement on TV violence and its effect on children: "TV viewing may affect aggressive behavior as long as ten years later. High exposure to televised violence at eight years of age was positively related to interpersonal aggressiveness in boys and girls aged nineteen. Clearly early exposure to aggressive models can have a long-lasting effect."[15]

SOME ACTUAL INCIDENTS INVOLVING VIOLENCE

The movie *Texas Chain Saw Massacre*, a violent, blood-spattered portrayal of a family that reveled in dissecting their victims in a manner that could only appeal to psychopaths or movie producers, was recently shown to inmates at the prison in Chino, California. One of these inmates was Kevin Cooper. Three days after viewing the movie, he escaped. The following day, the bodies of Douglas and Peggy Ryan, their daughter, Jessica (aged 10), and neighbor, Christopher Yuse (also 10), were found hacked to death in the Ryan home a few miles from the prison. The gruesome murder of these four innocent people was actually a reenactment of the violence depicted in the *Texas Chain Saw Massacre*.[16]

In view of such incidents, it is hard to cope with the fact that many children and adults (even Christian viewers) will willingly sit down and watch such abject *filth*. They openly *choose* to watch programs or movies that glorify perversion, sadism, and rebellion. Those who support the production of such debased spectacles (whether by buying tickets or watching it on TV) must realize that they share the responsibility for actions that come about as the result of such showings. If no one watched such productions, they wouldn't be made. Anyone watching them must share the blame for the consequences.

Another area of perversion of all normal standards lies in the popularity of westerns. Of course, the American western is a national (and international) institution. It has been called "the evangelization of violence," however, and with good cause.[17] Bandits are romanticized in western films. Hollywood has made no fewer than 21 movies about Billy the Kid. Such handsome leading men as Paul Newman and Kris Kristofferson have played this part. But was Billy the Kid a handsome and virile character in real life? Contemporary observers described him as a slight, short, bucktoothed, narrow-shouldered youth who looked like a cretin.

Do our children need such examples as heroes? What happened to the Lou Gehrigs and the Charles Lindberghs? Children need examples of character, commitment, discipline, and Godliness. While still innocent and impressionable, they will choose the models they will later emulate — whether for good or for evil. Unfortunately, there are practically *no* heroes of moral quality in the forefront today. Athletics is a sordid pit of alcoholism and drug involvement, and today's superhero (as exemplified by Spiderman) reveals a neurotic, girl-chasing young "swinger" who constantly laments the fact that he can't make any profit out of fighting crime. These are today's prototypes as heroes for our youth.

Physical violence is only one form of the violence to which young people are habitually exposed through television. There are other forms which, because they are more subtle, may present even greater problems than the more *recognizable* hostilities. Television characters, whether in comedy or dramatic series, habitually abuse each other verbally. Wives demean husbands, brothers "pull down" sisters, neighbors threaten neighbors, just about everyone (at one time or another) is insulted by someone else. Add to this the almost constant background of cheating, lying, and deceit that takes place constantly on television, and it hardly becomes an environment in which to leave your children for extended periods of time.

ALCOHOL IS PROMOTED

Although studies show that all crimes are exaggerated on TV, one crime-related area is *understated* — and this is the area of alcohol abuse.

Keep in mind that the TV networks receive millions of dollars in revenue from beer and wine accounts. It isn't surprising, therefore, that the problems associated with drinking are minimized on television. You don't bite the hand that feeds you.

The liquor industry has friends in Hollywood and at the networks (as they do in almost all major economic forces). In an interview with *The Evangelist*, Dr. Thomas Radecki, of the National Coalition on Television Violence, stated, "With the new research of the past two years, it is increasingly clear that TV advertising, and programmed use of alcohol, is playing a major role in the increasing abuse of alcohol." Radecki noted that the average child will see alcohol consumed 75,000 times on TV before he reaches the legal drinking age — when he must decide whether or not *he* will choose to drink. That's quite a subliminal influence to weigh his decision *toward* the "in folks" on television, who are bright, sophisticated, and inevitably holding a drink.

He also noted that the typical adult sees 5,000 incidents of alcohol intake per year. Ninety-nine percent of these cases of alcohol intake will be portrayed as neutral or favorable. Is that what life is like in the real world? Statistics indicate that 50 percent of real-life violence is associated with alcohol consumption, while only *one* percent of television violence is associated with drinking. Radecki believes that TV's portrayal of alcohol consumption is one of the major reasons why alcohol abuse and violence are the two most rapidly expanding causes of death in the United States.

A total of 90 percent of persons drinking *any* kind of beverage on television will be shown drinking alcohol. TV characters spend twice as much time drinking alcohol as they do tea or coffee. They consume 14 times more liquor and beer than they do soft drinks, and they drink 15 times more alcohol than they do water. Viewers will see an average of three incidents of alcohol consumption for each hour they watch during prime time. Those watching throughout the day will see *six* instances of drinking per hour. (Obviously, the soap opera characters belt it down more heavily than do evening characters.)

Contrary to what one might expect, it isn't the villains who do most of the drinking. The heaviest TV drinkers are well-known stars appearing in regular series. TV characters seldom refuse a drink, nor do they express disapproval of someone else drinking. In situation comedies, excessive drinking is often used as a method for "good naturedly" getting more laughs.[18]

CONSUMERISM AND THE CHILD

While perhaps not as blatantly harmful to the future welfare of the child, consumerism is another area of excess on television. Children see about 20,000 thirty-second commercials each year, or about three hours of TV advertising per week.[19] Advertisers spend over $800 million a year selling products to children on television.[20]

While individual salesmen formerly had to rely on the quality of their products and personal persuasion, today's electronic advertisement is a fantastic (and expensive) conglomeration of psychology, art, and action — designed to create wants where none exist. Production of the cheapest commercials cost thousands of dollars, and the more impressive ones are unbelievably expensive as they employ the services of top writers, scenic designers, models, actresses, and public figures to extol the so-called "virtues" of their products. On top of all this, psychological gambits are employed to leave the child (whose parents won't cater to their every want) feeling abused. If it's advertised on TV, *you've got to have it!*

How do they manage to effect this result? By targeting latent reflexes deep in the human brain. This is where the subliminal quality of TV selling comes in. They appeal to hidden stimuli within us (and within our children) to generate "want" reactions. They do it to adults with shapely models lolling on expensive cars. The subliminal message implies that if you had a car like that, you could probably have something like that lolling on *your* car. For children the method is the same, only the *details* are different. Here the subliminal message is, "If your parents *really* loved you, they'd buy you this." And if the parents don't think it's *good* for the child? A potential wedge is created between the parents and the child.

What do manufacturers promote to children on television? Primarily two products — food and toys. Not surprisingly, the items promoted to children in the food lines are the most heavily sugared and thus most desired among children. Among toys, the items that receive the heaviest TV advertising are frequently the shoddiest and least durable toys — those the manufacturer feels will need a considerable boost beyond their natural drawing power.

Let's look at the foods advertised directly to children via TV. Nearly 60 percent of all commercials during children's viewing time are for food products that conflict with one or more of the Dietary Goals for the United States, as established by the Senate Select Committee for Nutrition and Human Needs.[21] Less than *four* percent of food ads directed toward children are for meat, bread, fruits, vegetables, or dairy products.[22]

In a nation where 98 percent of the population suffers from tooth decay, more than *half* of food commercials directed toward children are for heavily sugared items — largely sugar-coated cereals and soft drinks.[23]

Another insidious by-product of TV is the frustration experienced by youngsters from less affluent families unable to afford luxury items promoted over the airwaves. Advertisers don't particularly worry about this, however; their advertising is also directed at the long-range effects it will have on potential *future* buyers.

According to statistics quoted on a CBS/FM national presentation, 12- to 17-year-olds possess the potential to spend $43 billion annually! Total teenage spending has increased by 53 percent over a five-year period.[24] Other surveys indicate that teenagers buy 57 million movie tickets *per month*.[25]

Television advertising agencies *exploit* the minds of susceptible young children. The vice-president of one of America's major advertising agencies callously commented, "Children, like everyone else, must learn the marketplace. You learn by making judgments. Even if a child is deceived by an ad at age four, what harm is done? He will grow out of it."

He further stated that there's no harm in the child becoming convinced that children on TV ads are his friends and not actors. His simplistic solution if irreconcilable differences are created between the child and parent? The parent has only to say, "Shut up or I'll belt you."[26]

THE BROAD PERSPECTIVE

As any rational parent reads the facts presented here, it should begin to be apparent that a great force for evil has been loosed on the American home. This force — which *did* have great potential for good at its inception — has been perverted into a force threatening the family, public morality, and Christian standards. It has literally become a "second god" in a great number of American homes — including *Christian* American homes.

It is also tempting to surrender to TV's sweet siren song of keeping kids off the street, quiet in the home, and supplied with entertainment. It's an automatic supplier of peace and quiet (for the parents) when the kids have "nothing to do." It is also the most effective device ever developed in all of history to retain all kids in one common spot on a Saturday morning.

It's a depressing fact, however, to think that on any given Saturday morning, nine million American youngsters are sprawled on the floor watching an animated world of meanness and mayhem. The only interruptions in this ongoing procession of bombs, dynamite sticks, and ugly "outer-spacers" are periodic and inevitable invitations to jeopardize the child's health (and the parent's pocketbook).[27]

They sit mesmerized as the electronic monster programs their little minds to become yet one more unit in a world that is rapidly becoming anti-God.

Not too long ago, Soupy Sales flippantly told his young viewers to "go into mommy and daddy's wallet and get all the dirty wrinkled green pieces of paper and send them to Soupy." He received hundreds of dollars in the mail.[28]

If this were all that was being programmed into those young minds, we might not have too much to worry about. Unfortunately, it doesn't scratch the surface. Like a thief in the night, the visual images and living sounds are stealing away the vestiges of all that was once considered good. In light of this fact, should you begin rethinking some of the policies on TV viewing in *your* home?

THEY BECAME FOOLS

"For the invisible things of him from the creation of the world are clearly seen, being understood by the things that are made, even his eternal power and Godhead; so that they are without excuse: Because that, when they knew God, they glorified him not as God, neither were thankful; but became vain in their imaginations, and their foolish heart was darkened. Professing themselves to be wise, they became fools" (Romans 1:20-22).

Clearly, we are becoming a nation of fools, and for this we can give full credit to the American system of public education. At this point in history, our educational system largely determines our future — both in terms of individual liberty and of international status. Its books, curricula, films, philosophies, and educators hold within their grasp tomorrow's citizens and, thus, our future. They will determine whether America will continue to be the land of the free and the home of the brave — or just one more great gray mass of socialist citizenry.

Despite the fact that 65 million Americans (three out of every ten) are directly involved in the educational process (which requires more than $130 billion each year to function), public education is a complete failure![1] Vast amounts of manpower and capital are invested in a system that fails to fulfill the true purpose of education and produces fools instead. However, public education is merely a reflection of the *general* condition of our decaying society.

The obituary notices for true education (which *should* be based on facts and morals) mirror the national humanistic trend:

- 1925 — Teaching of evolution is begun in the public schools.
- 1948 — Religious instruction is restricted in schools.
- 1962 — Court bans state prayer in public schools.
- 1978 — Caroling is prohibited in many schools.
- 1981 — Cross in public park is declared unconstitutional.
- 1982 — Church in Louisville, Nebraska, is padlocked.
- 1983 — Suit is made against the "Year of the Bible" proclamation.

The word "education" derives its meaning from a root meaning "to rear" or "to nourish." "Morality" comes from a root meaning "custom" or "measure." As such, the basis of education, which involves morality, would be to nourish or rear children according to the expectations and standards of society. Unfortunately, our public school system receives a failing grade because society's standards fail to meet God's design for educating its young.

From the earliest times, God commanded His people to teach their children to love Him and to follow His precepts. As the Giver of life, He instructs us how to live Godly, healthy, and fulfilling lives. God places a high priority on educating the young — primarily assigning this grave responsibility to parents.

In 1787, when Congress reserved two sections of land in each township for the specific development of universities, the learning of the *truth* was the very foundation of education. The universities of higher learning — Yale, Harvard, and Princeton — almost exclusively dedicated themselves to training ministers who, having pursued truth, would pass on their knowledge to others.

SEEDS OF DESTRUCTION

Nevertheless, only 18 years were to pass before the seeds of destruction were sown. In 1805, the Unitarians took over Harvard, making it a landmark event from an intellectual and educational standpoint. Samuel Blumenfeld says, "From then on Harvard became the Unitarian Vatican, so to speak, dispensing a religious and secular liberalism that was to have profound and enduring effects on the evolution of American culture, moral and social values."[2]

And this was just the beginning. Others who departed from truth began to dream of a new society in which man was supreme. One group known as the Owenites, a secret national society organized in 1829, determined to promote universal public education. One minister and adherent of the society wrote, "The great object was to get rid of Christianity and to convert our churches into halls of science."[3]

Their plan embodied the same strategies employed by humanists today. They would not openly *attack* religion, but they would conspire to belittle and ridicule ministers of the Gospel. They worked to establish national schools that would glorify *experience* (as perceived by the senses) and ridicule any knowledge of God.

Essentially, thinkers of this vein believed then (and still do) that the scientific method should determine what customs are best for a given time and place. They also aligned themselves boldly against Christians who trusted in divine law with its many absolutes. For them, science became the guide for establishing values and morals. The Owenites envisioned the school system as the logical place to make their converts since the law *compelled* parents to enroll their children.

In the early 1930s, a new ethic took shape in Germany when the German philosopher Hegel espoused a "Universal Spirit." His philosophy spread throughout the schools of Germany, convincing students — young and eager to learn — that all natural, cultural, and individual developments were a manifestation of the "Spirit."

Parallel with his philosophy came "situational ethics," which in essence states that whatever solves a problem on the practical level must be considered moral. If the results are desirable then the action is ethically right.

It was this philosophy, embraced by impressionable young students at all levels of Germany's educational system, that furthered Hitler's cause.

HUMANISM ON THE RISE

In America, humanism — fostered by both Unitarianism and Modernism — was on the rise. The Modernists particularly influenced the trend. Though they may have doubted God as a personality, they still believed in the concept of God. But they ran into a philosophical problem when they realized that their psychological dissection of feelings failed to produce anything analagous to God.

The stage was fully set for a new religion — one that would worship the creation rather than the Creator. Since orthodox Christians had, for the most part, abandoned leadership roles in public life (including public education), the secular humanists obtained strong footholds in the field of education. With little opposition, they made converts of educators and indoctrinated them into the philosophy of progressive education.

In 1933, John Dewey became the chief designer of the Humanist Manifesto, published in *The New Humanist* — forerunner of *The Humanist*. Signed by some of the leading humanists of the day, it sought to liberate humanity from the backwaters of "traditional and supernatural" religion. In addition, it provided a means and focus for many of the philosophies of that day.

Dewey's conception of intelligence dictated his practice as an educator. He viewed intelligence as a "social asset" to be used in the public interest. Therefore, the minds of scientists and industrialists are a collectively created social resource, as is the wealth these minds have made possible. Dewey concluded that America needed "organized action in behalf of the social interest" and "organized planning" of the economy — in other words, "some kind of socialism."[4]

When the country relinquished its halls of learning to Dewey's corps of progressive educators, it delivered its youth into the hands of the philosophy of pragmatism — that is, of animal reaction. Under this philosophy, our youth were to be reprogrammed to accept cause and effect as their new deity. It was the inauguration of the American "Enlightenment" — of the formal reign of Kant and Hegel — and not just among a handful of intellectuals but among the very leaders of American life.[5]

Basically, pragmatism states that the basic reason for anything's existence lies in its *consequences*. Although practicing pragmatists generally understood the ramifications of their philosophy, it caught the general public (businessmen included) unaware.[6] With subtle cunning, Dewey's philosophy was slipped into the schools of our nation, spilling its slow poison into the minds of our young. At this point, the stage was set for our destruction as a free society.

Coincidentally, it is interesting to note that John Dewey was born in the same year that Charles Darwin published his *Origin of Species*, the book that altered the very course of history.

Dewey's mind was a fertile ground for Darwinism. His system of ethics — which placed value on anything that *seemed* to solve life's problems — agreed nicely with Darwin's belief that man's ability to make moral judgments is a result of progressive, hereditary changes.

Like Dewey's, man's philosophies have always stemmed from one basic need: to make sense of his existence. But men who deny the reality of the very One who created them *won't* find truth. They are left with only the fancies and fantasies of man's own darkened intellect.

PROGRESSIVE EDUCATION?

Dewey, professing himself to be wise, fell into the error of all fools who say there is no God (Psalm 53:1). In essence, he believed that evolution had finally progressed to the point where man could now *control further evolution.*

Dewey viewed man as a "social animal." Therefore, he saw schools as social centers intended for the production of better social animals. He wrote, "The school as a social center means the active and organized promotion of this socialism, of the intangible things of art, science, and other modes of social intercourse."[7]

Ever since, the battle of creationism versus evolution has raged in our schools. Modern educators say that creationism is little more than a myth. But treating evolution as a "science" is the most unscientific charade that has ever been foisted on the general public.

The Bible tells us that *"In the beginning God created the heaven and the earth"* (Genesis 1:1). Because He did, the findings of true science — and the study thereof — harmonize with the biblical account. In fact, *true* science glorifies God and supports biblical truth.

It is true that we often "find what we're looking for." Some scientists, having been brainwashed by humanism, lose their scientific detachment and refuse to accept hard facts that contradict their previously instilled views. Even when confronted with unassailable proof, they are too spiritually blind to accept it. The problem is that man has taken a position of rebellion against God and then strives to understand a universe without God. It is impossible!

In a sense, "evolution" is just another word for atheism. "Atheism" literally means "without God" — without God in education, and without God in past, present, or future. Anyone basing his life on such a premise is doomed to follow a variety of roads — none leading to truth.

Still, evolution is taught as a scientific "fact" in the majority of schools throughout the nation. The saddest part is that little children are made to believe that man came from monkeys when there isn't a shred of scientific evidence to support this contention.

Evolution most clearly points to man's foolishness when he rejects God. The theory begins with matter, but evolutionists can't explain where matter comes from. They acknowledge that it began with *something* already in existence — but they can't explain where that came from either.

Some scientists hold to "the big bang theory." It states that all of the universe was created in an instantaneous explosion. The only thing they miss is, who lit the wick?

They speak of a "missing link" — as if all the chain of evolution from past to present is complete except for one missing link. In truth, it isn't a few *links* they're missing; it's the whole *chain*!

Evolution is a bankrupt, speculative theory (a *guess*) — not a scientific fact. And only a spiritually bankrupt society would stubbornly persist in such foolishness.

Such teaching will completely destroy our children. You start a child out in a dangerous position when you start with a foundation that is no foundation at all. Starting a child on a lie destines him for destruction.

The Bible says, *"In the beginning God . . . ."* If a child is not taught that, he remains uneducated despite everything else. Truth is the foundation of all education, of all training, and of all learning. Because God has been removed from the schools, the system is in a state of anarchy. Children complete school but they can't read, they can't write, they can't think logically, and, for the most part, they have no conception of why they exist or for what purpose.

If our nation — the greatest free nation on the earth — is ever destroyed, it will be because our children are fed a curriculum totally opposed to God.

IT DIDN'T JUST HAPPEN!

The story is told of a young Christian boy who attended class in a communist nation where evolution was taught. Of course, evolution is the bedrock of all Soviet teaching. It has to be that way, for unbiased education is impossible since communists insist on the theory of "no God."

Naturally, the teacher taught no God, no heaven, no hell, no Saviour. Man has no soul, no spirit — he just lives, breathes, eats, sleeps, and then dies. Everything happens by pure chance. In other words, "Nothing, working on nothing, by nothing, and for nothing, begets everything."

The boy made a model of the universe, and it was an excellent reproduction. All the planetary bodies, the stars, the sun, the moon, and the earth sat on a table when the teacher entered the room.

The teacher was stunned. The first question he asked was, "Who did this?" No one said anything. He was amazed at what he saw, and again he asked who did it. "This is the nicest piece of work I've ever seen. It's excellent." Everything was in its proper place and all to scale. It was a superb model.

Again the teacher spoke. "I want to know who did this." No one volunteered any information. At length, he turned to the class and firmly demanded: "Now I want to know who made this. It didn't just happen. *Someone* must have made it."

Finally, the boy stood up and said, "Teacher, that's what I've been trying to tell you. It didn't just happen. *Someone* had to have made it!"

Teaching rote knowledge without teaching God's original role reinforces the precepts of secular humanism — the religion that has raped the minds of millions of our children. And it has been a major influence in making the United States the cesspool of iniquity it is today.

THE HUMANIST PHILOSOPHY

In practice, humanists flatly oppose any instruction that allows a child to learn of God or that interferes with their atheistic, evolutionary doctrines. They manipulate young minds that are searching for answers to life's questions, they pollute the beauty of science, and they teach diabolical lies — all in an effort to create a substitute for God.

An excerpt from *Humanist Manifesto II* states, "A humanist outlook will tap the creativity of each human being and provide the vision and courage for us to work together. The decades ahead call for dedicated, clear-minded men and women able to marshall the will, intelligence, and cooperative skills for shaping a desirable future. Humanism can provide the purpose and inspiration that so many persons seek; it can give personal meaning and significance to human life."[8]

Humanists ridicule traditional moral codes, calling them false "theologies of hope,"[9] and deny their ability to meet the pressing needs of world realities. With missionary zeal they deify self-satisfied and self-indulgent men.

Secular humanism makes man the be-all and end-all of the universe. Its disciples believe that there is no source of knowledge beyond that which man can find within himself.

Thus, these fools — professing to be wise — are the enemies of everything that is good and wholesome. They purposely choose the school systems in which to spread their poisonous theories because they are the most effective arenas in which to make converts to their religion.

One statement made by one of these evil minds states, "Every child in America entering school at the age of five is mentally ill, because he comes to school with certain allegiances toward our founding fathers, toward our elected officials, toward his parents, toward a belief in a supernatural Being, toward the sovereignty of this nation as a separate entity . . . It's up to you teachers to make all of these sick children well by creating the international children of the future."[10]

Additional evidence of their intent to make converts to their religion is found in an article entitled "A Religion for a New Age." It states: "I am convinced that the battle for humankind's future must be waged and won in the public classroom by teachers who correctly perceive their roles as the proselytizers of a new faith: a religion of humanity that recognizes and respects the spark of what theologians call divinity in every human being."[11]

Think about *that*. American institutions of learning, orginally established to train ministers to teach and preach the truth, have now become strongholds of Satan to destroy our youth!

WHAT ARE THE TEACHINGS OF HUMANISM?

Here is what our children are being taught:

• *Evolutionary dogma* — Evolution is taught as unquestionable scientific *fact*.

• *Self-autonomy* — Children are repeatedly told that they are to be their *own* authority on questions of morals and values.

• *Situational ethics* — There are no *absolutes*. Right or wrong is dependent on the present situation.

• *Christianity denied* — Christianity is ridiculed. There is nothing supernatural in the universe (no God, no salvation, no heaven or hell, no Jesus Christ who rose from the dead). Many humanists claim that the only "deity" lies in man.

• *Sexual freedom* — Public sex education is pushed; a sex education without morals, modesty, shame, chastity, or abstinence. Sex is an animal function. Abortion, premarital sex, and homosexuality are all perfectly acceptable.

• *Total reading freedom* — Children shouldn't be supervised in their reading. They should read any pornographic material they choose.

• *Death education* — The concept is presented that there is no hope beyond the grave. The implication is that you'd better have your fun now; when you're dead, you're dead.

• *Internationalism* — The idea is stressed that world citizenship is more moral than national patriotism. They *don't* stress that world citizenship would no doubt occur under world *communism*.

• *Socialism* — Private ownership and the capitalist system are libeled while socialism is venerated.

Our children, by law, become a captive audience for the blatant perversion of truth. We submissively pay our school taxes to subsidize a platform for atheistic, humanistic educators to *brainwash* innocent children.

It's time we stop and think seriously about the implications and consequences of such a curriculum.

And if you really want to become infuriated, consider those things that are legally forbidden to be taught in our schools:

- The fact that God is the Creator.
- The deity of Jesus Christ.
- The teaching of creationism as a scientific subject.
- Moral absolutes.
- The biblical perspective on sexuality.
- That homosexuality is wrong.
- That there is eternal life, heaven, and hell (or judgment).

These subjects may not be addressed at any time within a school — even after regular hours.

Besides passing off their ration of socialistic internationalism as "education," some schools tend to be little more than mental health clinics in which the teacher plays the role of an all-knowing psychologist. These poor, misguided teachers feel they have been divinely appointed to guide children in discovering "their feelings and values." Many teachers see themselves as great humanitarians turning kids on to a world of self-awareness and deep, transcendental thinking. This is rot from the pit of hell, and it's destroying our children!

Let's face it, humanist "educrats" (educational bureaucrats) are determined to preempt the moral values of parents and forcibly teach our nation's children the bankrupt values of humanism — whether or not parents like it.[12]

INSTRUMENTS FOR SOCIAL CHANGE

Richard A. Baer of Life Sciences at Cornell University defends the position that teachers' goals are incompatible with parents' goals. Parents want to tell their children what the truth is and not allow them to search for it. Educators must challenge parental values. The schools have to have controversy.[13]

Part of the controversy involves using schools as instruments for bringing about social change. Students often spend hours in "rap" sessions discussing social and political issues and neglecting study of the basics. Because of this, many students — though knowledgeable about current events — are cut off from their historical and spiritual moorings.

We are also seeing a resurgence of Marxist studies. Back in the 1960s, there were hardly any courses promoting Marxism. Now over 400 such courses are being offered in U. S. colleges. It isn't surprising when we realize that the student radicals of the 1960s are now the Marxist professors of the 1980s.

Marxism in American schools is only one more evidence that "our halls of learning" have become "temples of humanism." But just remember: It is chaos, not peace, that is the ultimate end of humanism, as Dr. Francis Schaeffer warns.[14] Without God man is doomed to destruction. There can be no great and enduring civilization. If the truth were known, the communication of God's truth by His people is the only force that has prevented humanism from completely enslaving Western man.

Unfortunately, far too many parents refuse to believe that the anti-God, anti-family, anti-American religion of humanism is taught daily in nearly all public schools of our nation.

Parents, you may ask why educators feel that exposure to traditional value systems and creationism harms children while they place absolutely no restraint on a religion that says there is no God. I can tell you why.

The pride and rebellion of the sinful man's heart deceives him into thinking he is the center of the universe. He wars against anyone and anything that challenges his beliefs. Like all avowed atheists, he insists that "the nature of human beings is to seek their own good and that each individual has no purpose unless he is himself his own purpose."

A MORAL QUESTION

Theodore Roosevelt warned, "To educate a child in mind and not morals is to educate a menace to society." The bottom line is that the failure to instill ethical and moral values in public education contributes to juvenile delinquency, drug use, teenage pregnancies, et cetera.

At a time when our children require the transmission of a strong moral value system to harness their impulses and emotions, they are encouraged to seek values which are "entirely subjective and relative."[15] They are told that the only question to ask is, "Does it solve a present problem or meet a present need?" Anything that doesn't satisfy "needs" (or wants) has no value for the individual. Anything blocking the satisfaction of needs without offering the promise of even greater satisfaction later is bad and has a negative "value."

Based on this assumption, the student's personal tastes and preferences become his standard, thus permitting him to reject all other values — including those of his parents — simply by pointing out that these are "*your* values and not *mine.*"

Although humanists teach that the student must construct or choose his own values, they don't leave the process to chance. In a course called "Values Clarification," the student is forced to form his own values before he is capable of sound judgment. Teachers convince young children to reject values held by their parents or church, thus driving a wedge between child, parents, church, and even the authority of government.

In order to understand values clarification, let's look at the process the student follows.

First, the student must make his choice freely *without considering moral teachings of home or church.* Second, the student must investigate all possible alternatives. Third, the student, evaluating the advantages and disadvantages, must make a decision. It doesn't matter that the student is only eight years old and has no real knowledge of the consequences. Fourth, the student selects what he "prizes" the most. Fifth, the student makes a public affirmation of what he believes. Sixth, the student practically applies and acts on his chosen convictions and beliefs. Finally, the student may elect to make that choice a habit, or part, of his life.

Now the process itself may not alarm you, but the underlying assumption that defines a value should disturb you indeed.

Morals education is another instrument that has the capacity to achieve similar results. Unfortunately, even Christian schools, deceived by its title, become prey to it.

RATING THE SYSTEM

Edward B. Fiske writes, in the *New York Times* (March 20, 1977), that there is "a growing sense among parents, school board members, and others that the educational process has somehow gotten out of hand and that children aren't learning the way they should."

Where a diploma once signified application and achievement in mastering the requirements, it is now commonly given for "little more than twelve years of reasonably faithful and nonbelligerent attendance."[16]

David Hornbeck, Maryland superintendent of education, refers to this as "seat time." He says we use that as the measure of achievement rather than asking the more critical question of what students have actually learned.[17]

The alarm has been sounded and parents are finally becoming concerned. All major publications carry bleak accounts of the crumbled ruins of our temples of learning. Reports abound on functional illiteracy, plummeting test scores in basics, teacher incompetence, drugs, violence, and other disciplinary problems, questionable curricula — the list goes on. The facts are finally surfacing, but no one is addressing the root problem. The whole system can't help crumbling when its very foundation is corrupt. Any efforts made to improve the system are doomed unless basic humanistic assumptions are torn out at the roots.

Obviously, students are learning less and less. Statistics reveal that "the 1978 grades were decidedly lower than 1928s; in fact, even the best contemporary students did not perform as well as the best of 1928."[18]

Unfortunately, statistics of this nature aren't enough to divert the National Education Association from its course. Why? Because learning the basics is inconsistent with their policy and philosophy. What *is* their policy? Let's look at *their* literature on "Curriculum for the Whole Student."

"The curriculum must move away from an emphasis on the retention of facts to an emphasis on the process of inquiry, comparison, interpretation, and synthesis . . . . In addition to purely intellectual growth, the curriculum should regard emotions, attitudes, ideals, ambitions, and values as legitimate concern for the educational process."[19]

These philosophies, which pervade most of our public schools, rob children of the satisfaction of achievement. And academic achievement will contribute far more toward the building of self-confident children than any course aimed at "self-enlightenment." In fact, available research cites a "general decline in the teaching of basic fundamentals" as a key *cause* of achievement decline.[20]

Although parents are alarmed and demanding changes, many educators appear prepared to stonewall the opposition. While fighting for higher salaries and more benefits, their attitude toward declining test scores appears to indicate their determination to "de-emphasize the teaching of intellectual skills in favor of the inculcation *(teaching)* of social awareness and what can loosely be called the psychological enhancement of the individual student."[21]

As a result, Carol L. Schwartz, vice-president of the D. C. Board of Education, stated (in the *Washington Post* of May 17, 1977): "We are graduating students without the basic fundamental skills. We are employing some teachers who are academically deficient. We are so busy using our students as guinea pigs in the educational experiments of the day that their education is getting lost in the process."

Since we've been following the educational policies of our current elite, we shouldn't be surprised that many of our graduates can't read. Thirteen percent of them (in 1979) were considered "functionally illiterate."[22] We're told that the situation is *worsening*.

How could this happen when we employ over two million teachers and have truancy laws to ensure that every child in America is being educated? And yet, illiteracy in this country is turning into a blight that won't go away. While the United States has the highest proportion of young people in college of any major nation, it has not yet figured out how to teach tens of millions of its citizens to fill out a job application, balance a bank book, read a newspaper, or write a simple letter.[23]

The problem has reached such proportions that remedial reading and writing courses for freshmen have become a regular part of curriculums in our colleges and universities. If a child hasn't learned to read in 12 years, do you suppose a four-month course in reading will make him top student at Harvard?

There's not much hope for a society that stubbornly persists in supporting a system that turns out a generation of illiterates. And we are without excuse! Why should the world's richest nation with free, universal education have a reading and writing problem? There's simply no excuse for it.

TOO DEFICIENT TO DEFEND

I want to emphasize the seriousness of our present situation. It isn't a question of a "reading problem" at all. We're spending billions to produce a new mentality and new moral attitudes while our enemies across the sea train their young minds to wipe us off the face of the earth. Because complex ideas require complex vocabulary, they are gaining a decided advantage over us. As students become alarmingly incoherent in their writing — possibly indicating a decrease in their ability to think logically — our enemies gain more advantage. The decline in our math courses, especially, poses a major threat to American economic security and national defense.

A firm grasp of language is essential for clear, logical thinking and is an absolute necessity for written communication. The inability to grasp and use language hinders an individual in many ways. The lack of linguistic ability doesn't necessarily mean that the student lacks intelligence, however. Many students possess intelligence but have been cheated by our public school system of the opportunity to learn the use of *language*.

Professor Donald R. Tuttle describes the future for Western civilization if we continue to ignore the problem: "Words have been the channel of man's thoughts, the embodiment of his spirit, the interpreter of his emotions, the basis of his society, the chief of his weapons against the barriers of space and the ravages of time. Without language, man would be but the most miserable of beasts, his power of reflective thought, his greatest resource, as impotent as if it never had been."[24]

A *U. S. News & World Report* article cautions us that ability in mathematics is another problem area in our schools and is causing *technological illiteracy*. "Too few mathematically adept graduates are coming out of schools to develop technologies that hold the key to national well-being."

Russia requires *all* students to study subjects such as algebra and calculus — subjects essential to advancement in the "science race." Some of our schools require *no* math and others very little. Could it be that American high schoolers are "far behind their Soviet counterparts as the result of a strategy initiated in Russia more than a decade ago?"[25]

Don't be too hasty in brushing that possibility aside. At any rate, educators respond to math deficiencies in much the same way they do language deficiencies. Too often they casually ignore the problem while looking for easy solutions that deal with *surface* issues. Instead of struggling to learn basic computation, contemporary students rely on calculators to do their work for them — a recommendation suggested by a study conducted to investigate math teaching methods.

THE TEACHERS WE HIRE

It is obvious that public school standards must be upgraded. But the question is, can the teachers do the job? Recent reports of teacher incompetence have shocked the nation. Many of them are unable to pass simple competency tests in grammar, punctuation, and spelling. And if the *teachers* are incapable of teaching these basic skills, who will pass such skills on to the students?

We unquestioningly pay astronomical school taxes to support over two million teachers, but the return for this investment is *zero*! The system doesn't work!

And Americans, for the most part, are beginning to realize it. Americans have little or no confidence in those responsible for the school system.

Some of these not only want to put more stress on the basics, they "want a curriculum built solidly around the basics."[26] They seem to have faith that the public school system can be revitalized, but only by "embracing the old-time education." Their interest goes far beyond minimum competency exams; they call for totally revamping the system — putting it back on its *proper course*.

There seems to be some hope in that a "resurgence of traditional education has reached America's campuses. A third of the nation's colleges and universities are now reevaluating curriculums and undergraduate requirements in order to strengthen their once-thriving but recently faltering general education programs."[27]

THE CURRICULUM CORRUPTS

Prepared by the National Science Foundation under a government grant of over $7 *million*, "Man: A Course of Study" (MACOS) — a social science course taught to fifth-graders — indeed attempts to reduce man to the level of an animal.[28]

And what is taught in this course? It introduces adultery, wife swapping, cannibalism, murder, female infanticide, and senilicide. It promotes cultural relativism; that is, all truths or values are determined by the individual or culture in terms of the time or place of the situation. This is just another example of our "well-intentioned" educators planting beneficial attitudes in the minds of our youth.

Without doubt, God is a dirty word to humanists, while all manner of evil becomes an "alternate life-style." Is it any wonder that young people who hold traditional values are often ridiculed or ostracized for their beliefs?

What a contrast to the schools we knew *before* John Dewey and his humanistic mob of "progressive educators" took over! A study, investigating the moral and religious content of 1,291 American school readers in use between 1776 and 1920, clearly illustrates the shift from a biblical to a humanistic orientation in public education. The study found "100 percent emphasis on moral and religious content from 1776 to 1786, approximately 50 percent emphasis from 1786 to 1825, 21 percent from 1825 to 1880, and only 5 percent from 1916 to 1920."[29] At present the percent is so small as to be immeasurable.

We send our children to school to learn — to master knowledge. Since we pay the bills, we properly expect that only subjects constituting "an agreed-upon body of knowledge" will be taught. We don't need or want propaganda, political indoctrination, or pornography in our nation's schools.

Unfortunately, America is on the brink of destruction. Because she has taken God out of the schools and thrust her innocent children into the talons of the ugly god of humanism, our country has opened herself to philosophies repellent to traditional American values.

In effect, she sacrifices her children to a god that lustfully vomits out all that is good and righteous. Teaching a child that there is no god other than himself, that everything is in a state of perpetual flux, and that everything is relative to one's own desires breeds fear and uncertainty. Parents then wonder what has happened to their kids.

Once these kids find themselves hooked on drugs, living in the streets, locked behind bars, or pregnant outside of wedlock, it will be too late. Parents, wake up! The god of humanism literally *devours* those who follow him.

Anyone concerned about our children — our nation's very future — must resist this horrendous evil with every legal means at his disposal. Such resistance is crucial if our schools are to once again fulfill their traditional role of carrying on our cultural, historical, and patriotic traditions.

LAWLESSNESS IN THE SCHOOLS

Survival, rather than learning, would seem to be the order of the day at many public high schools. Realizing this, President Reagan declared that America's schools must be "temples of learning and not drug dens." He ordered the Justice Department and Department of Education to find ways of helping schools "enforce discipline."[30]

Certainly, if there is to be an element of learning in the schools, classrooms must be disciplined, orderly, and traditional. To encourage such an atmosphere, Neil Postman, the New York University professor who gained notoriety with his 1969 book, *Teaching as a Subversive Activity,* even recommends a dress code for students. He says it "signifies that school is a special place in which special kinds of behaviors are required [and] in which the uses of the intellect are given prominence in a setting of elevated language, civilized manners, and respect for social symbols."[31]

Compare the wide differences in the types of discipline problems occurring several decades ago and the types occurring now. In 1940, the top offenses in public schools were running in the halls, chewing gum, wearing improper clothing, making noise, and failing to put papers in wastebaskets. Today the top offenses are rape, robbery, assault, personal theft, burglary, drug abuse, arson, bombings, alcohol abuse, carrying of weapons, absenteeism, vandalism, murder, and extortion.

Some schools literally resemble "battle zones" where students and teachers both suffer the symptoms of combat neurosis.

Largely at fault for the lax discipline are the "theoretical educators" of the 1960s and early 1970s. Best-selling books of these years represented teachers (especially white, middle-class teachers) as outright villains who *deserved* any type of physical retaliation.[32]

The increasing number of student assaults on our embattled teachers is a commentary on how America has been "civilizing" its children. A generation ago, attacks on teachers were punished swiftly and severely. Even disrespectful language was unacceptable. Today? Our schools — the blackboard jungles — have become so dangerous that an all-pervading fear lurks in every corner.

As this was being written, the news carried a report on an English teacher in California who gave his freshman high school students an assignment to devise a perfect murder. He saw nothing sinister or improper in the assignment. The minds of men have become demented to a degree that they truly cannot see. They are indeed blind — at least in the area of *moral* vision.

ACADEMIC FREEDOM

Our educational system is intellectually bankrupt. The organization that once had a very simple mission — to educate our young people — has lost sight of its responsibility in a zeal to transform itself into an instrument for converting the political complexion of our nation. Marx advised that if you seize the minds of just one generation of children, you can take over a nation without a single shot being fired. We are almost at that point today.

About 20 years ago, the term "academic freedom" burst upon the national scene — seared into the national consciousness by liberal plotters in the information media and by supposedly respected educators. It was brandished aloft like a cherished American tradition that had been accepted since the early days of the republic. Ask the average citizen today where "academic freedom" is guaranteed and most will say in the Constitution, in the Bill of Rights, or in the Bible. The *fact* is that academic freedom is *nowhere* guaranteed, or even *mentioned,* in American tradition. It is a concept manufactured out of whole cloth a few years ago by those who wanted to be unfettered in their efforts to promote ideas repugnant to the average American.

There is, in fact, no such thing as "academic freedom." Teachers are not — and should not be — free to teach whatever they choose to the children *you* entrust to their care. Teachers are employees of parents and should teach what the parents *want* taught to their children.

Unfortunately, those who have seized the educational system by subversion knew that someday parents would grow restive and revolt, demanding that control be returned to them. They, therefore, arranged for an impenetrable jungle of rules and regulations, as well as tiers of bureaucrats, to stand between them and parental wrath. That's where things stand today. Your local atheistic principal, superintendent, and school board member can thus smile benignly and point over his shoulder and disclaim all responsibility, as blame is shunted to the next bureaucratic level. "It's not *my* fault — I just follow the regulations."

WHAT THEN CAN YOU DO?

Where can you turn for redress? Only the *elected* official turns pale when the voters grow angry. If you begin to put pressure on your elected officials and demand action, it will rapidly filter through to the *presumably* insulated bureaucrats. Beyond this? There is one other element (besides importuning prayer) that can turn the situation around. Mildew thrives in the dark. The one thing any fungus can't stand is direct exposure to sunlight. Satan can't abide exposure either. The more the *real* forces behind today's sordid educational practices are exposed before the bar of public opinion, the harder it will be for them to complete the job they're committed to. Talk to your friends. Recommend and pass along copies of this book, and books and pamphlets like it. Persuade parents to take an active interest in their children's schools, books, and curricula. This is the best single hope for cleaning up the mess in our schools.

And, finally, let's look at the *results* our schools are producing today.

Bill is a young man in his mid-twenties. He met the Lord in a personal relationship at the end of his junior year in high school. He couldn't wait to get to college where he wanted to become a minister of the Gospel.

When Bill enrolled in a "Divinity School" which was a division of an Eastern university, he was ready to have his Bible knowledge expanded — to lay down the broad base of knowledge that would make him a well-rounded servant of the Lord. Within six months he had dropped out of the ministerial program and was wallowing about in a mire of confusion and agnosticism. The "learned" theologians he had met had confused him with clever questions and snide allusions to "Bible myths" and "contradictions" within the Word of God. In less than a year these wolves in ecclesiastical clothing had robbed him of his God-given faith and had thrown him out into the world like a sheared lamb.

Today Bill is a lieutenant in the U. S. Army, fighting to reestablish the faith he lost just a few years ago. With God's grace and your prayers, I'm confident he'll find it again. He's basically a fine young man.

Our country is literally overrun with these disciples of evil who are robbing our young people of their relationship with the Lord. Are we going to allow this sordid situation to continue?

In the old days, in the Promised Land, the Lord God led His people in their fights against the forces of evil. Isn't it time that we stop hiding behind defensive walls and start moving forward on the attack?

The forces of evil are well-known, and their methods are well-documented. Theirs is a might that has been *subversively* built up in this country over a half-century. The only thing we have on our side is God's Word that He will render us *"mighty . . . to the pulling down of strong holds"* (II Corinthians 10:4).

How much more do we need than that?

SURVIVAL OF
THE FITTEST

"It may be that family violence is in fact on the rise in absolute terms, that social strains . . . and a spreading cult of violence are producing a sinister, growing pattern of abuse and death threatening the institution most critical to the survival of our and any society, the family."[1]

From the first raids on settlers' stockades to the most recent front-page stories of assassinations, terrorism, and mass murders, violence has been interwoven into the fabric of American society. Yet a new dimension in violence — a particularly frightening demonstration of man's inhumanity to man — spreads across our nation like a cancer. Like a malignancy (which depends on the host for survival but destroys the host anyway) this disease invades our homes and threatens to engulf our nation. We are speaking of family violence.

While most of it continues to lurk behind closed doors, its effects are nonetheless far-reaching. Its distinctive cruelty stems from its violation of the trust upon which all intimate human relations depend. It attacks those it supposedly loves — those nearest, most vulnerable, and least able to defend themselves.

A violation of trust is painful at any age, but in the infant or young child a basic sense of trust is essential for normal development. It is from this basic trust that the child's feelings about himself develop. It also plays an important role in how the child sees the world around him — whether it appears as a warm, friendly place or a cold, hostile, and threatening environment.

Whatever a person's early environment, it will influence him throughout life. To a large extent, it determines the amount of energy that will be free for creative pursuits, learning, and social relationships.

Michael Novack warns, "If infants are injured here, not all the institutions of society can put them back together. Familial strength that took generations to acquire can be lost in a single generation, can disappear for centuries. If the quality of family life deteriorates, there *is* no 'quality of life.'"[2]

Alberta Siegel, of Stanford, agrees. "Every civilization is only twenty years away from barbarism. For twenty years is all we have to accomplish the task of civilizing the infants . . . who know nothing of our language, our culture, our religion, our values, or our customs or interpersonal relations."[3]

Ideally, there's no better place for that process to begin than in the home, since it is meant to be a secure base from which to venture out to explore a whole new world. For this reason, violence inflicted here — especially by someone trusted as a guardian — is a special betrayal.

Scores of children suffer the pain and agony of that betrayal, yet we hear nothing about it. It would seem that our civilized society would not tolerate such cruelty. If an illness suddenly struck our households — killing thousands of Americans and costing billions of dollars a year — we would marshall the forces of the country to find a cure. If terrorists seized and plundered our homes, we would combine our hearts, minds, and energies to stop the devastation. On the other hand, family violence receives only the most minor of attention from public officials and is often given low priority in the budget planning of legislators. When media men do make it public, they select those rare cases in which "religious" or "Christian" parents conform to the caricature of the overzealous, fanatical, authoritarian ruler and disciplinarian.

Unfortunately, family violence — which infects every strata of society — often remains a family secret. It frequently takes on forms that would disgust and horrify all normal people — *if* they were aware of it.

One alarming aspect of family violence is its natural reproduction of itself. Like a poisonous plant, it sends out spores to propagate itself. Children of battered mothers — accustomed to the idea of family business being conducted with fists — often become battered wives or battering husbands. Worse, abused children grow up predisposed to abuse their own children. Sexually abused boys often become pedophiles and rapists while sexually victimized girls are more liable to become battered wives.[4] Undeniably, children imitate adults and *learn* patterns for family interaction.

Richard Gelles, a sociologist at the University of Rhode Island, described the grim ecology of a violent family: "The husband will beat the wife. The wife may then learn to beat the children. The bigger siblings learn it's O.K. to hit the little ones, and the family pet may be the ultimate recipient of violence."[5] Sadly, the youngest victims often have no one to turn to or cannot explain their dilemma, even if someone would listen and believe them.

A CULT OF VIOLENCE

The reasons for family violence are varied and perplexing. Some people attribute its growth to the unsuccessful struggle of humans to adapt to the rapid social and technological changes of a complex society. However, "coping with such pressures by rechanneling them through violence in the home may ultimately squelch our chances for survival at all."[6]

Nevertheless, violence remains a part of the American cultural scene. Impressionable children absorb violence through television and movies, newsmen give it a high priority in their reporting — and in sports, people pay to watch the violence that enlivens boxing, wrestling, and football.

In many ways, Americans actually idealize violence. An emerging body of scholarly literature indicates that violent methods are the ones used most frequently for goal attainment on TV programs. Most shows promote and encourage instant gratification. *Deferment* of gratification — often essential to a larger reward in real life — is generally belittled on TV. The prevailing attitude on television is, "I want what I want — and I want it *now*!" Of course, violence is the usual method for gaining goals on TV.

Regarding the bulk of current TV programming, Alberta Siegel asked some questions:[7]

• How many instances are there of *constructive* interventions to *end* disagreements?

• What methods (other than violence) are shown for resolving conflicts?

• How often is reconciliation shown?

• What strategies are shown for reducing hate?

• How often does the viewer see adults behaving in loving and helpful ways?

• What examples of mutual respect does he view?

• What can be learned about law and order?

• How many episodes of police kindness does he see?

• How often does the glow of *compassion* light the screen?

By using these questions to evaluate standard TV fare, we can understand how a civilized nation could be persuaded to resort to barbarianism and violence.

Recently, *Psychology Today* asked its readers the following question: "If you could secretly push a button and thus eliminate any person, with no repercussions to yourself, *would you press that button?*" Of the more than 650 readers who responded to the question, 60 percent said, yes, they would (if they could) send "that special someone" a *lightning bolt!*[8]

Yet there's no place as violent as the home. In his home in Houston a few years ago, second-grader Daniel Brownell, whose stepfather's attacks had left him paralyzed and permanently senseless, was found branded with cigarette burns that spelled out "I CRY."[9] What possesses a human being to brutalize a helpless child in such an inhumane way?

What is most disturbing is that little Daniel Brownell was not an isolated victim. Such inhumanity happens every day. Kentucky's Senator Wendell Anderson stated in the Congressional Record on March 16, 1978, "The fact is that while 39 thousand Americans died in the Vietnam conflict between 1967 and 1973, at the same time 17,570 Americans literally died on the home front — from family violence. Most of these were women and children."

"'Intimate Victims: A Study of Violence Among Friends and Relatives' conducted by the U. S. Department of Justice . . . published in January 1980 . . .showed that between 1973 and 1976, over three million incidents of violence among intimates took place. This study included *only those over the age of twelve*. In two-fifths of the cases, the results were bruises, black eyes, cuts, and scratches. One victim in every 20 was knifed or received a gunshot wound. A roughly equal proportion had bones broken or teeth knocked out, or received internal injuries, or were knocked unconscious. About 16% received burns, or had their hair pulled out."[10]

According to several psychologists, the estimated two million battered women and children each year are only the tip of the iceberg! Over 3.4 million children have been kicked, beaten, or punched by a parent at some time during their childhood. Between 1.4 and 2.3 million children have been beaten, and up to 1.8 million between 3 and 17 years of age have been threatened with a knife or a gun by a parent.[11]

"Despite discrepancies, research [figures] . . . portray a landscape dotted with casualties. They create a picture which would alarm us were the wounded reported among our soldiers on a foreign, rather than the domestic, front."[12]

CRIME ON THE HOME FRONT

If every assault made against another person were considered a crime (regardless of whether it occurred inside or outside a marriage or home), domestic assaults would undoubtedly be the single most frequently encountered crime in America today.

The FBI is aware of exactly 22,516 murders committed in the United States in 1981, a fifth of them killings of loved ones.[13] *Time* magazine reports that six million women are abused each year by husbands or boyfriends,[14] but an English law professor writes, "Once within the Family Court setting and a social welfare counseling orientation we may lose track of the fact that wife-beating may be a brutal criminal assault and not just the symptom of a troubled marriage."[15]

"One study by the Battered Women Research Center in Denver, Colorado, showed that 34% of the 400 battered women studied had been raped in their marriage at least once: 59% had been forced into sex, 49% more than once, 41% objected to being forced to insert objects into their vaginas, engage in group sex, have sex with animals, or play bondage games."[16]

The statistics are immensely disturbing:[17]

• Nearly six million wives will be abused by their husbands in any one year.

• Some 2,000 to 4,000 women are beaten *to death* annually.

• The nation's police spend one-third of their time responding to domestic violence calls.

• Battery is the single major cause of injury to women — more significant than auto accidents, rapes, or muggings.

• A 1979 FBI report stated that 40 percent of women killed were murdered by their partners — and 10 percent of men by theirs. (Many of these women acted in self-defense.)

Who would have ever thought that when the minister read "for better or for worse" they would experience the "worse" in the form of daily terror, vicious torment, bruises, broken bones, and even gunshot wounds.

One woman lamented, "Being married to this man was like being a prisoner of war. I was not allowed to visit my family. I couldn't go out on my own. He wouldn't even let me cry. If I did, it started an 'episode.'"[18]

We are told this selfish possessiveness and insecurity often increases during pregnancy. Psychologist Lenore Walker notes from her interviews with several hundred women, "Most of the women interviewed said the physical violence became more acute during pregnancy and the child's infancy. Men who are dependent logically become frustrated when the woman begins to pay attention to dependent infants instead of to them. More often it was a simple case of prenatal child abuse."[19]

The frequency of battering during pregnancy makes it particularly shocking. Of the women in shelters, 42 percent report experiencing it. In most cases, the man slapped the woman or punched her in the vulnerable abdomen or genitals.[20] It seems the intent to harm was directed equally at the unborn child and the wife.

A 30-year-old, middle-class housewife was first beaten by her husband when she was pregnant. Then last summer her husband, in a fit of temper, hurled a dinner plate across the kitchen at her. Instead of hitting her, the plate shattered against the wall, and a piece of it struck their four-year-old daughter in the face.[21] An innocent child became the victim of her father's infantile temper tantrum. In moments his temper no doubt subsided, but permanently blind in one eye, the child bears a constant reminder of the cruelty of family violence.

It's heartbreaking to consider the vicious web being woven by immature parents, many of whom are little more than children themselves. Psychologists, social workers, and sociologists agree that children exposed to violence grow up to become violent adults — both as mates and as parents. By being reared in a violent family, the young learn to be violent. In fact, parents who are most abusive to their own children received severe physical punishment, or were abused, as children.[22] We can't deny that children imitate adults and learn styles of family life from them — for good or bad.

One author reports that "one of the most distasteful aspects of human psychology is the fact that once violence has begun to be used against the helpless, helplessness not only loses its capacity to inhibit but may actually increase the use of violence. When animals of the same species engage in contests, the loser is generally allowed to go free, but men seldom let their defeated enemies escape."[23]

THE ATTACKER

Michael Groetsch, director of probation for the New Orleans Municipal Court, who sees scores of accused wife beaters every week, compares the male batterer to a two- or three-year-old: "His tantrums are very similar to those of a two-year-old. Like a narcissistic child, the batterer bites when he's throwing a tantrum. I have many women come in with teeth marks all over their arms and legs."[24]

Nine out of 10 wife abusers can be said to be violent individuals in general.[25] It appears that the problem isn't specific anger directed toward a wife, but rather an undirected *general* rage that *focuses* on the closest and easiest target — the wife. In many cases it is the abuser's own self-hate that is unleashed. When he finally vents his pent-up anger, wives, children, animals, and physical objects may receive the brunt of it.

The wife or child abuser must not be thought of as just someone reacting in anger, however. All too often, there may be no apparent "rage reaction." The abuser may attack with cold, cruel disregard for either the rights or feelings of his victims. It sometimes seems that he desires to create terror beyond what he may accomplish with simple physical violence.

Unfortunately, wife beating has by and large become an accepted practice among many men. Because men often believe that aggression or physical violence are acceptable ways to respond to stress and frustration, the problem of battered women continues to exist. How tragic that we aren't teaching the next generation that physical power and coercion aren't legitimate avenues for settling differences! Of course, to the person raised with constant violence (on TV and in movies), it's going to be a difficult job.

There's a certain irony in family violence. When it comes to fighting back the forces of communism which seek to enslave us, there is no desire to fight. Then we have only weak, complacent men wanting peace. Their aggressive tendencies seem to surface only when helpless victims are present.

A MATE — OR PROPERTY?

Another reason for wife beating's long history has been the common feeling among many husbands that a wife is an item of personal property and therefore subject to his whims and demands. Unfortunately, many have accepted this lowly view of the wife as a natural, howbeit unfortunate, situation.

One may expect to find this type of thinking among heathen cultures and pagan religions, but even in some Christian circles the woman is viewed as property. Christian counselors come equipped with unbelievable horror stories of wife abuse in Christian homes — even in homes where the abuser is a minister.

Maxine Hoffman, in an article in the *Pentecostal Evangel,* writes, "Statistics indicate that one of two women, *Christian or otherwise,* is battered at some time during her life."[26]

In fact, research shows that women from all socioeconomic and religious levels are abused at similar rates of occurrence.[27] It's been further suggested that in some cases religious opinions actually aggravate the problem. Primarily, this occurs when the wife is a Christian but the husband isn't. Feeling resentful or threatened by his wife's faith, the husband wants to eliminate it and regain control over her — even if he must resort to force.

Christianity Today declares, "There is a great deal of battering happening in Christian marriages, even in our churches, right under our noses."[28] Much of the current abuse seems to stem from a resurgence of strong teaching on the absolute submission of the wife to the husband. Some carry the teaching to the point of absurdity, making the Christian family a source of mockery in the eyes of the community.

C. Donald Cole, in his "Christian Perspectives on the News," writes, "Man's lordship over woman has been exploited to the point of physical degradation and beyond." He quotes I Peter 3:7, *"Husbands . . . be considerate as you live with your wives"* (NIV). Cole concludes, "If we participate in the institutionalized abuse of women . . . how much is our religion worth?"[29]

Of the thousands of wife beaters who happen to be in prison (almost all are there for some other crime), most regard rapists with contempt, while rapists look down on child abusers. But, in actuality, the three groups have many common traits.

They are often alcoholic or drug dependent.[30] In addition, they all tend to have low self-esteem. They use violence as a means of gaining power over those around them. Immature and impulsive, they want and demand *instant* gratification. Uncommonly isolated and virtually friendless, they are cut off from the mainstream of society.[31] From their narrow, private world they are constantly confronted by their own insecurities and inadequacies.

Unfortunately, women and children are the principal victims of these misguided, empty personalities. In 13 percent of wife abuse cases, children are assaulted.[32] According to a recent four-year study of a major metropolitan hospital, 25 percent of women's suicide attempts are preceded by a history of battering.[33]

Although men are *usually* the attackers in family violence, there are an estimated 282,000 *men* annually beaten by their wives.[34] In addition, domestic violence is also lethal to policemen. *Police* magazine reports that 40 percent of all police injuries — and 20 percent of all police deaths on duty — are the result of becoming caught in family disputes.[35]

Like the ripples of a wave, the repercussions of violence move out in ever-widening circles throughout society. A cold and hostile environment may make hardy survivors but it does little to produce the qualities that make for comfortable and serene living. Instead, it leaves the survivors devoid of normal reactions and conventional social skills. They become people who "slash their way through life *surviving* by hurting others, especially those whom they love."[36] And they, in turn, perpetuate the vicious cycle of violence by creating within their own children similar survival tactics.

IT CROSSES SOCIAL STRATAS

The problem of child abuse isn't restricted to special classes of people as some persons suppose. It cuts across all socioeconomic and ethnic lines.

Typically, abusive parents are young (between 18 and 35). They are likely to be experiencing financial, emotional, or marital difficulties. As mentioned earlier, they were probably abused themselves and lack satisfying outside social diversions — as well as the emotional support of sympathetic friends or relatives.[37]

This is where the church can come in. The problem of family violence begins with the individual. Through a relationship with Jesus Christ and a loving, supportive church family, the void can be filled.

Like wife abuse, child abuse is nothing new. Although a once-well-kept family secret surviving furtively in the shadows, it has emerged from behind closed doors to public awareness. In many ways, it remains an interlocking puzzle, fraught with mystery, complexities, and innumerable difficulties, but we can't ignore it. If we believe in the sanctity of human life, the horrible nightmare of child abuse must be faced.

Solutions are needed to break what appears to be a "family tradition" of epidemic proportions. First, however, we must be alerted to the tragedies occurring daily even in the finest homes and best neighborhoods. This enemy isn't *particular*; it's simply a matter of finding a victim who is young and vulnerable.

To the average person, the idea of a child being abused by those entrusted with his care is almost unthinkable. It violates our ideas of a happy childhood and the maternal instinct as well as our belief that children are always better off in their own homes.

For most of us, becoming aware of even the *existence* of child abuse is a painful experience. It hurts to think that childhood may be agonizing, that parents may torture their children, and that the traditional family may be, in fact, a chamber of horrors. It imposes on us a realization of the extremes of human suffering, helplessness, and sadism. Many people, finding thoughts of this nature too painful to entertain, prefer to just deny their existence.

We would do well to model our responses to life's tragedies after those of Jesus Christ. Children are the heartbeat of Jesus. He is touched by their tears, pains, fears, and loneliness. He doesn't ignore their problems — He deals with them head-on. How, then, can *we* turn away from the heartrending cries of America's little people?

SWEEPING IT UNDER THE RUG

Unfortunately, we have averted our eyes. Silence and denial have been the chief elements in maintaining this hideous violence.

There is often confusion over what *constitutes* child abuse. Professionals define child abuse in a number of ways. When we speak of child abuse, we mean the deliberate and willful injury of a child by a caretaker. Child neglect, on the other hand, can be the more passive (but equally harmful) treatment caused by a parent or guardian's lack of care or interest.

Although most parents have experienced fleeting moments of ill feelings toward their children or have had violent or aggressive outbursts at one time or another, they have been able to successfully control their impulses and substitute more appropriate reactions. All parents aren't able to perform in this way, however. Many adults can't adjust to the stresses and strains of society *or* of child care. As a result, many abuse their children physically or psychologically — often in ways too devastating to imagine.

The United Nations Declaration of the Rights of a Child states in Principal 2: "The child shall enjoy special protection, and shall be given opportunities and facilities, by law and by other means, to enable him to develop physically, mentally, morally, spiritually, and socially in a healthy and normal manner and in conditions of freedom and dignity."

For thousands of children these rights are grossly violated. Admittedly, the problem is a complex one and there is no simple answer. The breakdown of the family and rapid changes in society increase stress — no doubt contributing to an environment favoring child abuse. These are factors, however, rather than actual causes of abuse.

In any event, most experts seem to agree that the problem of child abuse, as it has been revealed, is only the tip of the iceberg. One report shows one million children abused in the United States in 1978 — 5,000 of these dying as a direct result of the abuse they suffered.[38] In the United States today, physical abuse is the number-one cause of death among children.[39]

In fact, in the year 1962, child abuse experts predicted that the battered child syndrome would be found a more frequent cause of death than such well-recognized diseases as leukemia, cystic fibrosis, and muscular dystrophy. They said that it would rank with automobile accidents and toxic and infectious agents as causes of disturbances of the central nervous system (the brain and spinal cord).[40]

THE VICTIMS

Frank Osanka, an authority on abuse statistics, claims that seven children die of abuse every day. Most of them are younger than three. In addition, brain damage (which may well cripple a child for life) occurs in *12* children per day as a result of abuse. He suspects that unreported cases would inflate these figures three times.[41]

Ray Helfer, another leading child abuse authority, predicts that "if changes aren't made in prevention and treatment, there will be millions of reported cases of child abuse in the next ten years — including 50 thousand deaths and 30 thousand permanently injured children — most with brain damage."[42]

In a society that supports the prevention of cruelty to animals, child abuse seems primitive and barbaric. For that reason, many recoil at the implications of child abuse for society as a whole.

A child abuse specialist points out that the rate of increase is geometric. If a woman has four children and abuses them, she has created a potential for *four abusive families*.[43]

A child can't escape the influences of his surroundings. In the case of the abused child, there is not only an inadequate and distorted parent-child relationship, but also an atmosphere inadequate to meet normal needs.[44]

Taken together, the entire home environment harms the child. His whole life is one of abuse and neglect, of family instability, and of parents too incompetent to provide the normal surroundings that go with growth and development.

A child *must* have a place of warmth and security where needs are met. In a cold or indifferent environment, he tends to "give up" and just survive. His growth — physical, mental, psychological, or spiritual — may be seriously retarded.

THE LONG-TERM RESULTS

Child abuse is a complex situation involving long-term consequences. The child's self-image is probably wounded as badly as his physical body. He feels the animosity directed toward him as much as he feels the physical blows. He perhaps feels cheated, if he is old enough to reason, because he knows he has done nothing to *deserve* it. The problem is basically the parent's, not his. He feels all alone in a world he can't control. If the abuse is extreme, actual physical damage to the brain and spinal cord may complicate the psychological wounds he has received.

Unfortunately, parents often confuse punishment with discipline. The child can't develop properly without correction and guidance. At times, discipline can require physical correction, but the intent must be for the child's good and not his harm. Spankings administered by a loving parent hurt, but they should not injure. When parents lose control and violently lash out in anger, actual physical and emotional harm can result.

It's wise to recall that "violence begets violence." In *Hide or Seek*, Dr. James Dobson comments, "Every day of his life, from the lonely days of childhood to the televised moment of his spectacular death, Oswald experienced the crushing awareness of his own inferiority. Finally, as it so often does, his grief turned to anger. The greater tragedy is that Lee Harvey Oswald's plight is not unusual in America today."[45]

A seven-year study reveals that the consistent element in the backgrounds of 1,800 delinquents was excessive parental punishment.[46] Furthermore, the degree of delinquency tended to match the degree of severity of the punishment endured. In effect, the study found that you can almost *predict* the degree of hostility that will remain with the child *throughout life* by seeing how severely he is punished as a child.

Such children end up with extremely low opinions of themselves — opinions imposed by parents while they were young. It may be that their compulsion to "get into trouble" is a continuation of the parent's dedication to "punishing them because they're bad."

As a result of living in a potentially explosive atmosphere, abused children learn to keep a "low profile."[47] They move less than normal children, explore less than normal children, and *speak* less than normal children. In effect, they become like chameleons, learning to blend into the background so they won't be noticed. Of course, such withdrawal prevents a child from reaching his full potential of development.

A typical abused child leads a predictable life divided into 13 stages:[48]

- Birth.
- Insecurity.
- Low self-esteem.
- Lack of trust in the adult world.
- Rejection in the family and peer group.
- Isolation.
- Rejection at school.
- Alienation (also incipient alcohol and drug addiction).
- Rejection by society.
- Inferiority.
- Helplessness.
- Exhaustion.
- Advanced alcohol and drug addiction.

Another problem typical of abused children is that their chameleon life-style causes them to cast off personal integrity early in life.[49] "If lying protects you, lie!" Not surprisingly, they don't trust *anyone* — let alone themselves.

Alcoholism and drug addiction create special problems for the abused child that need to be considered in view of the abuse of mind-altering chemicals. A study at the Washington Center for Addiction in Boston, Massachusetts, investigated the child care rendered by alcohol- and drug-addicted parents. All their children experienced *some* degree of neglect, but 30.5 percent were *seriously* neglected, 22.5 percent were physically or sexually abused, and 41 percent were *either* abused *or* neglected.[50]

Neglected children have been described as miserable, vermin-infested, filthy, ragged, near naked, pale, starving, and dying. The frequency of abuse or neglect from alcoholics and from addicts was about the same. Abuse was higher in alcoholics than in addicts, but neglect was higher in addicts. The point is that *both* alcoholics and addicts make very poor parents.

It was also found that 42 percent of these parents had been physically or sexually abused by *their* parents during childhood. Having *received* no mothering during childhood, they had no concept of how to *give* mothering.

Some correlation has been found between sexual abuse and drug addiction, particularly in adolescents.[51] Seventy to 80 percent of abusive mothers in a Parents Anonymous group were incestuously abused as children. Adolescent prostitution, suicide, and chronic running away also point toward incest.

Rape, family violence, and incest are still uncomfortable subjects in our society. But Miriam Ingebritson, a Minnesota therapist, says, "As long as incest has that secrecy [taboo], it has a potency and power it doesn't deserve. It has to be stripped of that power."[52] We will deal specifically with the subject of incest in a later chapter.

THE BATTERED PARENT SYNDROME

According to Dennis Madden, director of the Clinical Research Program for Violent Behavior at the University of Maryland Medical School, there is another widespread problem no one is talking about — it's called the battered *parent* syndrome. He says, "Parents are actually living in fear of their own children. Many hide the truth — because of the fear and embarrassment."[53]

It isn't a rare incident confined to one unfortunate family. It is happening in Baltimore where an 11-year-old pushed his mother into a door, breaking her coccyx, in Denver where a 14-year-old girl stabbed her mother with a letter opener because she was not allowed to go to a rock concert, in New York City where a 16-year-old broke his mother's elbow when she admonished him about poor grades."[54]

One child's excuse was, "It was his fault. He aggravated me. Hey, once they took away my room 'cause I wouldn't clean it up. They had no right to do that!"[55]

Still another type of family violence is becoming known as a social problem. It is called "granny bashing." It is the flip British phrase for mistreatment in which the elderly are abused by their children or grandchildren.[56]

Suzanne Steinmetz, of the University of Delaware, claims that "parent battering is the big problem confronting family-care professionals today."[57] Estimates indicate that it occurs at about the same ratio as child abuse.[58]

While some professionals disagree, Steinmetz sees a direct relationship between child abuse and parent abuse. "Our study showed that parents who are not violent toward their children stand only a one-in-400 chance of being on the receiving end. But if a parent is violent toward the child, the probability of attack goes up to 200 out of 400."[59]

Don Cuvo, a marriage and family therapist at the Family and Children's Services of Greater St. Louis, when speaking of young parent-bashers, observes, "I've never seen anything like it. These kids show no remorse. They aren't a bit sorry. Are we raising a generation without conscience?"[60]

NO EMOTION

An "absence of effect," as psychiatrists call it, is the most frightening aspect of all. We are now beginning to see this in our juveniles who have turned criminal. In the past, feelings of guilt or remorse generally followed a juvenile's explosive outbursts, but the "new criminals have been so brutalized in their own upbringing that they seem incapable of viewing their victims as fellow human beings or [in the case of murder, even] of realizing that they have killed another person."[61]

Increasingly, psychiatric reports on juveniles arrested for murder are filled with phrases such as "shows no feeling," "shows no remorse," "no discernible emotional reaction," and "demonstrates no relationship." A youth worker told a New York State Assembly subcommittee, "They seem to have no ability to distinguish between someone shot in a movie and shooting someone themselves. To them, everything is one big movie."[62]

THE RUSSIAN EXAMPLE

As early as 1919, Soviet authorities decreed that "the family has ceased to be a necessity both for its members and for the state."[63] In a few years the Soviet's great experiment began to fall apart. Men, feeling powerless and having lost a sense of responsibility, stepped aside and gave way to a more matriarchal type of society. Soon the solidarity of the family collapsed. Children raised primarily by mothers vented their frustration, giving rise to juvenile delinquency on a scale that had been previously unheard of. And the women didn't come out unscathed either. Far from elevating the status of women, the revolution robbed them of honor and demoralized them. We are seeing the same scenario unfolding in our country today.

Rates of violent crime and juvenile delinquency have been relatively stable since the mid-1970s but criminal violence remains extraordinarily high.[64] Efforts to reduce these rates have produced few results. It seems obvious that we must look at what was *right* a few years back and then see if there's still time to recapture some of the values that worked so well then.

When we allow TV to replace the family, church, school, and community, we subject impressionable young people to values which openly encourage self-interest and brute force. Our placid acceptance of the situation has begun to strip us of all the basics — to leave us a society where "might makes right."

No matter how we measure it, statistics show violent crime as a grave threat to our nation's safety and security. It occurs with ever-greater frequency and in ever-newer areas. All violent crimes — murder, assault, rape, and robbery — are up. And it isn't confined to crowded, impoverished inner cities or decaying slums and ghettos. It occurs both on the tree-lined streets of suburbia and on quiet country roads. Criminal behavior is endemic to every sector of American society. Many Americans actually fear to walk down the streets of their own neighborhoods.

At this moment, there seems little promise of improvement in the situation. In 1967, the President's Crime Commission estimated that a boy born in that year had a 62-percent chance of being arrested for some criminal offense over the course of his life.[65] That commission was just about on target.

Crimes of violence in the U. S. are growing faster than the population. As a result, our society is literally falling apart. In fact, sociologists calculate that if the robbery rate in large cities continues to grow as it did between 1962 and 1974, "by the year 2024 each man, woman, and child in a large city would be robbed by force or threat of force 2.3 times per year."[66]

"Last year, virtually one-third of all homes were victimized and a reported 23,000 Americans were killed by criminals. This was up from 16,000 in 1970 and was *four times* as many Americans as were killed in combat per year in the Vietnam War."[67]

Who commits these violent crimes? Almost 90 percent of those arrested for violent crimes are male, and most of these are young — more than half are under 25 years of age.[68] Another report shows that most crime is committed by school-age youth. Over *half* of arrests for violent crimes are of males between the ages of 13 and 20, while this group comprises less than one-tenth of our population.[69]

The most disturbing aspect of the growth in street crime by young criminals is its swing toward viciousness. One compassionate lawyer with a real interest in her young clients speaks of the "terrifying generation of kids" that emerged during the late 1960s and 1970s. She notes that at one time "adolescents and young men charged with robbery had at worst pushed or shoved a pedestrian or storekeeper to steal money or merchandise; members of the new generation kill, maim, and injure without reason or remorse."[70]

Today's street criminals are more lethally armed and more prepared to use violence.[71] They often kill for no apparent reason. While this phenomenon has surfaced during every known period of rampant violence, the current trend is frightening in its ferocity and in the fact that these vicious criminals are steadily growing younger.

Crime and delinquency cost at least $125 million per year, alter lives, destroy people, frighten and demoralize, and may even threaten our civilization.[72] While inadequate housing, unemployment, and poverty have long been blamed for crime and violence, they are not the *causes;* they are merely a convenient *setting*.

DOES CRIME PAY?

The increased violence in our society is, in fact, a reflection of many factors. It indicates a failure of the family, a failure of the schools, and a failure of all the social institutions responsible for transmitting values and generating character.

To reduce delinquency, there must be a willingness to get at the *root* of the problem. Here we're speaking of personal attitudes, values, and the problems that create criminal attitudes.

Every person, during the growth process, learns and develops methods for coping with life as it exists. We learn by both observing others and noting the results of their actions. We take our cues from what is rewarded — or punished — when others do it.

To reduce juvenile delinquency and crime, we must alter the examples shown to our young people. Ken Kelly, a member of the Board of Directors of the Prisoners Union in San Francisco, states: "In order to persuade juveniles or adults that crime is not acceptable in any society, the role models for that society must be untainted and free from lawlessness and corruption. This is certainly not true in any society that I am aware of and least of all ours."[73]

For at least two decades — ever since World War II, in fact — the weight of legislation (and federal court decisions) has been against the innocent victim to protect the criminal. As a result, the "bringing to justice" of court cases in America is unique in the world.[74]

• It extends over a longer period of time than in any other judicial system.

• It allows for more appeals and more retrials than any other system in the world.

• After all appeals are fully exercised, it allows — in fact, encourages — continued attacks on the conviction even though the conviction has been presumed final.

• In the final step — the correction stage — we seem to lose interest and our performance is a clear *failure*.

No other system in the world invites our kind of never-ending warfare with society — continuing long after criminal guilt has been established beyond reasonable doubt — with all the safeguards of due process. Nevertheless, there are 400,000 individuals in American prisons today, doubling the prison population of a decade ago.[75] The cost to imprison these offenders is bankrupting state budgets.

AMORAL AMERICA

The solutions to violent crime problems are as complex as the behavior of the criminals. Since human behavior is influenced by many factors — law, science, religion, education, social service, and labor must all be enlisted as avenues for reducing violent crime. Each of these areas can contribute something of value to help create a climate in which the family unit can prosper and grow. Strong families are a deterrent to crime.

Our crime problem is enormous because of the millions of young, impressionable children who have been desensitized and brutalized by family violence, or who have grown up in broken homes without guidance or control. Still others have undisciplined, drug-addicted, or alcoholic parents as their only role models. "The intrusion of drugs into the child's life not only dulls and incapacitates his emotional growth, but its availability and traffic creates disrespect for law itself."[76]

Somehow we must strengthen the institutions that encourage personal responsibility. Nothing will be gained by directing our attention to the symptoms. Obviously, the problem lies in a generation that is scornful of conventional moral behavior. It's like fighting a fire. You direct the stream of water at the *base* of the fire — not at the flames leaping in the air. If we don't "put out" the areas *feeding* the problem, the problem will only grow worse.

The law of the land, as well as all true law, is based on moral principles. From these values we evolve acceptable patterns to control our lives. Any society basing its laws and morals on God's laws has no problems. It is our departure from accepted Christian principles that has ignited the fire in our midst.

While there is little *public* awareness of research proving that religious institutions reduce crime, it is widely recognized by *criminologists* that religious institutions do, in fact, curb crime.

The United Nations 1977 World Crime Survey shows that countries in which there is a definite religious influence have low crime rates.[77] Consider how evil would flourish if the body of Christ were removed as a restraining force in our own society. I don't think we can imagine the horror of it!

Amoral America, a book published in 1975, summarized a study by political scientist George C. S. Benson and Thomas E. Engeman. Dr. Engeman says that Western society suffers from inadequate training in individual ethics. He adds that personal honesty and integrity, appreciation of the interests of others, nonviolence, and abiding by the law are examples of values insufficiently taught at the present time. There is a severe and almost paralyzing ethical problem in this country, Engeman continued. He believes that unlawful behavior is, in part, the result of the absence of instruction in individual ethics.[78]

On June 4, 1981, Mark W. Cannon delivered an address on the subject "Crime and the Decline in Values," which attracted widespread interest. The apparent reaction to his speech indicates a growing apprehension that crime is threatening all that is of value in our society. There is increasing concern about the deterioration of moral values that keep a lawful and responsible society under control. The more these moral standards are torn asunder by liberal thinkers and planners, the worse our American crime problem will grow.

Though it may surprise our present "educators," achievement is closely tied to moral values. The cream of our young people can be found among the names listed in *Who's Who Among American High School Students*. Here are results of a poll taken among this group:[79]

• Eight out of 10 belong to an active religion, and 71 percent attend services regularly.

• Nearly half don't drink, and 88 percent have never smoked.

• A vast majority (94 percent) have never used drugs, including marijuana.

• At least 80 percent don't think marijuana should be legalized, and 90 percent wouldn't use it if it were.

• Over three-fourths (76 percent) of these teens have not had sexual intercourse.

• Some 87 percent of those surveyed favor a traditional marriage.

• The majority (52 percent) watch less than 10 hours of television per week.

Integrity is required to be truly successful in life. A person of integrity is one who is at peace with himself and, therefore, free to direct his energies toward worthy goals. An individual *without* values, purposes, or goals tends to be at war with himself. Although he may *strive* to achieve, the bulk of his efforts will be dissipated. In effect, he is *shadowboxing* with success and is thus doomed to eventual failure.

God's Word says:

> *"There is a way that seemeth right unto a man, but the end thereof are the ways of death"* (Proverbs 16:25).

When man goes his own way, the road leads only downward. To put it simply, God's way is the only way. Only He gives the peace that men seek in this uptight, weary world.

SODOM AND GOMORRAH REVISITED

"Peradventure ten shall be found there . . . I will not destroy it for ten's sake" (Genesis 18:32). The fact that *not even ten* decent people could be found in Sodom and Gomorrah testified to the infectious nature of unbridled sex, perversion, and pornography.

The eighteenth chapter of the book of Genesis describes Abraham's efforts to preserve the twin cities of Sodom and Gomorrah. Abraham pointed out to the Lord that in destroying these cities for their sin, He *might* be destroying some innocent people included in their populations.

After an exchange in which Abraham winnowed the minimum number of righteous people down from 50 to 10, the Lord agreed to allow the cities to remain if even *10* souls out of their large metropolitan population were found to be decent and God-fearing. A short time later fire and brimstone leveled the site, and today a sheet of greenish fused glass is the world's only memorial to its first "sin city."

Over a period of time, the Bible recounts a number of additional nations (tribes and races) that the Lord ordered utterly wiped off the face of the earth because of sexual sin. Obviously, the Lord does not approve (nor does He condone) blatant, unbridled, and promiscuous sexual sin. As a nation, it would seem that we are in jeopardy of experiencing God's wrath. America is very rapidly approaching the depths reached in Sodom and Gomorrah just before they experienced annihilation.

How does an upright and moral nation find itself toppled from righteous standards to a level of unregenerate filth in just one generation? The whole battery of liberal thought-control forces in our nation focus obsessively on one goal — to tear down every moral influence that *formerly* kept us on an even keel. The press, TV, magazines, movies, the courts, and the "scientific" community present a united front to promote one thought — that *nothing* is too low, too vile, or too perverted to be publicized and "enjoyed" by individuals seeking sexual release.

In so doing they not only lower, but eliminate, any moral restraints that would normally control the excesses of the most debased elements within any society. Thus they allow the noxious excrement of the lowest element to spatter and infect the whole society.

Quite frankly, this very book uses phrases and describes sexual acts and situations that would not have been allowed in public print 30 years ago. I regret having to publicize them here, but we as Christians cannot take a head-in-the-sand attitude. Only by putting them into the glare of direct sunlight is it possible to reverse the relentless onslaught of these attitudes that come directly from the pit of hell.

WARNING: PARENTAL GUIDANCE RECOMMENDED BEFORE READING THIS SECTION

Magazines, movies, and playing cards feature little boys and girls, some as young as three, openly displaying their genitals and participating in coitus, oral, and anal sex.[1]

A seven-year-old girl (a cerebral palsy victim — retarded, blind, and unable to walk without assistance) is abducted from a nursing home and sexually molested. She is the second child in little more than a month. The first victim, a 14-year-old girl, was also retarded and blind.[2]

A pederast (approved as a foster father in Chicago) infects the throat of a 14-year-old boy with gonorrhea.[3]

Pornography drags woman to desperate depths. "She is used and abused in ways that can't even be mentioned in these pages. She is filmed and photographed having sex with one, two, three men. Legs spread, her genital area is shot in clinical close-up. She is filmed having oral sex, having sex with other women — even with animals. She is beaten in sadomasochistic pornography, and bound and defiled in bondage magazines. She is gang-raped for cameras and made to appear to enjoy it."[4]

Four male customers in a Massachusetts tavern seized and repeatedly gang-raped a 21-year-old mother of two children for two hours on a pool table. While she struggled and screamed, they sexually assaulted her again and again to the cheers and applause of at least 15 other customers and the bartender. No one tried to help her.

Five little boys, ages 10 to 13, gang-raped a five-year-old child — after watching pornographic movies on television.[5]

The Rene Guyon Society calls for new laws permitting children as young as eight to participate in sexual activities *with parental consent*. A "family-oriented" society, it provides counseling for doubtful mothers who are *reluctant to allow their young children to become sexually active!*[6]

Hospital emergency services report an increase in ripped colons, rectal abscesses, and intestinal infections in homosexuals. The increase is attributed to homosexuals forcing objects of larger and larger diameters into each other's anal canals. Doctors have removed "whiskey glasses, bananas, coke bottles," and "almost anything that will fit."[7]

FACES BEHIND THE MOVEMENT

When Hugh Hefner introduced *Playboy,* he barely hinted at what would follow. It was a marginally bawdier version of *Esquire*, but with a little more explicit language under the cartoons and with suggestive — but not blatantly pornographic — photos of scantily clad young women replacing airbrush paintings. Early issues were not in the execrable taste they would later demonstrate — as a steady succession of excursions to the borderlines of propriety eroded the limits of "public acceptance." With time, these "limits" (pushed back ever further by competitive excesses demonstrated by such new arrivals as *Penthouse* and *Hustler*) eventually *eliminated* any standards of print propriety in this country. By the 1960s and 1970s, *Playboy's* circulation outstripped those of *Time, Newsweek,* and *U. S. News & World Report*.[8]

In 1982 Hefner boasted, "Things are a lot better in the bedroom today than when I was growing up, and I think there is a clear recognition that *Playboy* played an important part in changing attitudes and values. It's the single thing I'm proudest of."9

Moral values don't change overnight; however, a relentless repetition will eventually dull the impact of even shocking or distasteful impressions. Old-fashioned words like "fornication" or "adultery" become outdated and bland. Instead, through careful imposition of new terms, sin is sugarcoated until not only is it acceptable, it even becomes desirable. In keeping with a new world view, sexuality gains acceptance among those who place men's physical drives over his psychological or spiritual ones.

Man, bent on satiating his passions at every turn, invents word games to soothe his conscience — thereby catering to his basest nature. He thus replaces guilt with pride in his sexual prowess. That marks him as a modern, "sexually liberated" individual.

What it all really means is that mankind has rejected the laws of God and replaced them with disobedience, relabeled to make it *sound* enlightened and progressive. The new permissiveness thus becomes "sexual freedom," and perversion becomes "an alternate life-style." Premarital relations become "trial marriages," and abortions are "terminated pregnancies."

Unfortunately, much as man may labor to make these practices sound acceptable, God still considers them sin. God still says that fornicators and adulterers will not enter the kingdom of God. They will burn in the lake of fire because God *still* says, *"Thou shalt not commit adultery"* (Exodus 20:14). Today, in the midst of America's "new sexual freedom," man finds himself not free but in *bondage*. Sinful man is, as always, a slave to his own pleasures and passions.

In the midst of a new moral vacuum, man sought to make himself acceptable, to change the standards that used to limit his excesses. He sought to pull God down to his level rather than raising himself to meet God's standards. Man desired gardens of grandeur— lush with forbidden fruit — but ended up mired in garbage heaps of ruin and decay. Today our whole society reaps the consequences of his unbridled sexual freedom.

OUR "JUSTICE" SYSTEM

While secular humanism set the stage, today's sexual revolution has been principally swept forward on a tidal wave of pornography. And it was our illustrious (and once respected) United States Supreme Court that opened the door to the free and easy production, distribution, and sale of pornography.[10]

In 1957, in *Roth* v. *United States*, the Court determined that material could not be considered obscene on the basis of its sexual content. The Court redefined obscenity: ". . . whether, to the average person — applying community standards — the dominant theme of the material taken as a whole appeals to prurient interests."

In 1966, in *Ginzberg* v. *State of New York*, the nation's highest Court further assaulted accepted standards by declaring that only material *utterly* without redeeming social value would be judged as pornography. The 1966 ruling was like a shot of adrenalin to pornographers. It was like the green flag at a drag race, emboldening even the most timid to *openly* peddle their wares.

Then, in 1973, any last vestiges of restraint were destroyed as the Court declared that to be pornography an item must be "without literary, artistic, political or scientific value" *(Miller* v. *California).*

Almost immediately, a flood of "adult bookstores" opened in almost every urban area. The demand for their books (turned out on pornography production lines in weeks for appallingly low fees), expensive slick magazines, and super-8 films (showing everything in "living color") caused porno dealers to make huge profits overnight.

The unprecedented growth of this sordid sex industry is made possible by two basic factors. The first (and most obvious one) is that aspiring smut peddlers — greedy for wealth — feed off the lusts of a generation bombarded by stimuli designed to provoke sexual interests. The second (and often overlooked) element is that our courts — supposedly the guardians of justice and morality — have made the whole appalling situation possible by overtly *promoting* everything *im*moral and *suppressing* everything Godly, decent, and honorable. They have done that by deliberately distorting and perverting the intentions of the United States Constitution line by line and paragraph by paragraph. Evidently, a secular humanist, liberal power bloc controls the courts of our land.

Ultimately though, we have a sex industry in this nation *because we want it!* If a substantial segment of our population didn't support such activities, they would go out of business! And it's not just the out-of-the-way, dingy bookstores on dark corners — it's everywhere!

Although the Supreme Court seems to have a great problem in deciding what constitutes pornography, those who seek it have little difficulty in recognizing it. Pornography is any material designed to arouse sexual appetites. And it should be noted that it doesn't just arouse, it literally *consumes* its victims. The porno addict becomes as helpless a victim of his "habit" as is the heroin junkie — and like the conventional drug addict, he finds himself with a raging need for ever stronger "fixes." Satan is, of course, the fundamental author of *all* pornographic material.

Satan lures his victims subtly. Beginning with risque humor, lewd suggestions, and erotic nudity, he baits his prospective captives initially with "socially acceptable" pornography. That is, he doesn't shock them into any rude awakening by overloading them with his more overt material in the beginning. The initial attack always comes by way of the more subtle material that most people don't consider outright pornography. Once they are "hooked" on that material, it is a short series of steps into the complete mire of outright porno addiction.

THE LONG, SLOW PROCESS

Over a period of time, the shocking becomes "socially acceptable." Modern value systems now accept a wide range of vices and evils that would have been considered unmentionable only a short time ago. And men, thinking they have been "set free," find themselves chained to a conveyor belt leading inexorably toward eternal damnation.

Unfortunately, it is impossible to limit pornographic movies and TV shows to "consenting adults" who wish to pay the porno industry for these services. It is impossible to separate the world of the child from that of the adult as it exists today via television. Those who think they can, delude themselves.

Videoporn will cost our nation dearly! It misrepresents sex to the detriment of an entire society. Our nation depends on the strength of the home, and pornography defrauds the home and distorts an honest understanding of sex. It presents a false "reality" that glorifies free sex — without revealing the *consequences* of such freedom.

It paints the "beautiful people" as supersexed men and women. It never shows the ugly scars of VD, personality destruction, and guilt that persist long after the "glamour" of the illicit sexual incident fades. It refuses to reveal its hideous and seamier side — the sadistic patrons, pimps, child abusers, and murderers of unborn babies.[11] Instead, pornography reduces human beings to mere animals or, even worse, to impersonal objects with value only as tools to be manipulated by *other* animals.

It weaves its insidious web gradually. The behavioral scientist, Dr. Victor B. Cline, conducted a revealing survey on the movies screened during a four-week period in a moderately conservative Western city of 25,000.[12] The city did not have any "porno" movie houses. In order of frequency, the following is a summary of the incidence of sexual actions or situations found in the 37 motion pictures shown during that period:

- Nudity (168 depictions)
- Kissing, embracing, body contact (90)
- Bed scenes with sexual connotations (49)
- In undergarments with sexual context (36)
- Seductive exhibition of the body (32)
- Verbalizing of sexual interests or intentions (36)
- Caressing another's sex organs while clothed (27)
- Caressing another's sex organs while nude (21)
- Undressing (34)
- Explicit intercourse (19)
- Suggested or implied intercourse (17)
- Homosexual activities (11)
- Oral-genital intercourse (7)
- Toilet scenes (5)
- Rape (4)
- Obscene gestures (4)
- Masturbation (3)
- Sexual sadism/masochism (3)

(And realize, this was the "acceptable" *public* entertainment.)

THE SICKEST OF THE SICK

What was once considered shocking and perverse seems tame compared to much of the pornography on the market in this country today. Dealing as it does with every imaginable perversion, it is virtually indescribable. Operating under a hideous law of diminishing returns, it resorts to increasingly bizarre stimuli to maintain a response that *demands* even greater *jarring* of the mental receptors. Therefore, it even caters to very specific depravities. It titillates and captivates the sickest of the sick and makes them slaves to their own consuming lusts.

God meant sex to be an expression of love and commitment. Pornography, in contrast, makes it a self-centered, mechanical manipulation. Since it depicts sex as something one does *to* someone, it attacks the whole spiritual basis of marriage — when the emphasis should be on giving and sharing. Based on a lie, pornography produces only "dissatisfaction, disillusionment, depravity, and degeneracy.[13]

PORNOGRAPHY — THE ENEMY OF THE HOME

Pornography strikes at the foundations of a society — marriage and the home. Besides corrupting innocent children (which will eventually weaken and destroy a nation), it conducts a relentless attack against women. Why women? No doubt because the producers and consumers of porn are almost exclusively male! "What pornography does to women," says Morton Hill, "is unspeakably ugly, evil and tragic. Scripture extols woman, pornography uses her. Scripture consecrates woman in marriage, pornography desecrates her. Scripture ennobles her, pornography degrades her."[14]

Men driven by lust and greed make merchandise of both women and children — deceptively presenting both as *willing* participants who *enjoy* the abuse.

Yearly profits for all pornography exceed $8 billion — a volume of business equal to that of the motion picture and record industries combined. In 1978 the top 10 "skin magazines" captured an audience of 16 million and earned $475 million. Adult films claimed well over two million admissions per *week,* with an average ticket going for $3.50. The nation's nearly 800 adult theaters thus generated a yearly income of $365 million.[15]

There is, of course, no way to put a dollar valuation on the *damage* done by this activity. Porno ensnares its victims in a living hell. It chokes out any semblance of normal life as surely as the "monkey" on the heroin addict's back. And just as the heroin addict begins his journey to destruction on softer drugs (as mentioned earlier), it is soft-porn that inevitably leads to a craving for even heavier material. The individual seeks ever greater depravity and perversion to meet the ever-deepening demands of his warped personality. Once hooked, the individual is lured ever deeper through the various stratas of the pornographic hell until his life is ruined, his marriage and family destroyed, and everyone for whom he cares contaminated.

A PROGRESSIVE DISEASE

Dr. Victor Cline explained in his testimony before a Texas legislative committee how pornography works to drag its victims deeper and deeper into the pit of degradation:[16]

- First, there is an addiction to pornography.
- Then, there is an escalation factor in which the person increasingly wants to see and be exposed to more and more deviant, obscene material.
- Next, a desensitization occurs; that is, what was originally shocking, antisocial, and distressing (even though still sexually stimulating) becomes *acceptable* with time.
- Finally, the man urges his sex partner or his wife (or sometimes even other members of the family) to engage in such sexual activities, many of which are extremely deviant and antisocial. (Parenthetically, one skin magazine claims to receive 65,000 pictures annually of nude wives and girl friends — many of them too lurid to be printed even in its filthy publication.)

A point should be made clearly and unmistakably. Although we've *alluded* to it, it should be stated clearly and specifically that we are *all* vulnerable to the corrupting venom of pornography. Even accidental exposure can prove deadly to some. Therefore we cannot tamper with questionable material and be assured of coming away unscathed. We must make a firm resolution that we will not *look* at materials that deviate from the pure, holy, and just. Pornography, without question, produces a conditioned reaction that eventually leads to acting out deviant sexual behavior.

Dr. Cline emphatically points out that sexual deviations are not inherited. They are always learned — in one way or another.

Pornography, and its accompanying criminal activities, could be quickly eliminated if people insisted that laws be enforced. But because most people haven't been exposed to the *horrors* of pornography, they lack the righteous indignation needed to take a firm stand against this destroyer. Ignorance allows liberty — and liberty rapidly becomes license.

Such ignorance has allowed even the meager obscenity laws now on the books to be further relaxed. If the Federal Criminal Code is revised (as some are now promoting), the importation, interstate transportation, and mailing of 90 percent of pornographic materials will be legalized.[17] The broadcasting of obscenity will be decriminalized.

And unless we protest as taxpayers, we will continue to subsidize the largest distributors of obscene material in the world — by allowing it to be mailed as fourth-class material.[18] We must fight against the legalization of pornography.

A recent study by John Court, contained in his book, *Pornography: A Christian Critique*, found that countries which relaxed regulations on pornography experienced dramatic increases in the rape rate in the decades following such relaxation.[19]

The United States	139 percent
England and Wales	94 percent
Australia	160 percent
New Zealand	107 percent

PORNOGRAPHY AND RAPE

Up until recently, the majority of rape victims have suffered alone. They have done so because of the social stigma attached to the fact of rape. Although rape remains one of the most misunderstood and underreported crimes, rape victims are beginning to fight back and demand justice. Nevertheless, only 3.5 to 10 percent of rapes are reported — according to an aggregate of surveys done by the U. S. Census Bureau, the FBI, and the National Opinion Research Center.[20] Using conservative estimates, experts calculate that a woman's chance of being raped at some point in her life is an appalling one in ten.[21]

In a study of rapists in Southern California, Dr. Michael Goldstein found that 57 percent of the study group admitted to trying out sexual activity that they had seen during exposure to pornography. Of a group of child molesters, 87 percent indicated that pornography had stimulated them to commit sexual acts with the children.[22]

Shirley O'Brien, in *Child Pornography,* reports: "A direct relationship exists between pornographic literature and the sexual molestation of young children . . . . Law-enforcement officers say they routinely find pornographic material when they investigate sex crimes against children. Supporting this evidence, victims say they were shown pornographic literature, films or photos during various stages of their exploitation."[23]

Experts confirm that sexual abuse may lead to a cycle in which sexually abused children become sexually abusive adults. When we consider the newest research, which shows that one of four males and one of three females are sexually abused at some time, we get some idea of the magnitude of the problem — both as it exists now and as it will expand in the future.[24]

In addition, there are an estimated 25 million *incest* victims in the United States who have been sexually violated by a parent, step-parent, sibling, uncle, aunt, grandparent, or other close relative.[25]

CHILD PORNOGRAPHY

As odious and bizarre as the sexual abuse of children seems to us, there is a long history of child pornography and child prostitution.

In ancient Greece and Rome, as they approached their downfalls, sodomizing of young boys was openly and blatantly practiced. Daniel 1:9-21 tells of Daniel and his three companions being literally "fattened" to become more sexually attractive — but they were spared this terrible consequence through God's intervention. In California, during Gold Rush days, runaway boys who had come to California seeking adventure were forced into prostitution and exhibited at "peg houses" where they were seated on greased wooden pegs.[26]

Although that account by Robin Lloyd, in his book *For Money or Love: Boy Prostitution in America,* seems almost unbelievable, we can't ignore the depths to which human depravity can descend. Many people have never heard of such exploitation — and others (if they have) obviously don't *care.* Still others are sexually excited by it — while some callously use it for profit. Some small percent may become disgusted and angry enough to take action against it.

This is because the laws of our land, in effect, provide "that children of any age, including infants, can be depicted simulating sexual activity including genital-genital, anal-genital, oral-genital or oral-anal sexual intercourse; or engaged in bestiality, masturbation, sadomasochistic abuse or lewd exhibitions of the genitals."[27]

Clifford Linedecker, in *Children in Chains*, reports: "By 1978, more than 260 different magazine titles featured juveniles engaged in sexual activities or otherwise posing lasciviously with other children or adults. Some of the better known titles were *Moppets*, a magazine featuring photos of wide-eyed little girls from three to eight years old; *Lollitots*, with child models from eleven to fourteen; and *Chicken Brats*, appealing to homosexuals, with young boys.

"Others incorporate violence and sexual abuse of children, or offer handy instructions for pedophiles. Magazines and books such as *Child Discipline*, which instructs its readers how to derive sexual pleasure from beating children, and *Lust for Children*, which among other things offers advice on how to avoid criminal convictions for molesting juveniles, are two. Other publications offer advice to child molesters on how youngsters can most easily and safely be lured from playgrounds, discuss the joys of incest, and instruct fathers on how to clip locks on the labias of their little girls to keep them 'all for you.'"[28]

In other words, children have become fair game for pornographers to include in their sordid sexual activities, to star in perverted movies, and to pose for magazine photos featuring all types of revolting sex acts with other children and adults. Children as young as five and six are solicited off the streets by "chicken hawks" who haunt bus terminals and railroad stations. "Pornographers starve, rape and otherwise abuse their young captives."[29]

Quick Press International, catering to this sick clientele, publishes a travel guide aptly titled "Where the Young Ones Are." It lists places where children can be found in 59 cities and 34 states. When Los Angeles police checked the areas suggested, they did indeed find places where youngsters congregated, and some were actively hustling.[30]

Some of the pedophile's collection may consist of colored slides, handled and traded like baseball cards. In one raid on a private nursery school, police found 4,000 such slides of nude children.[31]

Of all the vehicles used for child pornography, magazines are probably the most common. However, scores of pornographic paperbacks flood the market with such titles as *Chicken Chaser, Wynter's Tail, Jock Stud, Buddy's Butt, Do It . . . Son, Fun After School, Door-to-Door Chicken, Meat My Buddy, The Child Watchers, A Boy for Hire, Boy Nymphet, Boys for Dessert,* and *Male Incest.*[32]

The advertisement for one of these books asks, "What does a chicken cruiser — one who is horny, hearty, good-looking, well-educated, and stuck in a small East Coast town — do to change his life for the better? He goes to work at a boys' boarding school, of course, and lets it all hang out."[33]

Child pornography is a repulsive twist in child abuse. O'Brien says, "Without viewing child pornography, it is almost impossible to imagine. Only after one has watched a film in which an 8-year-old girl is sexually abused by two adults, manipulated manually and with mechanical devices, can one understand the powerlessness, defenselessness, lack of dignity and coercion inherent in these acts. The empty expressions and pitiful, searching looks seeking off-camera direction from the film's producers enable one to feel the helplessness of the child."[34]

THE LIKELY VICTIMS

Of course, *any* child can become a victim of pornography or abuse, whether he's from a conservative, strict, but loving family — or whether he's a "throwaway" from a family that doesn't care. Nevertheless, experts have identified some *general* characteristics of children prone to victimization:

• They are seeking attention and affection.

• They suffer from low self-esteem.

• They are young. It's their freshness, naivete, and innocence that appeal to adult clientele.

• They lack proper parental supervision.

• Some children give signals that they are trying to rush the growing-up process — therefore they seem to invite "adult" behavior.

• They lack recognition of right and wrong, of appropriate and inappropriate behavior.

• Most significantly — they do not have strong religious values.[35]

Once a young person becomes involved in pornography, he may be persuaded to recruit other young people. One such recruiter was coached as follows: "Find a boy who is having trouble in school and at home; if a boy likes school, forget him; if a boy tells you what a great family he has, forget him; forget also the uglies, the fats, the ungainly, the real toughs, the bullies — chances are they won't respond; forget it if they don't smoke a little grass; forget it if they're super studs with the women."[36]

A particular child pornographer — during questioning after a criminal conviction — explained what he looked for when sizing up prospects:[37]

• Whether the boy had any close church affiliation.

• Whether there was a strong father-figure or no father.

• The child's income level — did he need money?

• Whether he recently had undergone a trying experience — a family move, a divorce, or a death in the family.

These should supply some food for thought. They should certainly shed some light on what parents can do to help protect their children.

Child pornography damages children in ways no child should have to experience:[38]

• By awakening and provoking a child's sexual nature prematurely, psychological damage results.

• The child's image of himself as a person of worth is degraded or destroyed.

• The child is exploited but made to *appear* that he participated voluntarily.

• Children are made vulnerable to adults in unnatural ways.

• Sex is distorted and the child's development and future attitudes are therefore hindered.

• A child's privacy is forever invaded.

• The child's moral development is irrevocably complicated.

• A distorted sense of right and wrong — what is proper and improper — is produced.

The normal process of growing from childhood into adulthood is difficult enough in today's society, but sexual exploitation places a tremendous additional burden on the defenseless and impressionable child.

THE LIKELY PERPETRATORS

Child pornographers exploit and brutalize young children who are often seeking the attention and affection they lacked in their homes. So many young victims — scarred by divorce, neglect, abuse, and other factors prevalent in unstable homes — literally crave someone to care about them. Lacking a sense of self-worth, they are overly eager to please.

Unfortunately, the pedophile is driven by lust instead of compassion for the vulnerable child. He may go to great lengths to build the child's love and trust, but he does so for all the wrong motives — his deep-seated need to dominate and control. Too weak and sick for normal relationships, he stalks young children; and they become an uncontrollable obsession to him.

How chilling it is to picture a grown man courting a *child* in the same way a normal man courts a woman! How terribly, terribly sick! But then we should remember that the pedophile is just one sick element in a totally sick society. The loss of traditional values, the Courts' refusal to effectively define obscenity, our fascination with nudism, and parents too busy (or too disinterested) to provide love and proper parental supervision — all contribute to the exploitation of children.

It's especially damaging when the perpetrator is a person the child respects or looks to for leadership, as is often the case. He may be a Boy Scout or church group leader, a teacher, a camp counselor, or a friendly "good neighbor." He is not always the stereotype of "the nasty old man" looking for children to lure away. Although he may be exactly that, he may also be a respected member of the community — educated and wealthy. Some have been found to be millionaires. Their one *common* characteristic, of course, is that they are always found where the kids are.

Whoever they may be, experts tell us that little can be done to help or rehabilitate them.[39] Their arrogance, pride in their "trophies," and lack of remorse for their actions make them almost impossible to rehabilitate. The pedophile's lust for youngsters is the driving passion of his life. If the pedophile has his way, and age of consent laws are lowered or abolished, it will be like declaring open season on our children.

If this were to come about, we would see more organizations like the Rene Guyon Society, the Pedophile Information Exchange and NAMBLA (the North American Man-Boy Love Association). NAMBLA claims to have more than 20,000 members. Its spokesman, Bill Andriette, says the association has a "libertarian, humanistic outlook on sexuality."[40]

THE PLAGUE OF THE CENTURY

Today, due to the general permissiveness rampant throughout our nation, the homosexual community has "come out of the closet." Meeting places where one man can have sexual encounters with many other men in a single night are widely advertised. One physician stated that because of the filth of homosexuality, a situation similar to the plagues of centuries past could come upon us again. Sanitation is necessary to control epidemics. There is no sanitation in the homosexual life-style.

The deadly disease of AIDS (Acquired Immune Deficiency Syndrome) infects and contaminates the U. S. and the world, and we haven't a cure.

AIDS knocks out the body's natural immunity system, leaving its victims vulnerable to infection and a rare form of skin cancer. It is almost inevitably fatal.[41]

The establishment press is seeking physicians who are willing to prostitute their sacred trust by telling us not to be concerned about AIDS and not to shun its "victims." However, many doctors privately believe that this dreaded, fatal disease can be contracted by eating in a restaurant where the food is prepared, or handled, by AIDS carriers. It would seem that the establishment is persisting in its dedication to protect the sensibilities of homosexuals — even at the expense of the general public's health.

Ambulance drivers have been *ordered* — against their wills — to work on AIDS victims. Nurses and other personnel have been fired by hospitals if they balk at performing intimate duties for AIDS victims.[42]

On a more positive note, AIDS does seem to have taken some of the freedom out of the flamboyant homosexual life-style. Many homosexual bathhouses are closing, and the fear of death has forced many homosexuals to curb their promiscuous behavior. One medical director who works with "gays," comments on the low attendance at the baths. "Before AIDS, going to the baths had an aura almost like smoking. People knew it wasn't too *good* for them, but it was socially acceptable. Now it has the aura of shooting heroin."[43]

Bill Jones, owner of San Francisco's Sutro Bath House, shares the same sentiments. "Many gays are beginning to see that the party is over. You find more people interested in monogamy and their homes and their health. You go home and get on with your life instead of being part of the wildness that has been going in the last five years, the dehumanization."[44]

A San Francisco journalist expressed it well when describing the bewilderment many homosexuals are experiencing today. "Isn't it something that what *brought* most of us here (to the bath houses), now leaves tens of thousands of us wondering whether that celebration ends in death?"[45]

Until the left-wing politicians and establishment press began promoting "gay rights" — convincing even some normal people that it was a legitimate issue — the homosexual was at least as circumspect about his private life as his normal neighbor.

If a "glory hole" emerged, police would throw the participants in jail on morals charges. Gay bars, where homosexuals met in the back room, were shut down. But today this type of life-style is openly condoned and the appalling result is the disease called AIDS.

Almost half of all homosexual acts are performed in an orgy environment. Imagine, if you can, a writhing mass of humanity engaged in the most gross and despicable of actions. It would seem that the citizenry of this nation should, and could, do something to smash the homosexual movement and ensure that all such acts are criminalized. We're no longer talking about just a moral issue but a grave public health issue as well. If the homosexual isn't stopped, he will in time infect the whole nation, and the United States will be destroyed as other great civilizations have been destroyed — by corruption.

God Almighty, under the Old Testament laws, commanded that entire nations be exterminated. He did that because of the filth their citizens had engaged in. This is exactly what the United States is facing today.

You see, homosexuality involves a total life-style. It is completely opposed to the life-style of "straights" (heterosexuals). Therefore, the homosexual movement is campaigning for "gay rights." They want freedom to maintain their own society without interference or restraint.

"Homosexual rights is going to be the civil rights issue of the 1980s," declared Jean O'Leary, the militant homosexual appointed by President Jimmy Carter to the National Committee for the Observance of International Woman's Year.[46] O'Leary was the first publicly acknowledged homosexual ever to be appointed to a high federal position.

WE MUST BE PREPARED TO CONFRONT THE SITUATION

From all indications, the battle lines are drawn, as never before, for the moral confrontation of the century. We must be prepared to declare all-out war against the juggernaut of evil that tears apart families, drives the sexes in opposite directions, and irrevocably cripples children's growth and sexual development.

The horrifying level of overt homosexual behavior in our society reflects its *acceptability*. When a culture disapproves of homosexuality, its occurrence is low; when it is approved, it flourishes.

Homosexuals would like us to believe they are born that way. Some people assume that a hormonal imbalance produces homosexual behavior — in other words, that a lower-than-normal level of male hormones predisposes one to homosexuality.

It is not our goal to discuss the causes of homosexuality, however, but to expose a force that threatens our future. I've emphasized that homosexuality is a learned behavior so we may once again stress the importance of the family, God-ordained parental roles, proper emotional support, and discipline of the child. The Bible calls homosexuality a sin. It is an abomination to the Lord.

Because of *God's* view of homosexuality, parents must sear into their minds that it is a learned reaction and that it *can* be prevented by avoiding the actions that bring it about. By devoting themselves to playing proper parental roles, with God's help, parents can rear boys and girls to be men and women who will be comfortable and fulfilled in their God-ordained roles.

Those who have counseled hundreds of homosexuals will tell you that the homosexual is seldom satisfied in the role he has chosen. Despite all efforts to convince us that the homosexual life-style is "gay," in reality it is anything *but* gay. It tends to be one of frustration and an endless search for "the perfect lover" — the one who will finally fill the emptiness and take away the loneliness, soothe the internal conflict, and meet the wrenching need for love.

Of course, "the perfect lover" doesn't exist. Feeling loved means feeling *peace* — and perfect peace comes only through a personal relationship with Jesus Christ. No amount of one-night stands, bar-cruising, baths, parties, or even "homosexual marriages" can still the knowledge of being out of sync with the *real* world, a knowledge that plagues the homosexual. There is nothing "gay" about his situation. Actually, the one word to properly describe his continuing situation is *torment*. And the only solution to torment? To come *all* the way home to Jesus. A rejection of the errant path and prayer for God's forgiveness heals every torment — and it is the only way the homosexual will finally find peace.

OUT OF THE CLOSET

The media presents us with the image of the confident, brash, self-satisfied homosexual who wears his life-style as a banner. For the majority of homosexuals, the picture just doesn't fit. A 1982 survey showed that only 54 percent considered themselves "publicly out," and of these only one in five said his business associates knew he was gay. Four out of five still hid the truth from their families.[47] It would seem that the homosexual has difficulty in convincing even himself that his life-style is *gay* and one which should be as acceptable as conventional heterosexuality.

Homosexuals almost inevitably become masters of deception. Counselor's cite lying as a common characteristic in most homosexuals. "Their techniques of distortion or evasion are almost impeccable. They have learned the art of deception so well that they can look you straight in the eye and tell you a barefaced lie, while maintaining a look of complete innocence."[48]

Since the *majority* of Americans (according to a recent *Newsweek* poll) still disapprove of homosexuality as an alternate life-style,[49] homosexuals form their own "communities" and "networks."

Despite attempts made by the homosexual movement to present homosexuality as a normal — albeit alternative — expression of human sexuality, known practices of the homosexual clearly indicate that his sex drive is rarely satisfied. Consequently, new thrills and experiences are constantly being sought.

One of the most alarming practices that arises from an insatiable quest for increasing eroticism is sadomasochism. "In his quest for more, more and more erotic sex, the man with the cruel or sadistic disposition begins to experiment with pain-inflicting objects, from needles and pins to chains and icepicks. Only the imagination restricts the expression of a homosexual's 'sexual preference.'"[50]

Some gay establishments actually cater to this particular perversion. The Hothouse was legendary in gay San Francisco: a four-story,

10,000-square-foot "pleasure palace" filled with inviting private alcoves and the paraphernalia of kinky sex — harnesses, chains, and shackles. Owner Louis Gaspar saw the Hothouse as a sort of therapeutic playpen, a place where gay men could "live out their adolescence, sexually and playfully — because so many of us never got out of that phase." Recently, the Hothouse went out of business, a victim of the gay community's rising fears about the connection between promiscuous, anonymous sex and the AIDS epidemic.[51]

WHO'S PAYING FOR ALL THIS?

By and large, homosexuals are not content to keep to themselves. They want acceptance by the general public, and they crave certain rights. Where homosexuality was once considered clearly *deviant* behavior — an illness or a sin — it is becoming increasingly accepted.

While the homosexual movement continues to gain momentum, the American taxpayer continues to be its main source of funding. A recent report issued by Senator Jesse Helms showed that $640,000 of your federal tax dollars are being used annually to fund the Gay and Lesbian Community Service Center (a "resource and educational center" designed to indoctrinate the public in gay ideology). Last year, homosexuals received $41,000 from the CETA fund (which was *supposed* to provide job training for poor Americans) for a civic and community day parade known as Leaping Lesbians — and federal funding was given to 14 young homosexuals in California to put on a play called *Lavender Horizon*.[52] Besides being supported by our tax dollars, the movement has gained the support of political leaders; in 1984, prospective Democratic candidates openly bidded for the support of homosexual groups. The homosexual movement has become a force to be reckoned with.

In New York, Governor Mario Cuomo, fulfilling a 1982 campaign promise, issued an executive order designed to end discrimination against homosexuals by the state. The Democratic governor said that to allow government to discriminate against any belief or creed or private way of life would threaten us all.

It's certainly apparent that times have changed. While any political leader would have once *hidden* his homosexuality, even congressmen today unabashedly flaunt their life-style. Gerry Studds, the Massachusetts Democrat who took a congressional page to Portugal for a

2½-week fling, sees his behavior as a matter of "private preference without relevence to the public life of the nation."

When Studds was confronted, he defiantly spoke out. "The mutually voluntary, private relationship between adults, which occurred ten years ago, should not, by any conceivable standard of fairness, rationality, rule or law, warrant the attention or action of the House of Representatives of the United States."[53]

What Studds was saying was that he — like other homosexuals — wants special "rights" on the grounds of "sexual orientation." Dr. David Wood, Moral Majority chairman for the State of Michigan, points out, "There is no single issue on the political scene today that poses a greater threat to Christian families than the question of 'Gay Rights.' If we lose on this, we will have lost all, because homosexuals will have gained unrestricted access to our homes, our schools, and even our churches."[54]

Former Congressman Robert E. Bauman is another of our political leaders fighting for "gay rights." At an American Bar Association Assembly, he urged passage of a resolution barring discrimination against homosexuals. He said, "I am here to express my unqualified support for federal legislation extending civil rights protection to the 20 million gay and lesbian Americans who are my brothers and sisters."[55] Bauman, who served in the House as a Conservative Republican from Maryland, lost his reelection bid in 1980 — one month after being charged with soliciting sex from a 16-year-old boy.

During a 1982 newspaper interview, reflecting on the events which drove him from office, Bauman stated, "I suppose it's as Oscar Wilde said, 'The real crime is getting caught.'"[56]

THE GAY CHURCH

Deep within the heart of every individual is a cry for God. Though the individual may silence or ignore it, the heart still cries out to be right with God. When man rejects God, he must find some way to justify his deeds — and sometimes he tries to use religion to do so.

During Gay Pride Week in Hollywood, nearly 90,000 people marched to honor gays and lesbians. Interestingly, many community leaders and leaders of gay churches paraded the streets with signs proclaiming "Gay Catholics," "Gay Jews," "Gay Episcopalians," and so forth.

In addition, we have churches that are ordaining homosexuals to preach. The United Church of Christ has accepted a report affirming that the homosexuality of a candidate for ordination should not be grounds for refusing to admit that person into the church's ministry.

Homosexuality comes from the pit of darkness. It originated in hell and was birthed by Satan himself. Satan has always endeavored to take God's most cherished creation, mankind, and pervert him to nothing more than the soulless condition of the animal kingdom.

Because of their great wickedness, God destroyed Sodom and Gomorrah. If necessary, He will destroy *our* nation if men refuse to repent and turn from their wicked ways. But, in a greater sense, Sodom and Gomorrah were destroyed because of the shortfall in the number of *righteous* people. If there had been just *10 righteous people*, God would have spared these cities.

We, the people of God, can't ignore the cascade of filth being poured out upon us from the pit of hell. Sexual immorality, pornography, sexual abuse of children, and homosexuality — all reflect the depths of depravity to which America has sunk.

Alexis de Toqueville's famous words ring with profound truth: "America is great because she is good. When America ceases to be good, she will cease to be great."

America is being weighed in the balance and found wanting. The sexual revolution drains its poisonous consequences across the land like a pustulant sore. Unless America repents, the fate of Sodom and Gomorrah will surely overtake *us*.

The righteous must cry out to God to save our land and deliver us from the filth and the stench and the ruins of cities laid waste by sin!

TOO MUCH, TOO SOON

       Young people grapple, to an unprecedented degree, with pressures and problems far different than those of only a generation ago. Certainly, over the ages, other groups of young people have lived through difficult times — wars, invasions, and severe economic trials. But these crises usually passed with time and allowed those who survived them to get on with the business of making full and rewarding lives for themselves and for their progeny. In today's society, however, all too often the afflicted and overwhelmed don't get a *chance* to resurrect their lives that have been torn to shreds by existing conditions. And in many cases, there are no descendents to inherit the "better world" that is inherent in everyone's hope for the future.

       What's different today? Almost *everything!* The sexual revolution, today's emphasis on youth, the current preoccupation with success, and the almost hysterical obsession with pleasure, expanded knowledge, and experiences. It's one thing when adults *choose* to live their lives in pursuit of such temporal values, but quite another when they become *impositions* on the lives of children. Ultimately, young people become the victims of a society wound up to the breaking point. For this reason, many of them demonstrate all the symptoms of stress — headaches, ulcers, depression, and learning problems.

A startling result showed up in autopsies done on the bodies of youths (in their late teens and early twenties) who were killed in Vietnam. Although these were barely more than children (in years), pathological studies showed that an overwhelming number of them were suffering from arteriosclerosis — hardening of the arteries — a disease commonly associated with age and considered to be a result of stress.

Faced with too much, too soon, today's young people have lost the joy of spontaneity and the right just to be children. Today's youth culture demands that all young people be cool, be hip, be laid back. There is no room to be naive and innocent. To fit in today, you have to be skeptical, cynical, and old beyond your years.

Nothing in the atmosphere of our modern culture allows time to explore and savor the joy of discovery. There's no room for wondering about God and His purpose for the individual, or for the personal pursuit of individuality and creativity. Hence, many Americans and their children live day after day in a pressure-cooker society — one which reduces all individuals to components in the great gray stew of conformity.

Is it any wonder then that young people sound like little more than adults reduced in size? They aren't concerned with the things that *used* to matter to youngsters — today's concerns are dope, sex, and booze, just as they are (all too often) with their parents. Kids today, it seems, are recklessly committed to hurling themselves into the "pleasures" of the adult world before they've had the chance to experience the simple pleasures of youth.

Unfortunately, once cast into the "real world," all too many young people find themselves hopelessly ill-equipped to cope with the inherent pressures of that world. Although adolescence has always brought rapid physical, emotional, and social changes (making the teen years difficult in even the best of times), the uncertainty of the 1980s creates unprecedented havoc.

Teenagers need time to unravel their feelings and to understand them. They need love and forgiveness and patience in a secure environment. A teenager needs the assurance that despite his emotional outbursts, inconsistencies, and frustrations, he is still loved and accepted.

With few support systems (if any — for some youngsters), many have only their peers to turn to. En masse they march off to claim a place for themselves in the world, each as frightened and confused as the next one. It's difficult (and sad) to watch these "world-wisened" youth flounder around in the bog of uncertainty while attempting to maintain a "know-it-all" attitude. Unfortunately, today's average youngster just isn't prepared for the problems he must face.

Overwhelmed by "too much, too soon," 15 percent of the 65 million people under 18 have mental or emotional problems serious enough to require some degree of psychiatric help. At least 1.4 million minors have *severe* psychological problems.[1] Last year one of every 10 teenage girls became pregnant. The federal government estimates that there are now 3.3 million problem drinkers between the ages of 14 and 17. Suicide is the second greatest killer among high school students. Violence is increasing relentlessly. Trends indicate that these will increase.[2]

And it's not just the young people. Constant stress and unresolved conflicts keep many Americans in a state of depression. However, it is the *chronic* depression — long-lasting and usually resistant to treatment — that is viewed as the greatest danger.

MISPLACED PRIORITIES

The most common cause of depression is pent-up anger. Others include loneliness, a lack of self-esteem, a lack of intimacy with others, and a lack of intimacy with God. Resentments and bitterness are also culprits.

Many young people are continually angry today. Many feel they have been deprived of an important part of their lives. They feel old before they ever have a chance to be young. They feel used and abused. They adopt an "I don't care" attitude, and since they feel that no one cares about them, they refuse to care about anyone else — including even themselves.

When these young people were younger (six to 12), they wanted to please the adults around them. But as adolescence arrived and they began to review their childhood — what happened and what *didn't* happen — they became angry. Most parents can't understand why their teenagers lash out as they do. The outbursts often seem inappropriate to immediate events, but that's because the outbursts are really grand explosions stemming from long-pent-up anger and long-suppressed frustrations.

As members of a generation that focuses on selfish desires and personal gain, they've been cheated of intimate relationships and support from others. Focusing only on their own needs brings nothing but despair. Unfortunately, loneliness and depression make poor nourishment for emotional growth.

It's true that some young people, even reared under the direst of circumstances, seem to turn out fine. This is sometimes not as surprising as it seems on the surface. A child may be reared in the worst of poverty by an illiterate, widowed mother — and yet go off into the world to make a valuable contribution to society. This child, strengthened by tender love and faithful prayers and guided by judicious discipline, has a decided advantage over the kid from the other side of the tracks who *seems* to "have everything." Unfortunately, Americans for more than a generation have trusted a lie. We have misplaced our values and priorities. As a result, our children suffer.

Many counselors tell us that it is the perfectionist who is most likely to fall victim to depression. And how does one become a perfectionist? It begins in the earliest years of childhood, with parents who demand nothing less than perfection. They demand of their child more than he can possibly produce.

It is a vicious cycle for both the child and the parent. Both become caught up in a whirlwind of frustration, guilt, and, especially, anger. The perfectionist is obsessively neat, orderly, frugal, and reliable — positive characteristics when they *aren't carried to the extreme.*

The child growing up under that kind of pressure learns to live with constant criticism. It appears that he can do nothing right. Continually pushed and anxious, he eventually comes to lose heart. The children most able to cope with life's problems are those who grow up with a good sense of self-esteem. Feeling like a person worthy of respect and affection (rather than as a mere object), these children can feel secure enough to move out from their home base to explore the world. And a major part of their confidence comes in knowing that if they *should* fail, they can still return to a loving, stable home.

Who can fail to bleed in his heart for the scores of young people who wander our streets or weep in secret? It is man's rebellion against God and Satan's perpetual determination to steal, kill, and destroy that cheats children of the loving, stable, God-fearing homes they deserve. In such homes they could fulfill God's plan for their lives. But bound by a self-guilt imposed upon them by others, they remain caught in the grip of destruction, unable to forgive themselves — or even God.

Any way we look at it, our current social patterns of divorce, single parenthood, two-career families, and widespread economic and social stress cause long-term harm to youngsters. Most parents don't *intentionally* want to harm their children, but the fact remains: just because they are around, many parents vent their frustrations on them. From all indications, it appears that the problem will become more marked as parents continue to attempt juggling the demands of their jobs and the drive for personal fulfillment with the responsibilities of child-rearing.

Lisbeth Schorr, adjunct professor in maternal and child health at the University of North Carolina at Chapel Hill, observes, "It's not that people don't *care* for their kids, but that many are trapped between caring *adequately* for their kids and doing those other things — self-fulfillment, earning a second income — that they need or want."[3]

In any event, something is definitely missing in the lives of countless children. Today, many don't receive enough adult attention. They don't have opportunity for interaction. They lack the advantages of face-to-face discussion of feelings, values, and philosophical insights that are essential if they are to develop and mature properly. For all too many children, growing up in America has become an ordeal instead of a joy.

A MATTER OF CHOICE

The rearing of children requires sacrifice on the part of parents, and experts detect less willingness to sacrifice than in past generations. "Parents are caught in a crunch of conflicting values," says Edward Weaver, director of the American Public Welfare Association. "They value children, but they value other things as well . . . Given these conflicts, in a number of instances they neglect children or don't give them a fair shake."[4]

The Children's Defense Fund, a Washington group, says that about 5.2 million children of 13 and under, whose parents are employed full-time, are without supervision for significant parts of the day.[5]

Now unfortunately, recitation of these facts tends to impose a burden of guilt on those who are struggling, for whatever reason, to make ends meet and to hold their families together. It rains on the just and on the unjust (Matthew 5:45). Today, even the most well-meaning parent faces tremendous demands and difficulties. Fortunately, God is able to sustain us under even the most trying of conditions.

I wouldn't want to live in today's world without the power and presence of God to sustain me (and I feel that I am a seasoned adult *and seasoned Christian.*) How much more does the innocent child need God's sustaining grace in the home? We live in a time when Satan is waging unconditional warfare on mankind. Satan is a definite personality who is the enemy of God and of our soul. His aim is nothing less than to utterly destroy and kill each of us. We must be aware of his methods lest he gain a foothold in our lives — and our homes.

A study by pollster Lou Harris and Associates found that 52 percent of family members thought that the trend to having both parents working outside the home has a generally negative effect on families. If they had the option, many mothers would prefer to work parttime or at home.[6] Unfortunately, many *must* work, and they — like their children — suffer the consequences of juggling two full-time careers. Rearing children and maintaining a home is, in truth, a full-time job in itself.

A study by the Institute for Social Research (at the University of Michigan) found that working mothers with college educations tend to cut back on leisure time and sleep — to avoid "cheating" their children of the time they deserve with them.[7] They still try to provide their children with all the opportunities offered by a modern society — sports, ballet, art lessons, and so forth — while striving to maintain the perfect, idealized picture of a mother depicted in women's magazines and child-rearing books. The mother's attempts to be always "warm, witty, charming, dedicated, and so forth" can drive her to the point of distraction, despair, or burnout. And this happens *particularly* to the parent (men included) who *cares*.

BURNOUT

Unconcerned parents don't suffer from burnout. To "burn out" one must first be on fire. Essentially, burnout means that the *energy* available to the task fails to meet the *demand*. When the parent puts forth every effort to meet the demand and fails — or when the supply of energy runs out — he may be completely overcome by feelings of anger, guilt, depression, self-doubt, or irritability.

We are told that as many as 50 percent of parents experience at least the *early* stages of burnout.[8] Burnout happens mostly to highly motivated parents who face their child-rearing responsibilities with enthusiasm and dedication. They're usually the educated, middle-class people who are idealistic and whose personalities are oriented toward perfection.[9]

Overly committed parents may drop out of all nonparent-related activities in order to focus total attention on their child, or they may refuse to allow anyone else to care for the child. These parents deny their own needs for rest and recreation and feel guilty when they feel the need for a break.

Once the demands exceed the energy available, burnout is inevitable. "Parents who ignore the pain they feel and continue to overwork enter stage four — 'pulling away.' Unlike the previous stages, very few of the factors associated with pulling away are positive. Parents at this stage may even say they dislike their children. They become paranoid; they believe the children are out to get them. If the kids break a glass or get mud on the carpet, these parents might view that behavior as deliberate. At this stage, parents feel like a powder keg ready to explode, and they often do."[10]

The reverse is, of course, the parent who puts his own needs first. While the emotional needs of the parent are, of course, critical, the child who finds himself far down on the parent's priority list is a prime candidate for emotional problems. He is inclined to feel exploited and will often react to such presumed exploitation.

The key is balance. God never requires more of us than we are able to perform, nor more than He will give us the energy to perform. Still, we often impose burdens upon our*selves* that God would never expect us to bear. It's important always to be realistic, to take stock of our lives, and to pray for God's priorities and His direction in reaching these goals.

We should always find the time to listen to our children, to communicate effectively with them, and to manage our time. We should set aside time each day to *demonstrate* our faith in God, in addition to instructing them in God's Word. We should do something special with them daily — even though they could do it for themselves.

DOLLARS AND SENSE

It's been said that "there is an anti-child spirit loose in the land." Dr. Frederick Green, associate director of Children's Hospital National

Medical Center of Washington, D. C., says, "Children are becoming more expendable and are seen as more of a burden to families."[11]

The average family spends almost $150,000 through the first 18 years of a child's life. Many adults regard children as an economic liability.[12]

How unfortunate it is that we must assign monetary values to relationships, but the fact remains that it does cost money to rear children, and that this money *could* have been used in other areas.

But we must remember that people are infinitely more important than "things." We have to cherish and embrace those elements in life that make family life special and that strengthen and reinforce us to face all the challenges set before us.

SUICIDE

Suicide has become a serious statistical factor in the loss of life among the young, and one which is particularly odious because it is self-imposed. Although official figures are hard to obtain, it is clear that at least 7,000 teenagers commit suicide each year, with as many as 400,000 suicide *attempts* being made yearly.[13]

The suicide rate among young people 15 to 24 has increased 300 percent in the past 20 years.[14] Suicide rates among those 15 to 19 years old is the highest ever recorded in the U. S. Whereas suicide is the tenth leading cause of death in our nation as a whole, it is the *second* leading cause of death among youth. (The first leading cause is accidents — and experts believe that many of these are actually suicides in disguise, or are caused by subconscious death wishes.)

One expert estimates that a million children a year flirt with the thought of suicide at one time or another.[15] It can, unfortunately, appear to be "an easy way out." At this very moment, as many as 10 percent of our teenagers may be seriously considering suicide. Dr. Michael Peck, director of Youth Services at the Los Angeles Suicide Prevention Center, writes, "There are more youngsters thinking, obsessing, and worrying about suicide than ever before."[16]

That is evidenced by the influx of calls that come in to the 550 suicide-prevention centers and hot lines operating in America. One Chicago suicide hotline reports that it rings every 20 seconds.[17] Of those who do commit suicide, there are three to four times more males than females.

Up until now, the highest suicide rate ever established was during the Great Depression — a period when financial pressures and poverty became almost unbearable. Today, the majority of those who commit suicide are in exactly opposite circumstances. The high-risk suicide group today is the adolescent who has had every advantage.[18] Some parents have worked and deprived themselves to give their children everything — and these are often the children who end up feeling that life isn't worth living.

The surface reasons for suicide among the young may be many and varied, but a common factor is a sense of loss or failure. This failure may be only imaginary, but to the young person it can be very real. That's why parents must be careful to attend to the teenager who feels rejected and unloved. The introverted young person, who finds it difficult (if not impossible) to communicate his needs, requires special attention. He is the one most likely to commit suicide.

A Washington, D. C., psychiatrist says, "Parents sometimes are so busy working hard to provide the material things that they've neglected what the child really needs and wants — time, attention, love, and affection. The child acts out suicide attempts to get attention."[19]

THE FAMILY AS A FACTOR

Although studies show that suicide rates are related to economic conditions and social factors (such as drug abuse and alcoholism), a prime catalyst for suicide among the young is the breakdown of the family. Suicide is therefore more than an individual act by one who is bent on self-destruction. Though it may be prompted by feelings of hopelessness, depair, despondency, or anxiety, it is almost always the symptom of some malfunction within the family structure.

Most obvious perhaps is the escalating divorce rate, which some contend accounts in great measure for the increase in the rate of suicide among our youth. Carl Tishler, a psychologist at Children's Hospital in Columbus, Ohio, reports that even small children can be driven to attempt suicide if the parents "won't stop beating on each other" after the divorce.[20]

Other children have been made to believe — by being used as pawns by one parent against the other — that divorce or marital problems are really their fault. In their childish thinking, they reason that if they were dead, their parents would be able to reconcile their differences.

In the same vein, children of alcoholics or drug addicts may believe that they are in some way responsible for these problems. Similarly, they feel that ending their lives will end the parent's problems. This sounds like an overly simplistic solution, and it is natural to wonder how a young person can arrive at such a conclusion. The fact is, out of depression and despair, the person planning suicide enters a world of unreality. "Thinking that death will bring them peace, many begin to fantasize and romanticize about their death."[21]

To many young people death becomes a welcomed friend. Death seems to offer a cherished relief from memories of sexual exploitation, family violence, peer pressures, or unbearable loneliness. Dan Lettieri, a Washington psychologist, says, "If they see life as bad, and can't see shades in between, then the alternative, death, is not negative to them." Most don't actually think of death as permanent, as a state from which there is no return, but are only obsessed with "sweet relief."[22]

ISOLATION

Many young people reach depths of despair in which they feel completely unique, picturing themselves as different from all their peers. They don't see their friends as harboring the same insecurities that beset them, thereby reinforcing their sense of isolation. Today's highly competitive society makes it difficult or impossible for young people to accomplish idealized goals. Failure to achieve such impossible goals convinces them that they are failures as individuals. For this reason, city dwellers (under more pressure to achieve) are more prone to suicide than are rural dwellers.

It's been found that suicidal teenagers progressively isolate themselves from the most important people in their lives.[23] Also feeling ostracized from their peers, they eventually dissolve *all* meaningful social relationships. It's like a chain reaction that leads a person into complete isolation — where he can't reach out to others and they can't reach him.

This is the work of none other than Satan. He wants to get that young person — or anyone, for that matter — to the place where he can work on him unhindered by the care, warmth, and concern of others. In truth, Satan's ultimate motive is to separate people from God.

It may well be that at the root of most suicides is a sense of separation from God. In effect, suicide can become a weapon against God. Those contemplating suicide may not consciously consider themselves in rebellion against God, but their thoughts and actions demonstrate that they doubt Him and His ability to deliver them from the pits of despair.

A NEW HOPE

Emile Durkheim, nineteenth-century psychologist, said, "Human passions stop only before a moral power that they respect." The Bible says, *"The fear of the Lord is the beginning of wisdom"* (Psalm 111:10).

It isn't hard to see how someone who rejects Christ would look to suicide as a solution. A young person living in the 1980s, without Christ, may well think that life isn't worth living. And to be frank with you, without Christ it isn't. Fortunately, no one *has* to live without Him. He came to give us *"life, and that . . . more abundantly"* (John 10:10). When Jesus is Lord of a person's life, there is never cause for despair. He gives light that dispels the darkness; He gives joy in the place of mourning; He brings peace in the midst of confusion.

How depressing it is to see young people surrendering their lives and futures to the forces of darkness because they haven't heard the saving message of Christ! But what an immense joy it is to see those among them who hear the message and respond, receiving new hope and new life!

How often we see young people showing all the trouble signs: lethargy, loss of appetite, sleeplessness, and reluctance to go to school or even play with friends. These are young people dying because they have turned to Satan for leadership. Some may never actually commit suicide, but they are, in effect, progressively destroying their lives.

Satan's plan is always to weaken and destroy. Young people, thinking they are "showing the world," neglect their bodies, overindulge in drugs and alcohol, drive recklessly, or commit themselves to activities dangerous to their emotional or spiritual well-being. In all these activities, they are subconsciously crying out for help. Although the psychologists and sociologists give us many helpful insights, the problem is ultimately a spiritual one.

In order to better understand the young mind, we should realize that most teenagers live only for the present. They have difficulty in realistically planning for the future. They don't understand how things *can* change — and often for the good. Having come up against too much, too soon, these youngsters are desperate, unhappy, confused, and compulsive. And often they commit suicide because they think there is no other way out — which is a manifestation of their rejection of the one *true* Way, Jesus Christ.

AN EASY OUT

We must bring Jesus to those who are searching, and the hour is growing tragically short. The climate is ripe for destruction. The all-too-common attitude of disregard for the sanctity of human life is enough to give people a sense of social acceptance in the act of killing themselves. The pressures of growing up too fast and the low esteem generated by family breakdown push the young person farther along. Violence in the movies and on TV prime the pump even further. In fact, TV's quick and superficial endings have been cited as one reason for the inability of young people to cope with continuing problems.

Psychotherapist Margery Fridstein from Chicago's North Shore "suicide belt" (28 teenagers took their lives there within 17 months) says, "Kids don't like to read books — they'd rather watch television and see the story end quickly — and so they don't know how to deal with long-term frustration . . . . Because pills or a rope or even a gun is readily available, it is much easier to do this dramatic thing."[24]

Satan goes so far as to convince many young people that suicide may be a noble and heroic act. Those with very low self-esteem may feel that it is their *duty* to "spare others the burden of putting up with me." The most shocking example is perhaps that of the six-year-old boy who tried to hang himself because he thought he was a burden to his financially troubled family. Then there was the 14-year-old girl who knelt in front of a train after learning she was pregnant. Other suicidal young people just put themselves into a position to be killed — like the child who rides his bicycle into oncoming traffic.

Now, if you are a Christian, I want you to stop reading right now and pause for a moment to seek God. Think of the young people you may know: the perfectionists who are having trouble handling failure, the loners who have few (if any) friends and who feel that no one understands them, the angry who want to hurt and shock others, and the depressed who can see no light at the end of the tunnel.

Have *you* ever taken any time to tell these hurting souls about the One who cares and understands? Take a moment now and pray for these young people. Listen to their pleas for help *now*! For some of them, there may be no tomorrow.

"Linda was always the shyer one. Things seemed hard for her. Her sister, Peggy, was outgoing and cheerful, with boyfriends and medals in figure skating. But when Peggy was 16 something began to change.

"'She'd always gotten A's and B's, but now she thought she was stupid,' Linda says. 'She thought she didn't have any friends, but she had gobs of them. She said she was fat — but she was skinny as anything. I don't know what she expected — nothing she did was good enough.' All of her life Linda will remember the sunny winter morning when Peggy came out of the bedroom and put her arms around her father. 'I love you very much, Dad,' she said. 'Everything's going to be fine.' She walked back into the bedroom and shot herself through the head. In an instant her life was over." [25]

Here was a case where one more young person succumbed to the "quiet epidemic" of suicide. One more young life was wasted by Satan's seduction. But everything isn't "going to be fine." The rest of the family must cope with the most difficult bereavement crisis imaginable. The pain and the questions will last forever.

SPIRITUAL GUIDANCE

One last factor that should be mentioned in regard to suicide is guidance. Most modern families and much of our social structure are seriously lacking in guidance. They place on children pressures to excel, to mature, and to make decisions at a very young age, but they seldom provide the necessary guidelines and restraints.

Studies show that as guidance decreases (guidance provided through religious teachings and beliefs), the rate of suicide increases. [26] As mentioned before, suicide is the second leading cause of death among teenagers. Today, the sad fact is, three out of every four teenagers receive no regular instruction in *any* type of religion.

From 1954 to 1978 the suicide rate almost *tripled* for U. S. residents 15-24 years old. At the same time, church attendance (for those in the same age group) dropped from 48 percent (in the 1950s) to 28 percent in 1973. [27]

Dr. Steven Stack, a sociologist with Penn State University, states, "Religion regulates individuals. Apparently, if people have rules or moral codes to follow, they are less prone to suicide." [28] Involvement in an ongoing youth group has been viewed as especially positive in this regard. Our youth are less prone to turn to suicide when they belong to a group with common ethical values.

Dr. Mary Giffin, a Chicago psychiatrist who runs a clinic for teenagers on the North Shore, makes another point. "For a while," she says, "the spectrum was very clear. Catholics and Fundamentalists did not commit suicide. Now all that has changed because religious groups aren't as clear-cut in their beliefs as they used to be. There aren't as many absolutes being taught anymore."[29]

In other words, our young people need something *worth living for*! They need to dedicate their lives *to* something or someone — and that Someone is Christ! Their faith in Christ will support them through life's trials and lend meaning to their suffering. He alone gives hope where there seems to be none.

While many unhappy young people choose suicide as their avenue of escape, another two million a year take to the streets to escape an unbearable home life.[30] However, those who flee from their families soon find that the streets offer only fear, disillusionment, and want.

A NATIONAL EPIDEMIC

In our grim, pressure-filled economic climate, the number of runaways has increased to the point that we have a nationwide epidemic on our hands. Both boys and girls, some as young as 11 or 12 (the average age is 15), leave their homes in a virtual stampede. Almost half will never return home. They are confused and angry.

Many of them, from well-to-do families, simply disappear into anonymity amid the world of drug addicts and prostitutes. Most escape home only to become victims of others who will manipulate and abuse them.

Douglas Huenergardt, supervisor of the Runaway Youth Crisis Shelter in St. Petersburg, Florida, points out that the runaway of today is very different from those in the 1960s and early 1970s. He says, "During that time we had kids seeking alternative life-styles. That's not what's happening today. The child who's running is one who simply can't stand it at home any longer."[31] That makes them far different from "yesterday's flower children running *to* an inviting crash-pad Camelot . . . ."[32] These young people are running away *from* something — more often than not, a disintegrating family.

If the runaway should return home, an estimated 15 to 20 percent would leave again — some fleeing as many as 10 times. Cynthia Myers of the National Runaway Switchboard explains, "After a child has left the first time, if the reason that made him run doesn't change, I *guarantee* he'll run again."[33]

Besides the ones who have been physically or sexually abused, there are those who just don't feel loved at home for a variety of reasons. Their running away is a cry for help — a cry that says, "Please love me. I don't have what it takes to cope with these pressures, I feel insecure." Regrettably, many parents are so preoccupied with their own problems that they unconsciously drive their children from their homes.

One young runaway girl says, "There are few kids who will leave just for the pleasure of it, just to get out on their own. A lot of times things are really bad in a family . . . a person can only take what's been handed out to them for so long."[34]

Others complain of loneliness, of parents wiped out on drugs or alcohol. Some spend hours alone from an early age. Others wish they could find time alone as an escape from their pressure-packed, chaotic home situation.

According to the National Network of Runaway and Youth Service, a runaway can usually be spotted before he runs away. Ten danger signals are listed:[35]

• *Growing isolation* — The child avoids family gatherings (even at meals) and spends more and more time alone in his or her room.

• *Excessive blowups* — Tantrums are common in the turbulent teens, but watch out when the smallest things seem to trigger repeated explosions of temper.

• *Abrupt mood swings* — Take note if a normally sunny teen turns sullen, withdrawn, angry, or even manic without warning.

• *Increased violations* — Rules are the boundaries against which growing youth must lean or hurl themselves in the act of maturing. But take heed when "borderline" incidents turn to outright rebellion.

• *Increased sleeping* — It's normal for adolescents to sleep more than parents think is healthy, but beware of sudden marathons that can indicate depression or problems they can't manage.

• *Diminished communication* — Again, there may be a perfectly good reason why your children clam up. But if you can't think of one (and it persists), pay attention.

• *School troubles* — Plunging grades, truancy, class-cutting, disciplinary problems, sudden (and enduring) breakups with close friends. All or any of these can be cries for help that come before bolting.

• *Parental stack-blowing* — Are you, not the child, getting unreasonably upset over the smallest issues? Your subconscious feelings may be trying to tell you something — a subtle but significant shift in family balance that needs heeding.

• *Family crises* — Death, divorce, illness, the loss of a job, a major move — any of these can disrupt the family equilibrium and hurl your child off into orbit.

• *Unexplained money or possessions* — Even if they're not stolen, they may be stashed for an impending getaway. Obviously, individual circumstances should tell you when concern is called for.

THE "THROWAWAYS"

Of the two million young people on our nation's streets who are generally thought of as "runaways," the majority are in actuality *throwaways*. In other words, the majority of these don't *choose* to leave home, most are pushed out or abandoned. Sometimes unemployed fathers and mothers are unable to care for them, or single parents — struggling to make ends meet — have little time for them. They come not only from poverty-stricken families, but from the ranks of the middle-class as well. Homes, tormented by divorce, sexual abuse, and physical punishment use them up and then discard them.

Once the runaways are on the streets, survival becomes the name of the game in a jungle ruled by pimps, pushers, and thieves. With 80 percent of the runaways (or throwaways) coming from white, middle- and upper-class families, they need a crash course in survival tactics.[36] They fall quickly into the runaway life-style of sleeping outdoors, eating out of trash dumpsters, hitchhiking, shoplifting, panhandling, stealing clothes from Laundromats, selling plasma, et cetera. Before long they look like street urchins, aged far beyond their natural years.

Most often they fall into the hands of adults who hook them on drugs — and then use them for profit. They suffer from "malnutrition, drug-related disorders, sexual dysfunction and, having little access to medical care (runaways don't have health insurance), from disease."[37]

Many runaway boys die each year of rectal hemorrhage after engaging in prostitution to survive.[38]

In Chicago in 1980, 33 runaway boys and young men were killed. In Florida and New Jersey, at least 31 females were killed. In Houston, the bones of many runaways were found among the 27 victims linked to the operator of a homosexual torture ring.[39]

Unless runaways are rescued very quickly — experts say, sometimes within 48 hours — they are likely to be lost forever. Girls are especially vulnerable. Runaways need food, shelter, and clothing to survive; but they have nothing to exchange for it but their bodies. "What can a 13-year-old girl do but show her body?" asks a girl at a youth shelter.

With over 60 percent of the runaways being girls, and with most too young or inexperienced to obtain work legally, both boys and girls become victims. Pimps, exploiters, and drug pushers hang around bus terminals like vultures, awaiting the arrival of the hurt and disillusioned young boys and girls who have no one to turn to and nowhere to go.

They approach them with a mask of gentleness, concern, and a full deck of promises, but the deck is stacked. Before long the young will experience harsh demands and beatings that thrust them into the throes of drugs and criminal activity, prostitution, homosexuality, and pornography.

PROSTITUTION

Both male and female teenage prostitutes, some as young as 12 and 13, are among the 1,000 to 4,000 runaways to be found on Hollywood Boulevard on any summer night. On Santa Monica Boulevard, hundreds of young boys prostitute themselves in homosexuality daily while hundreds of girls sell themselves along Sunset Strip.

In New York, runaways keep the "Minnesota Strip" — a stretch of hooker's turf near Times Square — supplied with new prostitutes. Most of them, between the ages of 10 and 20, are runaways from other states.[40]

Dr. Judianne Densen-Gerber, a psychiatrist and lawyer who works in New York, says that it is not unusual to see male prostitutes as young as *eight years old*! There is one male prostitute for every four female prostitutes.[41]

In Chicago, call-in services offer hired "companions" at rates as high as $450 a weekend.[42] The service recruits boys in their early teens from runaways arriving at bus stations.

Although boy prostitution is not new, we will see more and more of it as homosexuals flaunt their life-style and push for gay rights. If our courts don't concern themselves with law enforcement and the protection of the public — rather than taking sides with civil rights issues — it will continue to increase. It will inevitably grow to the point where militant homosexual groups will literally *seize* the vulnerable young and make captives of them.

LOVE-STARVED

The truth is, many parents just don't care about their children — and the children know it. They are love-starved. For many young people, sex is just a trade-off for love and acceptance from adults. Many experts feel that it is a lack of love, stability, warmth, and caring (or simple morality) that lures both boys and girls into prostitution. However, some prostitutes grow up in reasonably healthy, normal homes. Therefore, we certainly can't blame *all* prostitution on parental neglect. There are other factors involved in the rise in prostitution, especially among the young.

The general decay in America's moral climate also contributes by making prostitution seem somehow more socially acceptable. Prostitution has even been compared by some young women in the business to shoplifting a generation or so ago.

Prostitution is a big business that brutalizes young people — especially the runaways or throwaways who depend on it for survival. Millions of customers believe that prostitution is nothing more than a victimless crime, a business deal between a buyer and a seller.

On the other side of the coin is the pimp who literally owns the prostitute. In the beginning he doesn't have to do much to lure the young, desperate runaway — frightened and lost.

Some pimps sell boys and girls, just like slaves, to other pimps. At a New York City "runaway auction," some were reportedly sold for as much as $10,000 each.[43] At other times, truckers pick up runaways, then sell them to pimps at designated drop-off stations. Two 12-year-old girls from Tennessee were reportedly picked up, raped, and sodomized repeatedly before being sold in California.[44]

THE AFTEREFFECTS

Even when these young prostitutes survive, they remain marked for life. The dehumanizing treatment they receive makes them hardened and cold.

Most of the young prostitutes don't feel young. They can barely remember what it was like to be a child. They view their wasted lives with little, if any, emotion. Nothing seems to matter anymore.

What's the solution to this virtual epidemic? According to the professionals, millions of unloved, unwanted, emotionally crippled young people will be loosed on the streets throughout the 1980s. Most of them will become involved in crime, either as perpetrators or as victims. Thousands will land in jail — many just because they're runaways.

Harry F. Swanger of the National Juvenile Law Center in St. Louis warns that, "Locking a child up certainly doesn't help. And in our opinion it's unconstitutional. It is a very serious mistake because it can increase the danger of harm to the child and it doesn't deal with the underlying issue of *why* he's running."[45]

On the surface, most runaways seem to have good reasons for leaving home. Of those who come before juvenile courts, over half left homes marred by alcoholism, violent physical abuse, or sexual abuse by fathers or other relatives.[46] Throwing them in jail only reinforces their low esteem and sense of rejection. And it *is* a dangerous "solution."

JUVENILES IN ADULT JAILS

An estimated 500,000 juveniles are held in *adult* jails; however, only one-fourth of them are there for serious offenses.[47] The other 75 percent exist under sordid conditions with little opportunity for recreation, exercise, education, or counseling because of *minor* offenses — property damage, breaking curfew, skipping school, or running away. And some of them — 20,000 a year — haven't committed any offense. They are jailed because, homeless and rejected, no one knows what to do with them.

One 17-year-old was arrested for failing to pay $73 in traffic fines and was beaten for 4½ hours by inmates. His stay was a short one, however. "On Memorial Day he was found dying in the exercise yard — apparently beaten, burned, gouged, and kicked to death by five other juvenile inmates."[48]

Another young person, serving time for underage drinking, was threatened with gang rape by his cell mates. He says, "You can scream bloody murder, but [the guards] can't hear you."[49]

Of the many runaways, over 44,000 a year do find their way to some type of shelter for runaways.[50] Some young people admit that if it weren't for shelters or a youth program, street life would have swallowed them up.

Programs like Teen Challenge, Holy Ghost Repair Service, and Centrum — knowing that only the love of God can restore the spirits, minds, and emotions of our nation's lost youth — take God's message of salvation right where they are. But is that the *solution?* At best they can only hope to *salvage* wrecked lives. Of course, this is not to be lightly dismissed; it is a great service and one that needs to be performed today. Every one of us should be in the business of bringing God's redemption to those who are lost and without hope.

But if the families and churches across the land were doing what they are *supposed* to be doing, there would be fewer runaways and throwaways *requiring* ministration. If we would *all* get back to the business of "building people" for the greater glory of God, our homes would be filled with God's blessings.

God gives us kids to nurture in the fear and admonition of the Lord. Anything less and we are responsible. Satan has sold the world a bill of goods, and we chase elusive dreams, waiting for the big jackpot. As a result, we are experiencing the consequences of God's law of sowing and reaping. If we sow *to* the flesh, we reap *in* the flesh.

Next time you see some young street urchin degraded by the filth and influences of the world, before you condemn him and go on your way, mentally peel away the layers of pain, rejection, loneliness, and fear. Look past the cold eyes, the rough manner, the harsh, bitter words, and the body marked by shame. Look, and you will find someone's child.

Allow the years to slip away. Look deep into that heart. There stands a child. And like any child, he was once trusting. He wanted to love and to be loved. God made him that way.

He may yearn for family and for friends. He may yearn for a good home life and for a comfortable living. Yet, he can't return. For him — as for many — there is nothing to return *to*.

But God loves him still — as he does all of them — and so very, very much. Allow yourself to become a vessel through which *His* love can flow.

A SEDATED
SOCIETY

"If we can enslave just one generation in any country, that country will fall to Soviet communism . . . The way to enslave that generation is by means of immorality, music, and drugs" (Joseph Stalin, 1935).

The scene was the Riverfront Coliseum in Cincinnati, Ohio. The day, December 3, 1979, was cold and blustery. The event was a rock concert featuring The Who,[1] a British group known for the volume of its hard-rock beat which was once clocked at a decibel level of 120 at a distance of 50 yards from the stage — an effect equal to standing behind an airline jet with its engines running. The crowd was made up largely of average American high school students and some reasonably disciplined and intelligent young housewives and businessmen in their twenties. In short, your neighbors' kids and mine. They shared one thing in common. This was the first generation to grow up with rock.

For five chilly hours before the concert, they gathered in the plaza of the coliseum to be sure of getting seats as close as possible to the stage. It was a long wait in the 34° temperature, but they were high on anticipation and excitement. The house tickets had been sold out over two months in advance, grossing nearly $190,000, and they had thought of little else since.

What *promised* to be a spectacular event — throbbing with The Who's unique beat and incisive lyrics — would *prove* to be one of the worst disasters in the history of rock music. There was nothing to suggest it was happening, and if it had been noticed, no one could have stopped it.

When it was over, 11 young people between 15 and 21 lay dead — victims of the tidal action of the crowd — the cause of death asphyxia . . . by compression of the chest.

Caught in the crowd's vicelike grip, they had found it harder and harder to breathe. With their arms pinned to their sides and all feeling gone below the waist, they had helplessly succumbed to the mesmerizing, dangerous sway of the crowd. Then, lost in an endless sea of faces, they had died quietly in the midst of the din.

The crowd hadn't been a rowdy one — most of them were not the violent type. Neither had drugs and alcohol presented a significant problem as with so many concerts. What occurred was a phenomenon that is as little understood today as it was 100 years ago, a phenomenon in which a large mass of people develop such an intense, obsessive loyalty to someone (in this case, a musical group) that they enter an almost trancelike state, losing full possession of their faculties. The "why" of the phenomenon is difficult to answer, and to pursue it is fraught with controversy. Those who are "into rock" defend it blindly, refusing to study objectively this and other phenomena associated with it.

MUSICAL APPRECIATION

Music — *all music* — is powerful. A skilled musician can entrance an audience. He does so by using the basic drives in music — melody, harmony, and rhythm — to move upon man's spiritual, psychological, and physical state. By carefully creating an imbalance in the music, he can subtly influence the listener who has been swept up in the flow of the music. By altering the tension and relaxation of the arrangements (such as is heard in the rise and fall of the music), the dissonance and consonance, the repetition and variation, he holds the power to create emotion: tension, frustration, confusion, rebellion, sensuality — even distraction, depression, or despair.

I recently read a statement that claimed that there's no such thing as a "devil beat." *All* music, it said, belongs to God. The writer argued that the only criterion for judging the propriety of music was the *message* it presented.

Although many sincere and well-meaning people — including Christians — disagree with me, I firmly believe that music (like many other good things of God) can be perverted and corrupted by evil. In fact, Scripture gives accounts of this very phenomenon in Daniel 3:5 and Exodus 32:18. These biblical accounts refer to instrumental music and singing. Good lyrics, no matter how Godly, can't override the influence of music based on ungodly composition. I believe, of necessity, that this concept must be grasped to develop a full understanding of music's potential in the world today.

THE MUSIC BUSINESS

Of all the unsavory influences operating in the United States, the music business has perhaps most widely affected the minds, morals, and overall direction of the young people of our nation. Anyone with even the briefest exposure to the commercial music industry can't escape the fact that it is an area that has been completely subverted by Satan. Why, one may wonder, would he exert so much energy on a seemingly minor part of our society? The devastating *results* supply the answer.

In 1955 a disc jockey named Allen Freid coined the phrase "rock 'n' roll."[2] It was a street term having sexual connotations. Today, it stands for a musical form which has literally swept our nation. While much disagreement exists as to what makes music "rock," art historian Carl Belz says, "Any listener who wants rock defined specifically is probably unable to recognize it." Because of its pervasive influence, we must learn to recognize it and understand the phenomenon it represents.

It has been, along with its associated life-style, the core element of a youth-oriented "counterculture" which is radically different from any force influencing our nation since its foundation.[3]

EARLY ROCK

In the beginning, it was an outrage. Parents — detecting suggestions of lust — rejected it and called it noise. Jerry Lee Lewis banged on the piano, Elvis grinned and gyrated his hips — causing youth to cheer and parents to grimace.

After the Beatles, the music business grew in its ability to influence its listeners. Relishing their new sense of power, they made bold and revolutionary social statements.

Today, it is an institution! A multimillion dollar industry, it is welcomed almost everywhere. It is the music *most* of the world listens to *most* of the time.

A person would have to be extremely gullible to think that the communists — masters of propaganda and psychology — wouldn't recognize a field with as much influence as music. Part of their plan to "rework culture" involves "reworking" through the subversion of music. The communists have made extensive use of music in America where they were markedly successful in capturing the field of folk music.[4]

They were able to do so because music is much more than entertainment. Music is the voice of the people, conveying messages — verbal and nonverbal — that one may hesitate to speak without music's support. It seems that the idea, the philosophy, the protest, and/or the mood are carried on the wings of music in a way that makes them more readily understood and *accepted*.

As such, music represents a powerful political force. Given a public platform from which to speak, almost any orator can pick up *some* adherents along the way. But add the soul-altering effect of music, and you have a *multiplication* of the word's persuasive power. Therefore, "forms and rhythms in music are never changed without producing changes in the most *political* forms and ways . . . . the new style quietly insinuates itself into manners and customs and from there it issues a greater force . . . goes on to attack laws and constitutions, displaying the utmost impudence — until it ends by overthrowing everything, both in public and in private."[5]

THE WOODSTOCK NATION

In June of 1967, in Monterey, California, 100,000 orchids were flown in from Hawaii and scattered over a field among crowds that had gathered for a weekend of music. Interspersed among the hippies and long-haired youth were 11,000 of the world's "communers" — newspaper and magazine journalists, critics, photographers, television, and radio reporters.[6] Without realizing it, they were witnessing the end of 70 years of popular music, and the beginning of what would become (in 1969) a sociological and musical phenomenon that would reflect the energy and vitality of an action-packed decade throughout the nation.

Later, the Woodstock Nation was born when 600,000 youth came together in a cow pasture in search of three days of peace, love, and music. These young people participated in what would come to be considered the countercultural event of the decade.

Just a short time after this legendary festival occurred, Woodstock became a symbol for all those who defied traditional values and celebrated the dawning of a new era with the exuberant sound of blaring guitars. The Woodstock Nation represented a generation built on the tenacity of rock music and the rage of a decade of revolt.

In the late 1970s rock took on a frightening new form. The moral dissolution and technological elevation of society profoundly influenced the evolving musical style. Rock lyrics were no longer crying out for peace and love; instead violence erupted from the wild new sound, beat, and philosophy of rock. The second half of the 1970s saw an increased popularity of groups featuring acts of gross violence and vain, egotistical lyrics.

Instead of outdoor festivals, indoor auditoriums gained dominance. These allowed "new wave" and "punk rock" groups to incorporate optical and laser effects to exert even greater emotional reaction from their music.

Earlier rock groups may have caused pandemonium, but such reactions were mild compared to the adulation greeting the gross displays of the punk rockers.

THE ANTHEM OF THE YOUNG

Rock has become the contemporary form of mass communication. One sociologist speaks of rock as "a new culture being born, and its lyrics serve as normative guidelines for youth in the process of defining and establishing a new order."[7] Listening to the music of youth reveals most clearly how they think and what they value — and such an excursion into the minds and thinking of today's youth is *frightening!*

Theodore Roszak, in *The Making of the Counterculture,* reiterates this theme by suggesting: "One is apt to find out more about youth by paying attention to posters and dance — and especially to the pop music, which now knits together the whole 13-to-30 age group."[8]

Even as early as 1972, children as young as eight were listening regularly to rock stations.[9] Over $60 million worth of rock recordings were sold yearly with the biggest group of purchasers being girls from nine to 13 years of age.[10] The average age of those tuned to rock-and-roll stations is 13. Now I want you to think about it. Boys and girls as young as 10, 12, and 13 are being led down a path of devastating destruction. Actually, some young people seem bent on self-destruction. Unable to cope with the pressures facing their generation, they gravitate toward activities that seem to promise escape. These young people, joined together by common fears and confusions, drown themselves in a blaring sea of sound.

Ralph J. Gleason, in *The Sounds of Social Change,* describes their need to escape from harsh reality in this way: "In a culture of noise — not just the jets roaring overhead and the trucks thundering on the streets, but the psychic noise of the crashing of institutions and assumptions and conventions, the whole crescendo of a collapsing civilization — the only peace seems to be in the middle of an even greater sound in which a special kind of sonic high is produced and a new kind of one-to-one communication occurs."[11]

MUSICAL SUBVERSION

Joseph Crow, perhaps America's number-one expert on musical subversion, believes that the changes in rhythm and other musical techniques used to sell attitudes and concepts are akin to brainwashing. "By changing the rhythm within a musical piece you can have a strong impact on the listener and the subliminal effect is to push the 'message' much more strongly."[12]

Switching a beat from three-four to five-four time produces a physiological response in some people. This type of "polyrhythm" — which is common in pop music — emphasizes the message. When lyrics are coupled with rock's rhythmic beat (noted by psychologists and scientists as related to hypnotism), mind-conditioning is made possible.[13]

A person in a hypnotic or semihypnotic state becomes highly suggestible. Therefore, the message contained in the lyrics is recorded and stored deep in the subconscious mind. It is then available for recall under proper conditions. For this reason, music can be dangerous whether the young person fully understands the words or not —especially when the lyrics promote illicit sex, drugs, rebellion, the occult, and all types of evil.

Rock's special allure is based on its power to play on real fears and emotions. But instead of *dealing* with them, it exploits them. "It provides only a 'manic moment of uplift' and plays with the psychological tensions of puberty."[14] It exposes young people — wrestling with sexual urges and their search for sexual identity — to perverted attitudes of sexual love. It paints an ugly and mechanical view, often to the point of becoming bizarre and perverted.

Rather than encouraging genuine commitments based on love, it advocates depersonalized sexual activity with an undercurrent of violence. The young person swayed by an illusion finds that his only recourse is the denial of his deepest needs. Over a period of time his frustrated need for true love and intimacy begins to express itself in hate and even violence.

Scripture says:

> *"[They] shall receive the reward of unrighteousness, as they that count it pleasure to riot in the day time. Spots they are and blemishes, sporting themselves with their own deceivings while they feast with you; Having eyes full of adultery . . . [they] cannot cease from sin; beguiling unstable souls: an heart they have exercised with covetous practices; cursed children"* (II Peter 2:13, 14).

God by His Holy Spirit gave the term "cursed children" to Simon Peter that it might be recorded for future generations. How well it expresses the specific character and blight of America today — *cursed children*!

All across America, parents throw up their hands in exasperation and despair, their universal complaint being, "We can't communicate with our teenage sons and daughters!" One reason they find it so difficult to get through to the "turned-on" generation is that today's young people, plugged in to blaring transistor radios, are *tuned out* to parents. Our youth appear void of intelligence because they're shell-shocked, immersed in a raging sea of rebellion instituted by the blast of sound blaring forth from the local rock station.

The impact of rock music stems from its complete association with the youth culture. Its exclusive identification with the young has given it a "purity" (from adult "contamination") that lends it authority in the child's mind — and *through* the young makes it a frightening power in our nation's future.

Rock singers *communicate* with young minds. They promote attitudes and ideas that would horrify parents if they were aware of the message. Because of their shared youth, audiences have a sense of camaraderie, "whether a general sense of generation or a specific sense of a particular cult."[15] Rock stars become the *focus* of this identification — largely because they too are young.

The adulation and sick preoccupation of young people toward rock bands and singers are nourished by a panoply of magazines aimed at teenagers. They "cover the lives, promote the attitudes, and sell the radical political views of the new 'gods' in hoary detail."[16] In other words, *rock music is youth!*

PORNOGRAPHY OVER THE AIRWAVES

In essence, all rock hinges on an exploitation of adolescent needs. Rock is a phony medium appealing to a phony culture. It is based on a contrived and commercialized appeal to a "need" *it* has created! Its false need is a lever meant to make a mass market vulnerable to manipulation by the forces that have created that market.

Some time ago, I happened to turn on a late-night television program. One of the late, late talk shows featured a particular rock group from England. Their answers to the host's questions were little more than a succession of grunts. They could barely string together four or five words, much less offer an intelligent answer to the questions being asked.

Their condition finally became so evident (and so disturbing) that the host shook his head and told them it was pointless to continue, allowing them to leave the stage. I watched them shuffle off — dirty, unshaven, with matted and filthy hair sticking out from their heads, their eyes glazed with drugs. "These," I thought as they shambled off the stage, "are the gods of our world today."

On another occasion, I flipped on the morning news of one of the major networks. A rock concert had taken place the previous night, and there had been a riot with several people killed. I watched the female anchor of the early morning news program as she spoke of the performing group with utter awe. She pronounced their name as if she were speaking the name of deity. It was as if she were speaking something sacred each time she mentioned their activities. I sat there in utter astonishment as this supposedly intelligent woman simultaneously deceived others and was herself deceived. I wondered if she realized what she was saying. She was treating these people as though they were gods.

Certainly she couldn't have realized that multiplied thousands of young people would be directed down the road to drugs, illicit sex, and rebellion because of their leadership. Some would die because of their influence, suffering the agony of the damned. Untold heartaches would be suffered by hundreds of parents — and all because of this group. Still, she was presenting them as something superhuman.

I listened to another newscast the other day. The announcer turned to the camera before a station break and confided, "We will be back in a moment and I will have news of . . . ." He named a rock group that had given a concert the night before. Again, it was as if something very special were about to be presented to the American public. What he was *really* doing — although I'm sure he didn't realize it — was acting as the Pied Piper of Satan's effort to lead multiplied millions to hell.

Today thousands of radio stations beat out the incessant pounding rhythm of top-40 rock. The beat has become so pervasive — and the lyrics so filthy — that they defy description. It is actually pornography over the airwaves.

The same can be said of cable television's rock-and-roll channels, except that they make it even *more* compelling because of the visual reinforcement of the musical beat. It is a definite possibility that the airwaves have become the greatest vehicle for the destruction of our youth.

Rock songs promote drugs, revolution, and the glorification of sexual union between teenagers. Just as the songs of revolution have served to condition many young people to accept the ravings of the new left — and the myriad drug songs were doubtless a factor in the drug epidemic — so the open exhortations to indulge in illicit sex are also a factor in the demoralization of our youth. They help to produce unprecedented numbers of illegitimate children and an unparalleled rise in venereal disease.[17]

Something about rock suppresses inhibitions and inflames youthful energies and desires. It arouses listeners from fatigue, boredom, or apathy and moves them to *action* — even though it is a counterproductive sort.

In the 1970s rock concentrated on the sexuality of youth. It was a natural development. From there it was only a question of focus. Traditional morality was the target. Then the only question was how to best demonstrate your complete *disdain* for it. What could be more personal, if personal liberation was the creed, than liberating your sex organs as an expression of rejection of everything that had gone before? This would be the logo of the 1970s — the "mooning" of everything the older generation viewed with respect.

And so the sexual revolution erupted with full force. Sex became every man's stairway to power and glory.

PUNK ROCK

Rock-and-roll music literally breathes the essence of erotica. Its perverted stimulation is intended to "turn you on." But sin can never be satisfied with just one step — it always has to go farther. While acid and hard rock were oriented toward sex, drugs, and satanism, punk rock concentrates on rebellion against parental authority, anarchy, and bodily perversions more extreme than routine pornography. The whole punk style is an improvisation on themes of death, rape, sadomasochism, and bondage.

Punks are obsessed with sex, especially violent sex. Self-mutilation remains the most emphatic trademark of punk rock. It was sadism and masochism (the torturer and the tortured), featured by punk rockers, which moved sex into the area of power games. Games are what rock performers play onstage — and rock managers play *off*stage.

Most people can hardly imagine the depths of depravity to which punk rock sinks. Below is an excerpt of an article by Lois M. Reed. When I first mentioned the article on our Telecast, some station owners and managers reacted in disbelief. However, after contacting Ms. Reed for her sources, we found the original materials were far worse than that which she had included. She had written:

> *In both punk rock lyrics and punk literature, frequent reference to corpses, blood, scabs, phlegm, etc. takes precedence over erotic and standard four-letter obscenities. Many punk rock bands hang out in cemeteries. The Los Angeles Voodoo Church band gets its ideas for new songs by sitting in a graveyard.*

The articles, photos, and illustrations in a publication called "No-Mag" are more disgusting and obscene than any found in Hustler *or* Penthouse, *yet it is sold at record stores such as "Roads to Moscow" which are frequented by children.*

In one published interview, a band leader talks of a future system of masters and slaves, a pending blood bath, and the earth being regurgitated. According to another, their purpose is to tell kids the truth — "that America sucks" —and to encourage kids to go against the police, the establishment, and the so-called preachers and Christians. The same issue contains an article about a 40-year-old female pornographer who is intrigued and obsessed with castration and fondling teen-agers, accompanied by graphic photos.

Two pages are filled with illustrations, photographs, and discussion of keeping food costs down by cooking high-protein fetuses with "amniotic fluids and membranes" cooked in a special sauce.

"Life Sentence" ridicules education, comparing life with being a "chained-up dog fenced in a yard." One titled, "The Equalizer" maligns the work ethic, and splashed all over a sheet distributed by Thunderbolt Record Distribution are the words, "Life is so ugly why not kill yourself?"

It's very difficult to accept the fact that multiple thousands of boys and girls listen to such putrid rot, often through headphones for many hours each day. It's even more difficult to accept the fact that the parents of these youngsters actually buy this filth for their children through generous allowances, plus their failure to investigate and supervise what's being purchased.

Many of these groups, made up of avowed homosexuals, advocate homosexuality. Others can scarcely be categorized as homosexual or heterosexual, apparently accepting the bestial concept of "if it feels good, do it." This is the type of example being held up to our youth today.

These rock groups advocate every type of perversion and filth, as well as satanic worship, witchcraft, and necrophilia (the performance of sex with a dead body) until the perversion has become so gross that the minds of millions of young people are literally being destroyed. Their music makes the perverse seem glamorous, exciting, and appealing.

THE ESTABLISHMENT

Youth searching for a separate identity rebel against authority and the establishment, or society, created by outdated, outmoded adults. Little do they realize that this very establishment owns and operates the stations, magazines, and record companies that promote rock as a powerful force in American life. It was the establishment that dragged the Beatles up from their dingy Liverpool cellar and made them multimillionaires.

Paul Wolfe, in *The Sounds of Social Change,* points out that LSD would be nothing more than three letters of the alphabet and marijuana would be a minor problem reserved for jazz musicians if it had not been for the establishment's promotion.[18] Therefore, it shouldn't surprise us that the same establishment that uses the media to push their ungodly philosophies would use it to lure the youth of the world into acceptance of these philosophies.

I believe the major establishment record companies are right in the middle of the drug scene, the counterculture, and the counterrevolution. It isn't uncommon to find in the "underground" newspapers (squeezed between the pornography, drug pushing, and shouts for revolution) full-page spreads purchased by major record and broadcasting companies. These vicious anti-American, underground newspapers are, in fact, *supported and directed* by the very establishment they claim to oppose.

Why? Because it is basically the establishment that takes in the *gold* produced by illicit drugs, illicit sex, and the "revolution."

Wolfe issues a solemn warning. "Our teenagers would do well to ask why the establishment would finance those claiming to seek its own demise? — unless what is happening is all part of a single revolutionary thrust, of which America's youth is to be the ultimate victim."[19]

Gary Allen, also in *The Sounds of Social Change,* asks a provocative question: "Is it possible that record producers have been fooled by the jargon of the songs — have put out such discs not knowing what they mean? It is unlikely because it is impossible to be in the music business long without seeing pot smoked . . . and the terminology of narcotics is widely known and understood in the industry both by artists, recorders, and producers.

"Some publishers shrug off the drug song by saying, 'These songs are a reflection of our times.' In songs meant for children of 12 or even younger they proclaim that it is wise and hip and inside to dissolve your responsibilities and problems of a difficult world into the mists of marijuana, LSD, or heroin."[20]

These men are wallowing in one of the most sordid, filthy businesses in the history of the world. Everything they produce pollutes the youth of our nation and glorifies a life-style of adultery and fornication. They are, in fact, more guilty than the rock groups and individual performers who create the original product. The company owners, producers, distributors, station owners, and all who are active in distribution are demonstrably individuals of intelligence and capability. They know full well what they are doing and can't escape the basic fact that they are doing it *strictly for money!*

No wonder the Bible tells us (I Timothy 6:10) that the love of money is the root of all evil. In other words, these flesh peddlers are comparable to a pustulant sore, draining out a satanic poison that will corrupt the hearts and lives of untold millions of young people and cause the worst type of life (and death) imaginable.

Record company executives and producers who sit in ivory towers in the major cities of New York, Los Angeles, and Nashville — along with radio station owners and TV cable companies who play that malignant rot — are as morally corrupt as mad scientists deliberately loosing a plague on a nation.

They are, in effect, pimps who pander, solicit, and distribute a basic evil. They are the mortal enemies of American society, the home, the younger generation, the American way of life, and all that is noble, pure, and holy. They know about drugs — the suffering, the pain, and the heartache — but they apparently *just don't care!* They don't care about the millions headed for hell. They make their decisions based on one thought — *keep it rolling!* If they can keep the music playing and the cash registers ringing, nothing else matters. It's just one more example of the modern philosophy of life — "What's in it for *me?*"

Politicians in major cities routinely provide motorcycle escorts to "honor" rock stars performing in their areas. They frequently give a hero's welcome to those who are (almost without exception) so bombed out on drugs that they probably couldn't even name the city they're appearing in. In turn, these "heroes" routinely aid in the destruction and death of untold thousands of young people mesmerized and enchanted by their music. It seems senseless, but the spirit of this present world caters to those who love darkness.

Despite this, my heart breaks for the thousands of performers who have been led into the paths of darkness by Satan, most of them knowing little or nothing about God. While performers are trying to find popularity, the brass ring, riches, and fame, Satan weaves a web around them and uses them to damn the souls of untold millions. Many of them have no idea of what they're doing. In truth, they are little more than pitiful victims who barely comprehend their own actions. They're just grist for Satan's mill.

ROCK-AND-ROLL FATHERS THE DRUG SCENE

My men were unloading our equipment from our vehicles to set up for a night service in a giant coliseum. It happened to be a service dedicated to young people, and I will never forget what transpired.

Equipment was sitting all over the sidewalk (as my men prepared to carry it inside) when a young man approached. I asked him to come to the service, and I could see he was even then high on drugs. He gazed vacantly around at the equipment, thinking it would be a rock-and-roll concert. To him, all that musical equipment could only mean one thing — rock-and-roll.

He turned his gaze to me and horror suddenly registered on his face. He almost shouted. "No, I don't want it. I can't go it anymore. I've taken all I can take. If I go to another one, I'm afraid I'll kill myself."

I'll never forget the despair registering on his face. Satan had just about taken him the last mile, and it was a mile that Satan meant to end in death.

I believe God ordained our meeting that afternoon. I put my hand on his shoulder and said, "This isn't a rock-and-roll show. It will be a Gospel service where Jesus Christ will be glorified." He looked startled for a moment and then bowed his head and asked for prayer. I prayed for him then and there.

How many others have traveled down the same road — a road characterized by a wasted life and culminating in confusion and despair? Alvin Toffler, in *The Third Wave,* says, "Throughout the affluent nations the litany is all too familiar: rising rates of juvenile suicide, dizzying high levels of alcoholism, widespread psychological depression, vandalism, and crime. In the United States, emergency rooms are crowded with 'potheads,' 'speed freaks,' 'Quaalude kids,' 'coke sniffers,' and 'heroin junkies,' not to mention people having 'nervous breakdowns.'"[21]

How many hundreds of thousands (perhaps millions) started on drugs — the second greatest rot of hell — because their "gods" of rock-and-roll set the example? Rock-and-roll has fathered the drug scene as has nothing else in the world.

Serious drug taking has always been part of the rock-and-roll scene. Rock people who take drugs for fun rarely stop at one kind. Most become poly-drug users, taking combinations of drugs to see what the new effect will be. The restraining barriers of illegality and fear are soon overwhelmed by fascination with new highs and new experiences. Users are easily ensnared in the trap of addiction and self-abuse — often ending in death.

As early as the 1920s, many small-time and second-rate musicians claimed marijuana improved their ability to play hot music.

MORE THAN A YOUTHFUL FAD

"The sprawled body of a young girl lay crushed on the sidewalk the other day after a plunge from the fifth story of a Chicago apartment house. Everyone called it suicide, but actually it was murder. The killer was a narcotic known to America as marijuana . . . It is a narcotic used in the form of cigarettes, comparatively new to the United States and as dangerous as a coiled rattlesnake."[22]

That account was recorded 35 years ago. Today the "age of pot" is upon us and the "day of the reefer" has dawned. Though much of the extreme abuse of LSD and the other dangerous hallucinogenics has subsided, marijuana use continues to climb.

Although the Marijuana Tax Act, enacted in 1937, was intended to eliminate the use of marijuana in the United States through harsh criminal sanctions, the number of marijuana users has never fallen below the number that existed at the time marijuana was prohibited.[23] The reason? The drug problem in our nation today is not a problem that can be legislated away; it is a *sin* problem!

Marijuana use now cuts across all social and economic barriers. "At least 65 million Americans — more than 30 percent of the adult population — have tried marijuana.

"By 1982, there were estimated to be more than 30 million *regular* marijuana smokers in the United States . . . . Marijuana arrests increased from 18,000 in 1965 to over 400,000 in 1973. Since 1970, there have been more than five million marijuana-related arrests in the United States."[24]

Though marijuana remains a top-ranking drug among young people, its fashionability has somewhat subsided. Drug experimenters of the 1980s have developed a more expensive taste — cocaine. Touted for the exhilirating, seemingly harmless high it offers, cocaine's popularity has grown quickly in recent years.

In 1976 cocaine — which has a long history of use in the United States — became the drug of focus with an expanding volume of books, articles, court cases, drug busts, and arrests of the famous and infamous attesting to "coke's" popularity. As a result, cocaine's price increased, its quality decreased, and it became a standard item in the "recreational drug culture" of the 1970s.

The net effect of all the endorsements by musical idols and wide-ranging media publicity was to legitimatize the illegitimate. It no longer appeared an illicit drug or an odd habit of the rich. It became the high of the "stars," and the fans stampeded to become a part of it.[25]

THE MONEY BEHIND IT

The picture of our nation's drug problem isn't complete without considering its business aspects. It is *big* business. There's no business like it for being able to promise such incredible profits for such a small investment — and in such a short period of time. A young adventurer can become a multimillionaire overnight. Retail sales from the illicit marijuana market are estimated to be over $25 *billion* a year. But the costs are staggering.

Dr. Edward Brandt, Jr., assistant secretary of Health and Human Services, pegs the total cost of drug abuse in America at around $100 billion. Between $10 and $16 billion is drawn out of the health care system, the law enforcement and judicial systems, the unemployment market, and the welfare and social service systems. "Another 70 to 80 billion dollars in annual costs," reports Dr. Brandt, "result from the association between drugs and crime."[26]

Drug taking is a symptom of disillusionment and dissatisfaction. It reveals a basic search for something of worth in a society that has chosen to wander down the "value-free" path. If the durable American dream has suddenly transformed itself into a nightmare, it won't be restored by turning to stupefying drugs. Use of drugs will at worst *kill* the user, and at best *postpone* the inevitable day of coming to terms with the real world as it actually exists.

Actually, it is very difficult to assess the long-term impact of the drug culture on our nation. The sudden inundation of a society by a completely new mood-altering agent like marijuana isn't something that happens every day. Such an event is a revolutionary occurrence, and only time will reveal the ultimate, long-term consequences.

What we do know is that America's political system can't continue to evolve under a culture based on escapism. Traditionally, great empires have met the challenges imposed on them by the political considerations of their world and day. Hiding behind a marijuana cloud or a cocaine high won't turn back the challenge of Russian imperialism.

The dissolution of our society is apparent, but still there is an "enlightened" element within our nation that calls for the legalization of marijuana. While we tremble at the behavior patterns of our youth that signal moral and mental decay, these "intellectuals" bombard us with insane propaganda. Even some supposedly reputable scientists and "authorities" suggest that marijuana — far from being a *threat* to our youth — may be the *solution* to many of the ills of modern society. Such thinking demands payment of an enormous moral price. Decriminalization is neither a practical nor an acceptable solution to the marijuana problem.

ALCOHOL

Another serious problem is that of alcohol. A leading cause of deaths for adolescents is currently abuse of alcohol and marijuana.

Another study attributes alcohol abuse and violence as the two most rapidly rising causes of death in the U. S.[27] Fifty percent of real-life violence is associated with alcohol consumption.[28]

It is time that we realize the seriousness of the alcohol problem in our nation. It is ironic that the Tylenol scare — in which *seven* people died in *three* days —was given tremendous publicity. The public was warned, federal agencies intervened, and all potentially contaminated products were removed from store shelves. If the killer had been found, he would have been tried for murder.

But what about alcohol? Even though 25,000 people die each year (almost 70 *daily*) from alcohol, the news media gives no national attention to this story. The public isn't warned, federal agencies do not intervene, and the products *identified* as harmful are *not* removed from the shelves. Further, those who produce, sell, advertise, and promote the product (which kills) aren't held accountable for the damage done by their product.

Dr. Ernest Noble, former director of the NIAAA (U. S. National Institute on Alcohol Abuse and Alcoholism) states, "We have a devastating problem with alcohol among our youth in our country. We feel that the problem is at epidemic proportions."[29] Statistics would certainly confirm this. There are an estimated 12 million alcoholics and nearly 25 percent of these are teen-agers.[30] Alcohol is responsible for 80 percent of home violence, 30 percent of all suicides, 60 percent of all child abuse and 65 percent of all drownings.[31] Sixty percent of all divorces are alcohol-related.[32] It is estimated that when a woman is an alcoholic, her husband leaves her in nine out of 10 cases. When a man is an alcoholic, his wife leaves him in *one* out of 10 cases.[33]

The alcohol industry, worth over $30 billion yearly, spends $250 million on *advertising*.[34] America produces 4.35 billion gallons of beer each year, about 21 gallons per person.[35] Seventy-three percent of all Americans keep beer in their refrigerators.[36]

The National Safety Council figures that automobile accidents in 1981 alone cost the U. S. $40.6 billion. Half of these can be attributed to drinking drivers. Consider the statistics:

• Car wrecks caused by alcohol are the most frequently committed violent crimes in America today.[37]

• Drunk drivers claim the lives of 70 Americans every day (about one every 20 minutes, or 26,000 each year) making it our nation's fastest-growing epidemic.[38]

• Every single day 25 young Americans are killed and nearly 125 are disfigured as a result of alcohol-related auto crashes.[39]

• Over the past decade, drunk drivers have killed more than 250,000 Americans — more than five times the number killed in Vietnam during the 10 years of fighting there.[40]

• One out of every two of us will be a victim, passenger, or driver in an alcohol-related car crash during his lifetime.[41]

• Drunk drivers cause more deaths, injuries, and destruction than smugglers, robbers, rapists, thieves, and murderers.[42]

IS THERE AN ANSWER?

Drug and alcohol abuse can seem like an abstract social problem until it involves someone you care about — like a son or daughter. Dr. Edward Bloomquist states, "One of the biggest problems where marijuana is concerned is that adults and youths have a remarkably different set of values. A young person needs a reason not to smoke pot, other than to be told, 'Because I said so.'"[43] Drug prevention starts in the cradle. Young people don't avoid harmful substances because they've been warned about them; they avoid them because of the *example* they grew up with.

Drug abuse can be prevented, but it means that the very core of society must change. Perhaps one problem is that life is too *easy* for our youth today. If they were worried about where their next meal was coming from, they wouldn't have so much time to sit around talking about how *bored* they are.

Once a young person has begun drinking or using drugs, recovery means more than just stopping. It means a whole new life-style, which means facing life — rather than running away from it.

Reginald F. Mattison says, "The most successful cure for drug dependence . . . is a miracle of God through conversion. It involves a number of factors:

• A desire and a decision on the part of the individual to accept Jesus as his personal Saviour and to obey His instructions as revealed in the Bible.

• Daily renewal of his relationship with God through prayer, which means asking God for help to accomplish His will in his life for that day.

• Helping others with needs by sharing how God has helped solve his problems.

• Daily study of God's Word for constant growth in knowledge and inspiration for continuing the experience.

• Association with others who have similar aims and experiences for group strength."[44]

I would agree that there is no more successful program for drug dependence than this. But I might add, "An ounce of prevention is worth a pound of cure." Parents who listen to their children, make reasonable demands, respect their individuality, show their love, encourage constructive activities, provide their children with a sense of roots, and explore their life goals with them provide the most realistic *preventive* measures by promoting *responsible living*.

But for scores of young people, it is too late for prevention: many of the "cursed children" cry out from the agony of the damned. Yet there are a great many others who remain on earth, wandering our streets like the living dead. It is not too late to save these.

We have a responsibility to reach out to this generation's *cursed children*. Many have become entirely too complacent about the drug epidemic in America, but I feel certain they would be far less complacent if they could grasp the true extent of Satan's damage.

At this moment the cursed children may scream for more drugs, but the time will come when they will scream for relief from a devil's hell where the fires of pain and torment are unquenchable. No drug will soothe them then. As children of darkness, they will suffer eternal damnation.

Harry Anslinger, America's first great anti-marijuana crusader, fought against the destroyer of youth without fear or retreat. We, as crusaders for Christ, must also relentlessly crusade against the forces murdering our youth as we "snatch them as brands from the burning" (compare Zechariah 3:2).

Perhaps most ironic of all is the fact that our youth — considering how they rebel against all the traditions and values established over the years — aren't going to hurt the *older* generation with the "new society" they seek to impose. They are the ones who will have to live out their lives in the bleak, ungodly world of "I deserve."

AMERICA: ON THE EVE OF DESTRUCTION

"My people are destroyed for lack of knowledge: because thou hast rejected knowledge, I will also reject thee, that thou shalt be no priest to me: seeing thou hast forgotten the law of thy God, I will also forget thy children" (Hosea 4:6).

America. How much time does she have left? The prognosis appears grim. It seems that a whole generation has lost contact with reality. Mankind wanders forlornly about, looking to human institutions for answers to celestial questions. All the time though, they are being propagandized, deceived, and taught to trust illusion as if it were reality. This futile search for utopia, mixed with the advance of communistic thinking, has brought this mighty nation to the eve of destruction.

By and large, the American people have been lulled, pacified, and transported to a fantasy world. Communism, socialism, and humanism have been made to appear as "acceptable alternatives." The fuse is burning down on the powder kegs in our storerooms, but alien philosophies and ideologies have rendered us all but helpless to stand against the forces of darkness that are *already* enveloping us.

You and I are the keys to America's survival! Together we can drive back the enemy. But first, we must *recognize* the forces arrayed against us. Throughout previous chapters I have attempted to expose Satan and his tactics. Now, I must point out Satan's human disciples, those who are doing the actual nuts-and-bolts *assembling* of the forces and influences that will eventually *bring us down!*

Much of what I will say deserves more detail than space will permit, but I will try to show how man's *philosophy* dictates his *practice*. Doing this will, I believe, alert Christians to the imminent danger facing them — a subtle, pervasive influence that could subvert the very foundation of their beliefs.

FREEDOM OF RELIGION

Until now, we have been free to worship God after the dictates of our hearts. Unfortunately, we are even now in the process of *losing* this freedom. It won't happen overnight, but it will happen *of a certainty*.

If there is one point I would like to make, it is this: freedom costs! As Americans we are abundantly blessed. We live in a free country. But we must never forget that this freedom has been bought at a great price. Countless men have fought and died for *our* freedom. You see, freedom is not man's "natural state." Every man is born in bondage to his own needs and desires. Given the opportunity, man will demand *his* absolute freedom — but all too often at the expense of freedom for others.

For that reason, history records few free societies. Even today, most people labor under one form of tyranny or another. Many perils threaten our liberty. Unless we realize that freedom has always been won and kept by effort and sacrifice, our complacency will result in the ultimate erosion of our great, free society.

THE LAW OF THE JUNGLE

We can't allow the "natural" laws of the jungle — prevalent in contemporary society and promoted by current philosophies — to dictate standards of conduct for individuals or for society as a whole. Although fundamental beliefs in equality, liberty, and justice are to guide our relationships with each other, it takes uncommon individual maturity to sustain a democratic way of life.

Basically, democracy depends on much more than a collection of political principles. It must have, as its base, respect for the dignity of man. When such respect is recognized and practiced, such desirable traits as courtesy, kindness, honesty, and generosity become an all-pervading standard that promotes and supports the rights of every man. When immaturity and an attitude of "me first" replaces this enlightened attitude, the stage is set for *destruction*.

America is on the brink of destruction because many have shrugged off the basic Christian values espoused by our Founding Fathers. Although many mouth allegiance to God, they embrace concepts, value systems, and ideologies which render them vulnerable to influences intent on their destruction. And the *source* of just about all of these influences is atheistic communism.

COMMUNISM VS. THE FREE WORLD

Abraham Lincoln's observation that a nation can't exist "half slave and half free" applies equally well today. The communists warn us, as they always have, that they will coexist only at the price of our eventual surrender. They have a definite and widely declared plan to defeat us. Therefore, unless we understand how communists think, act, and organize, we will surely live to see them victorious.

The struggle between democracy and communism is, without question, the key issue facing mankind today. Still, Americans fail to grasp the seriousness of the conflict. If we are to avoid abject slavery, it is crucially important that we be awakened and alerted.

We *must* alert those who care about America's future. Amid the din and clamor of those who cry for peace at any price, we must make the voice of reason heard. When political leaders proclaim that they are willing to sacrifice "anything" for peace, what they are actually saying is that they are willing to sacrifice our *freedom*. I would ask you, since when do nations under bondage live in peace?

Communism is the absolute and ultimate expression of bondage. The final (and, I might add, tragic) aim of communism is to create mechanical puppets trained to do exactly what the communist party desires. Once you allow the camel's head of socialism into the tent, then, the ultimate condition will prove to be slavery.

In 1958 J. Edgar Hoover, in *Masters of Deceit*, gave a preview of what a nation can expect under communism:

> *"The press would be muzzled, free speech forbidden, and complete conformity demanded. If you expressed an opinion contrary to the party line, you should have known better and your 'disappearance' would serve as a lesson for others. Fear becomes an enforcement technique. Movies, radio, and television would be taken over by the government as agencies for government propaganda. Churches would probably not be closed immediately, but they would be heavily taxed, their property seized by the state, and religious schools liquidated. Clergymen would be required to accept the party line.*
>
> *"'God does not exist. Why worship Him?' say the communists. Children would be placed in nurseries and special indoctrination schools. Women, boast the communists, would be relieved of housework. How? Huge factory and apartment-house kitchens would be set up, so that women would be 'free' to work in factories and mines along with the men."* [1]

Does that sound like the type of society in which *you* want to live?

While faint hearts cry for peace and disarmament, the communists concern themselves with victory. They see only black and white in the conflict between communism and democracy. Only one side can win, and only one side can emerge dominant in the philosophical battle for men's minds.

THE COMMUNIST PERSPECTIVE

In 1927 Stalin sketched his perception of the future. "Two centers of world-wide scope will take shape: the socialist (i.e. communist) center, drawing to itself the countries which gravitate toward socialism — and the capitalistic center, drawing to itself the countries which gravitate toward capitalism. The struggle of these two camps will decide the fate of capitalism and socialism all over the world." [2]

In 1930 communist Dimitry Z. Manuilsky bellowed to a group of students at Moscow's Lenin School of Political Warfare:

"War to the hilt between communism and capitalism is inevitable. Today, of course, we (the communists) are not strong enough to attack. Our time will come in 20 or 30 years. To win, we shall need the element of surprise. The bourgeoisie (economic middle and upper classes) will have to be put to sleep. So we shall begin by launching the most spectacular peace movement on record. There will be electrifying overtures and unheard-of concessions. The Capitalist countries, stupid and decadent, will rejoice to cooperate in their own destruction. They will leap at another chance to be friends. As soon as their guard is down, we will smash them with our clenched fist."[3]

In 1955 Nikita Kruschchev declared, "We must realize that we [the communist world and the West] cannot coexist eternally, or for a long time. One of us must go to the grave. We do not want to go to the grave. They do not want to go to the grave either. So what can be done? We must *push* them to their grave."[4]

Then, in 1957, before a nationwide American television audience he stated with calm assurance, "I can prophesy that your grandchildren in America will live under socialism (communism). And please do not be afraid of that. Your grandchildren will . . . not understand how their grandparents did not understand the progressive nature of a socialist society."[5]

COMMUNISM DEFINED

The term "communism" comes from the Latin word which means "in common." It was first used over a century ago to signify a political creed. Its proponents felt that by man having things "in common," social ills such as poverty, low wages, misery, and so forth could be cured. Today, communism is more than a political creed; it's a philosophy, an economic system, a matter of psychological conditioning, an educational indoctrination, and a total way of life.

The first revolutionary communists were Karl Marx and Friedrich Engels. They drew up a 50-page pamphlet, *The Communist Manifesto,* published in England in 1848. It explained their scheme to overthrow the existing order and to create a communist state. Under their plan, a new Soviet man — one completely responsive and subservient to the masters of the universal state — would emerge.

Part of America's downfall is either ignorance of the plan or a refusal to take it seriously. Communists always use obscure language to confuse their opponents and to impress and attract followers. In actuality, though, communism rests on a few simple and easily understood propositions, each of which is falsely based and can lead only to error and destruction. They are:

• *Atheism* — They deny the existence of a Supreme Being and His divine design, purpose, and law. To them nature is the only force; because of the ceaseless motion among the forces of nature, matter came into being. Communism, deprived of all its flowery distractions, is militant atheism.

• *Dialectical materialism* — They see no basic difference between man and the brute beast. In fact, human beings are considered to be only an advanced state in the evolutionary process. Their completely reckless disregard for human life stands out as the primary characteristic of their doctrine. Taking their philosophy a step farther, they say that nothing exists except matter. If something can't be weighed and measured, it simply doesn't exist.

• *Naturalism* — They deny life after death. They deny the existence of an eternal moral law. They see all actions as related to the spread of communism. Whatever furthers the cause is good. Whatever hinders it is evil. They say man must be ready to lie, steal, torture, and murder if necessary. Since they believe there is no life but this one, they are concerned only with the present. Future rewards and punishments do not exist for them, therefore nothing is innately right or wrong.

• *Class struggle* — All history is considered to be merely a record of class wars. In other words, the competition and conflict between the various socioeconomic classes serve always to advance civilizations. Because of this, they feel that religion should be overthrown. Religion inhibits the desire for revolution. The first proponents of communism recognized that deep spiritual convictions hinder people from accepting the communist philosophy and rule. This fact should be particularly noted. We'll discuss it more fully later.

After reading the four major premises of communism, some will say, "So what? How does this affect *me*?" Cleon W. Skousen, in *The Naked Communist,* states, "Such attitudes have practically been our undoing. These beliefs can *hurt* us."[6]

And hurt us they undoubtedly have. Listed below are 45 communist goals as they appeared in the Congressional Record of January 10, 1963.[7] They serve as a checklist for evaluating the *progress* of the communist conspiracy in our nation. As you read them, notice how many have *already* been accomplished in the last 20 years — while we, like ostriches with our heads in the sand, refused to believe it could happen here. Well, believe it or not, it is happening here and now. It is almost too late, but there is still time if America will only *wake up!*

CURRENT COMMUNIST GOALS

• U. S. acceptance of coexistence as the only alternative to nuclear war.

• U. S. willingness to capitulate rather than engage in atomic war.

• Development of the illusion that total disarmament by the United States would be a demonstration of *moral strength*.

• Encouragement of free trade between all nations — regardless of communist affiliation.

• Extension of long-term loans to Russia and Soviet satellites.

• Provision of American aid to all nations — regardless of communist affiliation.

• Recognition of Red China and admission of Red China to the United Nations.

• The setting up of East and West Germany as separate states, *despite* Krushchev's promise in 1955 to settle the German question by free elections under the supervision of the United Nations.

• Prolongation of the conference to ban atomic tests, because the United States has agreed to suspend tests *as long as negotiations are in progress*.

• The permitting of individual representation in the U. N. for all Soviet satellites.

• Promotion of the U. N. as the only hope for mankind. If its charter is rewritten, demand that it be set up as a one-world government with its own independent armed forces.

• Resistance to any attempt to outlaw the communist party.

- The elimination of all loyalty oaths.

- Continued Russian access to the U. S. Patent Office.

- Capture of one or both of the political parties of the United States.

- The use of court decisions to weaken basic American institutions by claiming their activities "violate civil rights."

- Control of the schools. Use them as transmission belts for socialism and communist propaganda. Soften the curriculum. Get control of teachers' associations. Insert the party line in textbooks.

- Gain control of all student newspapers.

- Use student riots to foment public protests against programs or organizations which are under communist attack.

- Infiltrate the press. Gain control of book review assignments, editorial writing, policy-making positions.

- Gain control of key positions in radio, TV, and motion pictures.

- Continue discrediting American culture by degrading all forms of artistic expression. An American communist cell was told to "eliminate all good sculpture from parks and buildings, substituting shapeless, awkward, and meaningless forms."

- Control art critics and directors of art museums. "Our plan is to promote ugly, repulsive, and meaningless art."

- Eliminate all laws governing obscenity by calling them censorship and a violation of free speech and free press.

- Break down cultural standards of morality by promoting pornography and obscenity in books, magazines, motion pictures, radio, and TV.

- Present homosexuality, degeneracy, and promiscuity as "normal, natural, and healthy."

- Infiltrate the churches and replace revealed religion with "social religion." Discredit the Bible and emphasize the need for intellectual maturity which does not need a "religious crutch."

- Eliminate prayer or any phase of religious expression in the schools on the ground that it violates the principle of "separation of church and state."

• Discredit the American Constitution by calling it inadequate, old-fashioned, out-of-step with modern needs, and a hindrance to cooperation between nations on a worldwide basis.

• Discredit the American Founding Fathers. Present them as selfish aristocrats who had no concern for "the common man."

• Belittle all forms of American culture and discourage the teaching of American history on the basis of its being only a minor part of the "big picture." Give more emphasis to "modern" Russian history (since the communists took over).

• Support any socialist movement that promotes centralized control over any part of the culture: education, social agencies, welfare programs, mental health clinics, and so forth.

• Eliminate all laws or procedures which interfere with the operation of the communist apparatus.

• Eliminate the House Committee on Un-American Activities.

• Discredit and eventually dismantle the FBI.

• Infiltrate and gain control of more unions.

• Infiltrate and gain control of big business.

• Transfer some of the powers of arrest from the police to social agencies. Treat all behavioral problems as psychiatric disorders which no one but psychiatrists can understand or treat.

• Dominate the psychiatric profession and use mental health laws as a means of gaining coercive control over those who oppose communist goals.

• Discredit the family as an institution. Encourage promiscuity and easy divorce.

• Emphasize the need to rear children away from the "negative" influences of parents. Attribute prejudices, mental blocks, and retardation of children to suppressive parental influence.

• Create the impression that violence and insurrection are legitimate elements in the American tradition, that students and special-interest groups should use force to solve economic, political, and social problems.

• Overthrow all colonial governments before native populations are ready for self-government.

- Internationalize the Panama Canal.

- Repeal the Connally Reservation so the United States can't prevent the World Court from seizing jurisdiction over nations and individuals alike.

It's certainly alarming to observe that the communist conspiracy never rests from its labors. With its imposed emotional fervor, communism's adherents cling to its totalitarian doctrines much as believers cling to their religious faith. To entertain any beliefs but their own is unthinkable.

Therefore, under a totalitarian regime, allegiance to the basic doctrine is *demanded* of every citizen. This doctrine — a definite, official, and exclusive one — imposes conformity through every facet of public communication. However, conformity is not just a negative element depending on censorship and control. The totalitarian regime doesn't confine itself to *opposing* ideas it doesn't like, but actively *imposes* the positive content of everything it *wants* the nation to think.

At the very core of this doctrine is the conviction that the state or the government is better qualified to plan and direct the lives of individuals than they are themselves. And acceptance of this concept demands further acceptance of the premise that surrendering your liberties to the government for their control will lead to security, happiness, and prosperity.

Communism directly opposes every concept of democratic life, democracy emphasizing the importance of the individual and the need for him to develop in an environment of freedom. Totalitarianism recognizes only the absolute power of the state.

CATCHING THEM WHILE THEY'RE YOUNG

Soviet children begin a persistent indoctrination program at an early age. They are taught that their first duty is to the Soviet state — not to God or parents. They must reject God and *be willing to betray parents* — for the good of the state.

Americans simply cannot comprehend a universe in which there is no room for reasoning, compassion, kindness, or tolerance. Americans, who are used to compromise, reason, and ethical behavior, can't conceive of a system under which men are pawns and puppets to be ruthlessly used in creating a socialist world — usually by violent revolutionary means. And it should be noted here that the basic difference between socialism and

communism lies only in the *method of takeover.* Communism employs
violence while socialism doesn't. Some people tend to forget that the
U. S. S. R. stands for the Union of Soviet Socialist Republics.

Communism is a reality which must be faced and dealt with. Not
only does communism see no limits to its goals, it recognizes no limits to
the *means* it employs to impose them. Convinced that the end justifies
the means, communists view propaganda, imprisonment, terror, slave
labor, brainwashing — and even the total destruction of entire nations —
as legitimate means to achieve their purposes. It is a morally bankrupt
system that is "planted in human blood, nourished by human blood, and
forever dripping with human blood."[8]

THE MINDS BEHIND THE SCHEME

Of course, Satan is the primary force behind communism, but he
chooses as key leaders those who have consciously rejected all conventional
ethics to accept the brutal premise that "the end justifies the means."
Despite all their rhetoric about the "masses," each has demonstrated an
unbridled lust for power. Marx, Stalin, Lenin — each saw annihilation as the
perfect solution for those who might oppose them. That particular trait
seems "inseparable from the character of the modern totalitarian dictator."[9]

The first major architect of communism was Karl Marx. Marx was
born of Jewish parents; his father was a Jewish lawyer — decended from
a long line of rabbis — and his mother was a devout woman. Marx grew
up in a religious home environment, but the general political and
religious environment was said to be in a state of crisis, much like today.

Many explanations have been offered by historians as reasons for
Marx's radicalism. Some have mentioned his anger against the raw, ruthless
industrialism of his day. Others have mentioned personal experiences in his
life which embittered him and left him with a sense of failure. Among the
explanations, one stands out from all the rest: "It was his proud rejection of
the only Being whose Love could have quieted his restless spirit and brought
him peace. Marx let the reservoir of hate be filled to the brim and then
flood his heart until there was no room in it for the love of mankind."[10]

Friedrich Engels, the second major planner of communism, was
Marx's intimate friend who worked with him for some 40 years. He, too,
turned away from his belief in a Supreme Being to become an atheist,
thus intensely grieving his conservative and religious-minded father.

Lenin made a definite display of his complete break with God at the age of 17 by tearing from his neck the cross he was wearing, flinging it to the ground, and spitting on it. We can only guess what brought him to that decision, but it was perhaps "the first outward expression of a hatred of God which later on would obsess him so violently that the mere mention of God's name would cause him to fall into a spasm of uncontrollable fury."[11]

Next came Joseph Stalin, whose father died when he was 11, leaving his Christian mother with the responsibility of caring for him. Her meager earnings from menial tasks contributed to the bitterness of young Joseph, a somewhat sickly child, pockmarked, with a webfoot, and a partially crippled arm.

Bitterness and hatred were the driving forces that propelled him to a unique position: the most feared and hated man of the twentieth century — loving no one and apparently loved by none. It was Stalin who shepherded Marxism to world power. Before long "the Soviet Union soon found that it had slipped from the iron grip of the Red Dictator (Lenin) into the steel fist of the man whose last warm feelings for the human race had, according to his own testimony, faded with the death of his first wife some twenty years earlier."[12]

Such were the men who made Russia into a world power. The essential characteristics of the men — utter brutality, bitterness, and ruthlessness — are still with us today.

What happened to these men? Pascal says that when men reject God, they choose between two courses in life. Either they set themselves up as gods and try to behave as such, or they seek to find happiness and satisfaction by catering to their appetites for pleasure.[13] Once man denounces God, His Holy Word, morality, eternal judgment, the reality of the immortal spirit of man, and the sanctity of individual human life, he begins to worship himself.

WHERE DO WE STAND?

Despite communism's man-centered orientation and destructive methods, there *is* something we could learn from them. Communism stands *for* something! It is evil beyond imagination, undertaking to replace Christian morality with a complete *absence* of morals. But the fact remains that it steadfastly and unremittingly *pushes forward to achieve its goals!*

Of course, they can't make the world over in their own image *unless* accepted ethics and morals become obsolete. The moral vacuum, created in America when God was "pronounced dead" by modern man, provided Marxists with their most effective weapon. Because man is a physical-spiritual being, he can't tolerate an emptiness in his soul — a vacuum created by rejecting God. He must find a substitute to *fill* this soul-vacuum.

America is the fourth-largest nation in the world, both in population and in area. But of the 332 million Americans, only one-half claim any religious profession. And even though one-half claim to belong to a church of some kind, only one out of four attends church with any degree of regularity! An uncommitted, spiritually weak people can't hope to stand against the forces of darkness that are committed to destroying our nation.

Remember, the American ideal of liberty is rooted in God. The American republic was established to protect man's God-given dignity and freedom. "Separated from God, it can no more survive than heat separated from fire."[14]

PHILOSOPHY DICTATES PRACTICE

Harry Conn, in *The Four Trojan Horses of Humanism,* states, "The greatest problem we have in the United States is not ignorance; it is believing things and concepts that are not true."[15] He cites sociology, psychology, politics, and theology as the four Trojan horses responsible for bringing certain untruths into popular belief. Each of these Trojan horses is based on a certain philosophy of man and the universe. That philosophy dictates how man defines his existence, origins, and purpose.

Any philosophy which pervades a society will determine the spirit of that society and its institutions. To truly understand the erosion of a society and its future, it is necessary to look beyond institutions and culture to the underlying doctrines directing the *thoughts* of that society.

The communists, aware of this principle, attack the foundations of our nation through ideological warfare. To achieve their mission, they denounce every other ideology. Therefore, to destroy America, they must attack her faith in God. Russian Commissar of Education, Anatole Lunarcharsky, declared, "We hate Christians and Christianity. Even the best of them must be considered our worst enemies. Christian love is an obstacle to the development of the revolution. Down with love of one's neighbor! What we want is hate . . . Only then will we conquer the universe!"[16]

Lenin confirms their philosophy: "We must hate — hatred is the basis of communism. Children must be taught to hate their parents if they are not communists."[17]

Another disciple declared, "God will be banished from the laboratories as well as from the schools."[18] With a certainty, they did begin to make inroads into the schools and laboratories in the 1930s, known as the Red decade in America. The schools became platforms from which to infiltrate the rest of the nations.

Agnes Murphy, in *An Evil Tree,* points out, "The most fertile soil in which to hide Red seed is in the mind of the teacher and in his textbook." She says that in 1935 American communists received explicit directives from the Kremlin concerning the ideological warfare that was to be waged in the schools: "Red instructors were told to create a Marxist-Leninist atmosphere in the classroom. They were ordered to write textbooks and to rewrite history from the Marxian viewpoint." They were to conceal their true political orientation. "They were to become masters of deception." No level of education, from the kindergarten to the university, was to be neglected in the plot to make America a Red Socialist state.[19]

The communist strategists, recognizing that everyone will not be convinced of the perfection of their system, see the mind of a student as the major battleground. Students can be either trained to *propagate* the communist doctrine or prepared to *swallow* it if they realize they've been made a victim of subversive activities.

Our youth are our future society. For the communists to conquer America, they must involve themselves widely in converting "intellectuals" to their way of thinking. Of course, some will remain unconvinced; but if they don't have the weapons to *protect* America, they will eventually be subdued. Murphy says, "The enemy has been making use of progressive education to reduce America to a country of illiterates, unable to read, write, think, or refute. The task of conquering an illiterate, uneducated people is much easier than conquering a well-educated and cultured people."[20]

Abraham Lincoln once said, "If this country is ever destroyed, it will not be from without but from within." By winning the child of today in the schools, the communists capture tomorrow's leaders. Nevertheless, the schools are only one area in which they work to prepare America for their doctrine. They infiltrate all organs of public opinion: the media (radio, movies, television, newspapers, and magazines), important governmental organizations, labor unions, military establishments — even churches.

By internal subversion, they intend to silence opposition and to destroy America. By ridicule and irony, they attempt to destroy all patriotism — the glue that holds a nation together. By establishing "fronts" — organizations, committees, groups of people, or printed publications — they steadily chip away at America's strength while simultaneously planting seeds of destruction.

In essence, a new group can't win the support of a society without systematically preaching its theories, doctrines, opinions, notions, and beliefs. Of course, seeds of discontent can always be found somewhere in every society. The trick is to draw them out and intensify them.

One of the favorite tactics of this clever and unscrupulous force is exposing the *wounds* of society, then working to intensify these areas of pain. They know what the people want and are quick to promise them things, all the time assuring the victims that the only lasting solution lies in the socialist society they promote.

Americans have been fooled for too long. We think revolution involves bloodshed in one cataclysmic explosion. In reality, through careful strategy, a revolution begins long before its true impact becomes apparent. Lenin saw revolution as a *prolonged* conflict. To him, even the interim between capitalism and communism was part of that revolution. However, even though control is won through espionage and subversion and by ferreting into key positions, violence becomes necessary to *maintain control*.

Actually, Lenin was the one who instituted infiltration as a standard communist tactic. Conn stated that "all religious, political, psychological, and sociological systems are based on philosophical presuppositions, theoretical bases or assumptions."[21] If these theories are false, all conclusions developed from them are false and will cause frustration, confusion, and eventually the collapse of the society that tries to live with them. Lenin and others like him recognized the value of this theory and seized every opportunity to invade the institutions which provide strength and stability to the American way of life.

Listen to the exhortation by Georgi Dimitroff, General Secretary, before the Seventh World Congress of the Communist International: "Comrades, you remember the ancient tales of the capture of Troy. Troy was inaccessible to the armies attacking her, thanks to her impregnable walls. And the attacking army, after suffering many sacrifices, was unable to achieve victory until with the aid of the famous Trojan horse it managed to penetrate to the very heart of the enemy's camp."[22]

Communists today are not shy about using similar tactics. Hoover says, "The Trojan horse has enabled the party to wield an influence far in excess of its actual numbers."[23]

TROJAN HORSES

Malcolm Muggeridge writes, in *The End of Christendom*: "The whole social structure is now tumbling down, dethroning its God, undermining all its certainties. All this, wonderfully enough, is being done in the name of the health, wealth, and happiness of all mankind."[24] The philosophy he was discussing? We know it today as secular humanism.

The happiness of man *now*, not some vague promise of life after death, is always the promise of humanism. In other words, momentary happiness is viewed as an end in itself. Whatever is necessary to achieve that happiness is of *value* to the individual. Sound familiar? It's just another version of "the end justifies the means."

Throughout preceding chapters we've mentioned secular humanism time and again. We have done so because it's at the very heart of the philosophy by which the majority of Americans are now living — whether they realize it or not. It has been insinuated into the mainstream of our culture and influences vital decision-making. Most individuals wouldn't *call* themselves humanists, only because they've never made the effort to understand what school of philosophy they actually follow. So, like puppets, they pay homage to a doctrine which, based on false assumptions, can only produce frustration and confusion — and ultimately the eternal damnation of their souls.

It is only natural that human beings desire to find "meaning" for their lives, to relate their personalities to some grand view of existence. They want predictable and established patterns to provide acceptable solutions to their problems. But of more importance, and of greater consequence, is developing a life philosophy that is based on a *correct* view of the universe.

Although some may contend that *any* philosophy brings clarity and meaning to individuals, nations, and civilizations, it is pure folly for man to attempt to define reality apart from God — *the only eternal reality*. But that is exactly what humanism does.

The philosophy of humanism — the Trojan horse of our enemies — is destroying America. It is slowly but surely stripping us of our

American heritage. Unfortunately, the American public has, by and large, bought a bill of goods that aims to destroy them — despite its claim of being "the ethical ideal of concern for all men." When humanists speak of democratic faith in the "worth of the individual" or "the welfare of all humanity," it *sounds* promising. But if we delve into the philosophy *behind* these statements, we find nothing more there than the same old tissue of lies espoused by Marxist communists.

Of course, humanists say today that they do not advocate socialism — or any other particular economic system, for that matter.

And now, let's read an excerpt from the *Humanist Manifesto II:*

> *"The next century can be and should be the humanistic century. Dramatic scientific, technological and ever-accelerating social and political changes crowd our awareness. We have virtually conquered the planet, explored the moon, overcome the natural limits of travel and communication; we stand at the dawn of a new age, ready to move farther into space and perhaps inhabit other planets. Using technology wisely, we can control our environment, conquer poverty, markedly reduce disease, extend our lifespan, significantly modify our behavior, alter the course of human evolution and cultural development, unlock vast new powers, and provide humankind with unparalleled opportunity for achieving an abundant and meaningful life."*[25]

THE REAL AUTHOR OF HUMANISM

How does the preceding quoted excerpt from the *Humanist Manifesto* compare with Satan's bold declaration found in Isaiah 14:13-14?

> *"I will exalt my throne above the stars of God; I will sit also upon the mount of the congregation, in the sides of the north: I will ascend above the heights of the clouds; I will be like the Most High."*

And for those who might be feeling discouraged after all we've brought forth thus far, we shouldn't miss God's answer to this attitude, as expressed in the next verse:

"Yet thou shalt be brought down to hell, to the sides of the pit."

It is plain to see that the same proud, arrogant spirit runs through both declarations. That's because Satan *still* pursues his clearly stated goal: to gain universal supremacy. He hasn't deviated for a moment from his original intentions. Although his vicious struggle — or, more appropriately, his war — against God continues to be a hopeless one, he persists in attacking those who love God and in luring those who don't to damnation.

Satan is incorrigible. He will never abandon his pride or cease his efforts to dethrone God. And he, the archenemy of God, will use anyone who rejects God to carry on his diabolical schemes.

Behind the communists, the socialists, the fascists, and the humanists — behind the followers of all humanist religions and doctrines, for that matter — stands Satan. Adherence to any one of these false doctrines is as damnable as idolatrous worship. When men don't worship the one true God, they *will worship something*. And some have chosen to worship self — the creature rather than the Creator — but they are monstrously deceived. In actuality, they worship Satan. They devote themselves to him — such devotion being the basic aim and desire of his heart.

Although Satan is the biggest fool who ever lived, he is not without cunning. He knows what he's doing every second. He possesses great intelligence shaded with diabolical craftiness. When man, created in God's image, follows God's plan for his life, Satan is no match for him. But when man rejects God, he becomes a pawn in Satan's clawlike hand.

The ultimate result of Satan's obsession with power and divinity has been demonstrated time and time again in the lives of those who fall prey to self-idolization. We see this spirit in the deeds of Napoleon, Peter the Great, Stalin, and Hitler. We hear him speaking through atheists, the humanists, modern ministers, and the communists.

Today, as his last-day program tries to counterfeit that of God, we find him lurking in the shadows behind psychologists, social workers, sociologists, social action leaders, philosophers, politicians, educators, and religious leaders — all those to whom society looks for guidance. Without God, men wander about in a malaise, vulnerable to every "wind of doctrine" that promises to bring "peace and happiness."

But do these institutions have any valid answers to give? Or are they Trojan horses designed for our destruction? They *could* have answers *if* their theories were founded on God's truth. Unfortunately, that is rarely the case.

For example, government in America was established by our founding fathers to *serve the people*. Government is not inherently evil. It is government's philosophical *base* that determines its orientation toward good or toward evil. Because we have strayed away from Godly ideals and purposes, our politics has become *perverted* and has now ended up serving as another Trojan horse.

OUR PERVERTED SOCIAL INSTITUTIONS

And what about the other social elements mentioned, such as psychology and sociology?

Several years ago, a U. S. Supreme Court Justice said, "When a man kills his wife and four children, we should not blame him for what he has done but look into what caused him to do it."[26]

If you understand the many false assumptions behind this unbelievably asinine statement, you can begin to understand how the enemy uses sociology and psychology as Trojan horses to pervert and manipulate the attitudes of our citizens.

Sociologists view man as a product of his environment. Therefore (they say), man can't be unfairly expected to assume full responsibility for his behavior. While there's no question that environment does *influence* behavior, it still isn't an immutable *cause*. If we follow the thinking of sociologists, we must change the environment to produce any improvement in man's character. Man's responsibility thus disappears, and he is responsible for nothing he does.

Contrary to current sociological and psychological thinking, man can't find happiness just because he *wants* to find happiness. True happiness comes only when we seek to serve others for Christ, rather than thinking primarily of ourselves.

The world must realize that most social problems result from faulty personal choices. Unfortunately, the personal *ethical* position of the individual determines how he will view himself. In today's philosophy of "worry only about yourself," few will find real happiness.

Conn states, "We can accurately state that what is caused cannot be free . . . . It can also be said that what is free cannot be caused."[27] God created man with a free will. It is *man* who chooses the influences he will accept and those he will reject. Although consistent decisions become habits (and even with time, ingrained characteristics), God still holds man responsible for his decisions. He is free to choose, therefore he remains accountable for his choices.

If environment were the *cause* of behavior, man would have no freedom of choice and would bear no burden of responsibility. Essentially, he'd become a permanent "victim of circumstances." But what does God say? Scripture emphatically *denies* that man is a robot controlled by the principles of cause and effect.

Psychology, perhaps even more than sociology, provides a camouflage of acceptability from which the enemy can work to infiltrate the minds and spirits of individuals and the nation. Insidiously promoted as an "exact science," opinions and theories are foisted on the public as facts. And what is behind this reverence for the "scientific method"? The realization that it can be used to make almost *anything* seem logical and rational, and to mask imposed *ideas* with the appearance of scientific proof.

J. P. van Praag, in *Foundations of Humanism,* admits: "The fact that all psychology is based on man as a natural being, which means that he is produced by nature and is culturally oriented toward that nature, makes psychology a humanist-oriented science."[28]

Some psychologists would argue that they've moved away from psychology's scientific orientation to an essentially human-oriented approach. They've stretched the boundaries of psychology to include growth, creativity, values, peak experiences, self-acceptance, and transcendence. They stress the positive rather than the negative, the healthy component rather than mental or emotional weaknesses. Progress? It may *appear* to be so until we recognize that this outgrowth of psychology — humanistic psychology — operates on the philosophical assumption that "the total *humanity* of man . . . must be the basis of psychological thought."[29]

Don't for a moment think the enemy doesn't know exactly what he's doing. Humanistic psychology carries the potential to influence people and affect their lives in ways that the basic, statistic-oriented study of psychology never could. And Christians — laymen, ministers, and counselors alike — are swallowing the enemy's bait hook, line, and sinker!

Some well-intentioned Christian counselors would have us believe that "mental or emotional problems" should be viewed as nothing but a disease process just as we would view a cold, a case of the flu, or mumps. However, only five percent of the people in mental institutions are there because of *physical* factors influencing their minds.[30] The vast majority are there because of "problems in living" — often willful *refusal* to make the accommodations that allow living in harmony with society. It's about time we accept some cold, hard facts. People have problems because they've rejected the Life-giver, neglecting to learn (or to follow) His principles for abundant life. They inevitably end up mentally, emotionally, physically, and spiritually impaired.

The philosophies of men serve no more purpose in dealing with man's real need than would a Band-Aid on a pustulent sore. Man must be purged of sin and selfishness before he can find peace, health, and happiness. That isn't to say there's no place for Christian counselors. But it does imply the importance of a thorough understanding that a spiritual foundation is essential for the counseling. All too often, Christian counselors make unsuccessful attempts to reconcile man-made philosophies (learned in their psychology courses) with the *true* guidance found in God's Word. They thus end up with an unworkable hodgepodge of God's promises mixed with the self-actualization of Goldstein, Maslow's hierarchy of needs, and Roger's self-concept. These *aren't* compatible.

If the church would get back to the Bible (and to calling sin what it *is*), fewer people would be running to psychologists and sociologists to seek help in "coping" with their rebellion and disobedience. It's appalling that the church has integrated the doctrines of men into its structure, to the point where we spout the teachings of humanistic psychology while attaching scriptural references to them.

Clearly, we must become aware of the tactics of Satan and remain alert to the seeds of destruction he thus plants in the framework of our beliefs. Our philosophies *do* dictate our practice! No matter how much we may try to expand ourselves spiritually, or how sincere we are in our commitment to helping others, bad trees (errant philosophies) can *never* produce good fruit.

RELIGION

Humanist philosophers point an accusing finger at the churches and mock them for their lack of power and their spiritual weakness. Christians are *supposed* to have the answers. We are to be candles in the darkness, salt for healing, power against evil, and the earthly representatives of God's grace and glory. Instead, all too many have only *"a form of godliness, but denying the power thereof"* (II Timothy 3:5).

By viewing Christ as "just a good man" rather than the very Son of God, or by recognizing His love but not His wrath, they miss the cosmic point! Their religion — infiltrated by humanism — ignores the Cross, the blood, the suffering of Christ, and the sacrificial nature of His death. But without *these,* there is no forgiveness of sin, no victory, no peace, and no help for those in need.

Apostasy and religiosity have become the norm in many churches and denominations across the land. This should be a matter of deep concern for all Bible-believing, practicing Christians. America is being weighed in the balance and found lacking. She teeters on the brink of destruction because God's people have rejected knowledge and turned to the arm of flesh for instruction and support. Christians have become entirely too tolerant and passive while the enemy uses the Trojan horse of *religion* to further destroy us from within.

Although we hear much about humanism, we must remember that it is nothing new. For quite some time it has insinuated itself into the churches until it is barely distinguishable from Christianity.

For several decades now, modernism (or Christianity invaded by humanism) has made great inroads into our churches — until the whole of society gropes in aimlessness and spiritual apathy. If those who profess to know God have no answers to give, to whom can man turn?

Ineffectual preachers, burdened by their inability to meet the needs of their flock in terms of modern society, are responsible for the increasing humanist influence in both the liberal and traditional churches.

These ministers, once converted to humanism, used Christianity as a disguise or as a camouflage for their endeavors. Lucien Saumur, in *The Humanist Evangel*, says, "They argued about religion, defending those aspects of religion which served to promote humanism against those aspects which threatened it."[31] Somehow, they even denied the Christian ideal of suffering, and contemporary Christians failed to recognize it as a humanist plot. In retrospect, it *should* have been evident.

Saumur indicts Christians in America for providing a "haven of tolerance to humanism — thus weakening Christianity and launching the 'Enlightenment'": "It is the spirit of the Enlightenment which has lasted to this day and which constitutes the presence of humanism in the West."[32]

The willingness of Christians to *compromise has* robbed Western Christianity of its vitality. One thing is clear: there can be *no* compromise if we are to follow Christ's mandate to convert the world. We can never link arms in "unity" with those who are willing to tolerate modernism. Our very existence depends on a fervent *intolerance* of everything that opposes God and His will!

The Trojan horse of *religion* is a subtle ploy that is wreaking havoc in our nation. A Christian doesn't have to reject God and deny salvation to become trapped in the mental maze of humanism. Initially, he must be predominantly pro-man, though not necessarily anti-God, and primarily concerned with the affairs of this world rather than those of eternity. In time, through absorption of *small* doses of the humanistic attitude, the transformation is completed. Direct recruitment by humanists was never necessary.

Whether the new humanists stay in the church or leave, their new confusion acts as a catalyst in their own downfall, and in the downfall of those with whom they come in contact. They now question the inerrancy of Scripture; they question God's wrath and a literal hell; and they accept liberal social attitudes. Their new view of man with his do-it-yourself approach to "successful living" makes them effective tools of Satan — and of the communists, who consider the church as one of their best *fronts* to neutralize religion!

In effect, many churches have become Satan's most effective weapons to promote his diabolical scheme to overthrow God.

Communism is the primary tool of Satan. Communists, in their diabolical shrewdness, have imposed an attitude upon the nation that anyone who's afraid of communism is "some kind of a nut." Intelligent people don't see "communists hiding under every bush." *Intelligent* people realize that communism is only a minor, fringe philosophy held by a handful of ineffective people who don't have a *chance* of changing our way of life. *Therefore,* anyone who *speaks out* against communism is a certifiable screwball *and not worth listening to!*

Well, the truth of the matter is that communism is an awesomely successful force, one that has already conquered two-thirds of the world (in just 50 years) and massively influenced the *entire* world.

Almost without exception, Americans parrot communist doctrine daily — never suspecting the *source* of these views or their consequences. This nation is literally riddled with subversive and clandestine communists. They occupy principally bureaucratic (but key) roles within every important institution of this nation. While their names are not known in most cases, their results are apparent in everything that influences our thinking.

The time is short. If we don't start recognizing the undercover communists in our midst, exposing them, and routing them out, we will shortly become a Soviet satellite. Ridiculous? I wish it were. Unfortunately, that's exactly the attitude they *want* us to take. There's nothing easier to club down than an ostrich with his head in the sand.

A PLEA
FOR SANITY

"It is time, O God, for Thee to work, for the enemy has entered into Thy pastures and the sheep are torn and scattered. And false shepherds abound who deny the danger and laugh at the perils which surround Thy flock. The sheep are deceived by these hirelings and follow them with touching loyalty while the wolf closes in to kill and destroy. I beseech Thee, give me sharp eyes to detect the presence of the enemy; give me understanding to distinguish the false friend from the true. Give me vision to see and courage to report what I see faithfully. Make my voice so like thine own that even the sick sheep will recognize it and follow Thee" (A. W. Tozer).

Without question, America teeters on the brink of destruction. We can blame this deplorable circumstance on communism, socialism, secular humanism, or any number of additional philosophies that bid for man's attention. Ultimately though, the responsibility falls at our own feet. We are being "sucked into a vortex of atheism and self-destruction" because we are unprepared (or unwilling) to counter the attacks of our enemies. Like the characters in the recent comic strip *Pogo,* "we have met the enemy and they is us."

Of course, throughout the ages Satan has commissioned emissaries to infiltrate society — and the church — with perverted spirits, motives, philosophies, and doctrines. That's still no excuse, however, for the religiosity and apostasy that have cast many of God's people into a drunken stupor, while the world dies and goes to hell all around them.

Any way we may choose to view it, evil prevails because we, the church, have *failed!* Our people have allowed the corrupt doctrines of man to degrade the morals of our citizenry and chip away at the very foundations of American society. It is certainly time that we come to our senses and become totally involved in the affairs of our nation. But tragically, even that will not be enough because the problem goes so much deeper than that.

How can we extend our religious faith into the community if our own hearts are contaminated by the very philosophies we are supposedly warring against? Today's culture merely *parades the evil that has long been lurking* in the hearts of its citizens. If we are ever to effectively challenge the philosophies which encourage and promote a diseased society, we must first rediscover *our* roles as the salt and the light to preserve and illuminate that society.

In Isaiah 30:1-3 we find the awesome consequences of following after *man's* wisdom instead of God's:

> *"Woe to the rebellious children, saith the Lord, that take counsel, but not of me; and that cover with a covering, but not of my spirit, that they may add sin to sin: That walk to go down into Egypt, and have not asked at my mouth; to strengthen themselves in the strength of Pharaoh, and to trust in the shadow of Egypt! Therefore shall the strength of Pharaoh be your shame, and the trust in the shadow of Egypt your confusion."*

A few verses down we read:

> *"For thus saith the Lord God, the Holy One of Israel; In returning and rest shall ye be saved; in quietness and in confidence shall be your strength: and ye would not"* (30:15).

What a solemn warning from God! Our only hope today is in returning our full allegiance to God and resting in His wisdom and truth — quietly and confidently receiving His strength for the battles we must face.

It's time for a purging among God's people. We have been guilty of looking to "Pharaoh," to "Egypt," and to "experts" for counsel and strength. And now we reap the consequences of such spiritual adultery.

AWAKE!

The enemy wreaks havoc in our midst while many God-fearing Christians stand by in fear and frustration, wringing their hands and wondering where it will all end. Don't you know how Satan *loves* this? Can't you envision the humanists and the communists relishing every moment of it? We *allow* them the freedom to smugly promote their poisonous beliefs, all the while manipulating us with their power to influence and sway our minds. Isn't it time that we finally break our silence and stop allowing these onslaughts against us by the God-haters of our day?

We are entirely too tolerant — too complacent — despite the fact that we have been commissioned by Jesus Christ to serve as His witnesses in the world. That's quite a responsibility. In essence, we are to represent Christ to the world. And one can't help wondering what kind of images we are projecting.

We have no right to be mere onlookers. Our witness must permeate every area of human life. We must actively engage ourselves as extensions of God's service to all mankind. It may take the form of ministering and caring, or it may mean donning the armor of spiritual warfare in the battle for men's souls.

God said, *"Live peaceably with all men,"* but in the same Scripture (Romans 12:18) he also said, *"If it be possible!"* It is *not* possible to be at peace with those who are enemies of the Cross, who attack God's people, and who attempt to thwart God's plan through insidious subversion! Our passive acceptance only gives them unrestricted freedom to accomplish their purpose. The end result will surely be chaos and destruction of all that is still good in this land.

Francis Bacon reminded us, "It is not what you eat, but what you *digest* that makes you strong. It is not what you earn, but what you *save* that makes you rich. It is not what you preach, but what you *practice* that makes you a Christian."

What are we practicing? In the midst of a national moral crisis, are we boldly *demonstrating* what is right and wrong? Without such evidence, we are not acting as examples of the strength needed to stand against the enemy. That's why Lenin said we'd fall into the communists' hands like overripe fruit.

Why are Americans adrift without principles? It would seem that the whole world wanders about in a great social malaise — swept along and interested only in the latest fads and follies. Mankind looks to social institutions, but after pursuing every new and untried course, he finds himself empty and confused. That's because "the counsel of Egypt" can never bring peace, strength, contentment, or enduring wisdom.

Man, in all his vaunted knowledge, has not been able to slake the thirst of a dry spirit or soothe the hurt of a broken heart. Social institutions, for all their attempts to "mend" broken lives and decaying foundations, have contributed little (if anything) to improving man's condition. They often deceive and distort and keep him in his miserable and fallen state by diverting his attention from the real *answers* to his needs.

As a result, almost two out of every three marriages today continue to end in divorce (totaling 47 million divorces since 1960);[1] and our prisons maintain one of the highest rates of occupancy, with the longest sentences. Despite all this, crime increased dramatically in the past two decades.

Homosexuals, looking for something new and exciting, become more militant and sadistic. Not satisfied to keep their sexual activities private, they lobby for special privileges and rights until their influence is being felt in every political, economic, social, and even "religious" arena.

Twenty-three million youths and adults trip out on drugs while others sedate themselves with alcohol[2] — all the while our enemies make steady progress in their plan to conquer the world.

While this cult of the new morality flourishes, legalized murder robs innocent victims of life through abortion; and the incidence of teenage pregnancy, VD, herpes, and AIDS keeps climbing.

Man blatantly wears the pockmarks of his rebellion against God. Our once-mighty nation lies in moral ruins. Is there no hope for healing?

AMERICA'S GREATEST SIN

Oddly enough, America's greatest sin isn't homosexuality, the breakup of the home, or the difficulties our children face in their school systems. Although all of these are factors, it becomes more and more obvious that our nation is headed toward destruction because Satan has taken over every agency and force that brings truth and information to our citizens. And bad as this is, the *sin* of America is that we have *accepted* these forces. We, every one of us (and this includes the Christian element in our society), have accepted (and even *relished*) an environment of sin — an environment in which we are *willing* to live!

The social and political issues that confront us today are really *sin* issues. The deplorable conditions we accept daily are, in actuality, the outward manifestations of a state of mind that pervades the very foundations of this nation. The roots go much deeper than the degradation, the iniquity, or the spiritual adultery. It's far more than just a matter of rejecting God or disobeying Him or breaking His commandments.

America's greatest sin is that she *ignores* God — as though He doesn't exist! For the past two decades (especially the last one), America has charted her course without any consideration of God or His laws. And since, in many circles (especially in many influential ones), God *doesn't* exist, man doesn't even realize that as a nation we stumble and stagger on the precipice of catastrophe.

Of course, tragic as the fact is, more Gospel has been preached in this land than in any other country in the world! We're not without knowledge, but still man acts in a deliberate, determined, and diabolical manner. Like lunatics gone wild with power, the masses shake their fists in the very face of God and then declare there is no God. Such individuals do not want God; they will not have God; they will have nothing of God. As a result, with premeditation and conscious planning, they work to remove Him forever from their minds and from their lives.

It's not coincidental that humanists and communists are militantly hateful of God, promoting the thought that He doesn't exist. That is central to their very philosophy of life. The amazing part is that they fight as hard as they do against God, yet claim all the time to be atheists (who deny His very existence) rather than agnostics (who do not know if He exists). In any event, they are the ones who pass laws saying that His commandments are no longer welcome in our schools and that His Word — under the guise of the separation of church and state — can no longer be exhibited in our schools.

Because America ignores God and conducts her daily affairs as though He doesn't exist, every type of perversion rages unchecked across our land; the stain of communism gets darker and darker; and the unbridled powers of our august lawmakers doom our churches to complete state control.

The question *must* be asked: *What are we going to do about it?*

THE CHURCH SLEEPS

Consider Solzhenitsyn's comments on Russian churches fallen prey to the enemy: "Orthodox churches were stripped of their valuables in 1922 at the instigation of Lenin and Trotsky. In subsequent years, including both the Stalin and Krushchev period, tens of thousands of churches were torn down or desecrated, leaving behind a disfigured wasteland that bore no resemblance to Russia such as it had stood for centuries. Entire districts and cities of half a million inhabitants were left without a single church. Our people were condemned to live in this dark and mute wilderness for decades, groping their way to God and keeping to this course by trial and error."[3]

Solzhenitsyn recalls that, as a child, he had heard a number of older people explaining that great disasters had befallen Russia because "men have forgotten God, that's why all this has happened."

He says further, "Since then I have spent well-nigh fifty years working on the history of our revolution. But if I were asked today to formulate as concisely as possible the main cause of the ruinous revolution that swallowed up some sixty million of our people, I could not put it more accurately than to repeat: Men have forgotten God; that's why all this has happened."[4]

Today, in the twentieth century, the main reason for all our major upheavals is still the same: Men have forgotten God. However, lest we become condemnatory, we need to examine *our* hearts, *our* motives, *our* dedication, and *our* commitment as God's children — as His witnesses to the world. Have *we* allowed *them* to forget God?

Could it be that, as Christians, we've so separated ourselves from the social order that our presence is no longer a threat to the enemies of God? Have we divorced ourselves from the everyday affairs of our nation until we've lost all *influence?* Have we, by abandoning the political, economic, legal, and scientific arenas, relinquished power to those of the opposition? Have we surrendered our beliefs to a "kangaroo court" by default? Have we allowed these nihilists and know-nothings to take over because we have held ourselves *above* the "earthly" matters of politics and everyday life? It would seem that we have done so, and by so doing we have given the world irretrievably over to the hands of Satan.

Of course, in a pluralistic society the humanists can no more "force" their views on society than we as Christians can force ours. But they have competed in the marketplace of ideas, expressing their viewpoint in ways that are legitimately available to all in a democracy. We, on the other hand, have for the most part kept to ourselves. Because we have allowed men to forget God — by not constantly making our presence felt throughout society — America has moved away from the Judeo-Christian values upon which our nation was founded. We have abandoned our young minds and our unformed personalities to the influences that great wealth has bought and controlled with the absolute plan to use it against everything that is moral and Godly!

G. K. Chesterton once wrote, "The trouble when people stop believing in God is not that they thereafter believe in *nothing;* it is that they thereafter believe in *anything.*"[5] That "anything" has been (in our case) a completely new mind-set called secular humanism, and a whole new life-style called liberalism.

This deceptive monster of liberal humanism has made such inroads into our society that the average church across this land has become a citadel of *self*-worship — rather than a place where man can commune with God. While the church sleeps, rape occurs in the midst of the sanctuary. Supposedly holy men of God commit spiritual adultery without shame or remorse. Is it any wonder that souls are not saved, addicts not delivered, and the sick not healed? Such "holy" men are truly whited sepulchers, filled inside with dead men's bones (see Matthew 23:27). And you can be sure that this debauchery rises as a stench to the very nostrils of God!

The problem is that traditionally this country was *formed* under a system where *spiritual* influences dominated secular matters. Today, the opposite is true — secular influences *control* the spiritual aspects of our nation. The church of Jesus Christ is allowed to function today in this nation only as a weak, ineffectual, and completely harmless *sop* to whatever spiritual thoughts an ineffective minority may have. The moment anyone has any thoughts on moral or spiritual matters, our commentators, editors, reporters, entertainers, and left-wing judges intrude and tell us that this is not a proper subject for discussion under the "separation of church and state doctrine." What they don't tell us is that there is no such thing as a "separation of church and state doctrine" within our Constitution. There is one line in the Bill of Rights which states that the Congress shall make no laws *imposing* their atheistic doctrines on the *majority* of the people. And how did we react? By doing *nothing!*

In other words, the spiritual has been secularized. Men have changed the rules to conform to whatever is right in their own eyes. Having removed the restraints of God's law, they pursue their carnal inclinations to the full. "Modern thinkers" and "liberated Christians" overrule the former Christian consensus until the very processes of society and family life are affected. For this reason *"God gave them over"* (Romans 1:28); and their religious views have become just "one among many," rather than being known as the truth that sets men free.

Church, we're losing time. We stand on the brink of destruction. Surely the Christian church must have an answer for the multitudes lost in a malaise of confusion. It will not be easy for us to recover our influence, but we must rise to the challenge of the hour. If we remain silent and passive, we fail to fulfill our calling as witnesses of Christ.

But first we must repent for our blindness and smugness. What we need is a heaven-sent, God-anointed revival that will put fire in our souls and burn up our dross. The unfortunate part is, of course, that revival must start with *us,* instead of *them.*

Unfortunately, all too many Christians have soaked up the blessings of God until they've become fat and lazy. We all enjoy being saints on the receiving end. We all love the rapture, but how many of us would be willing to sign up for the *Colosseum?* God loved the Christians who strode in there, singing as they faced the lions; but how many of us today would have the stomach for that? How much nicer to picture ourselves at the banqueting table where His banner over us is love. And all the time we don't love our own children enough to stand up and demand reform among the forces that inflict immorality on them.

There's only one thing that's going to save us — and save our nation — and that is the renewed presence of God in our midst. God is willing to pour out of His Holy Spirit on this country as never before, *but he must first have a receptive people who see more than their own personal interests!*

God is interested in the salvation of souls. Nothing we have is of any value in God's economy unless it can be used as a tool to bring about His ends — to rescue the perishing and to care for the dying. All our efforts and energies will come to naught unless they are dedicated to that purpose.

According to the late Austin Sparks, there are two classes of Christians in the church today.[6] There are those who have so organized Christian activities that they've made it a corporation that moves along under its own momentum. They mistake unceasing activity for life and power. Regrettably, drive and ambition ride roughshod over the essential "waiting on the Lord." There seems to be little or no interest in the matter of spiritual depth.

We can all become so involved, so committed, so driven that the unhurried, still, small voice of the Holy Spirit can't penetrate all the noise and confusion. Our fury and our zeal can actually cancel out the *input* we should be *receiving* from God.

The second group of Christians is comprised of those who are so settled in tradition and an inflexible position doctrinally, that it's impossible for the Holy Spirit to lead them into fuller revelations of Jesus Christ. Unfortunately, there is no such thing as a spiritual status quo. If we aren't climbing, we're *slipping!* This happens every time we lose the white heat of the fervency of the Holy Spirit. The Pentecostal movement has just about lost it today. We're becoming another "denomination" all wrapped up in forms and rituals. We've lost our vision to win the lost, and we've become insensitive to the urgency of the hour. We're working against a deadline, and the sad thing is — we don't know it! We must be about the Father's business while it is yet day. God expects us — the church of Jesus Christ — to call men to repentance. With each act of transgression and with each display of licentious filth instigated by hell, America slips closer to absolute destruction. The hour is indeed late.

That's why I preach as I do. I'm trying to sound the alarm to sinners. And I'm trying to tell Christians that they're too comfortable and at ease in Zion. A lackadaisical, complacent Christian religion won't work. Without the presence of God, you won't be able to stand in the heat of battle. You can mark it down, the battle is on — but it's going to get a lot worse. God will purge His church. He's going to separate the wheat from the chaff.

THE CHURCH FAILS TO TOUCH GOD

We've seen such great revival in the past 20 years as God has poured out His Holy Spirit; but even in the midst of this great Charismatic movement, there has been a passive attitude toward sin. Some have become so enamored with the *blessings* of God that they've neglected to learn His *ways* and His *character*.

I don't care how many Charismatics raise their hands and dance in the Spirit, or speak in tongues, or see visions, or dream dreams. If they're passive toward sin, they will be destroyed. They are falling into moral decay because God's blessings don't give us license to *do what we want*. God hates sin, and we'd best not forget it.

Somehow the "world" has so infiltrated the traditional bounds of spirituality that a new breed of immature Christian clamors after happiness, wealth, and security. This new theology — which is almost universally proclaimed from behind pulpits and in the electronic church — implies that Christians have the *right* to all things. This can be a snare.

Shouldn't our primary concern be to do the will of God? (See Matthew 7:21-27.) We needn't seek to be *happy,* we need only seek to be *holy.* Then, if we're holy, we'll have true happiness added unto us.

God demands holiness from His children, and we are without excuse. What *His* holiness demanded, He provided at the cross of Calvary. In Christ we can live holy lives, but the problem is that our focus and our priorities are all too often wrong.

Caught up in the pursuit of happiness and success, we sell out for less than God's best. When we accept the world's values, think its thoughts, and adopt its ways, we put to shame the glory of God about us.

God is looking for men who will *separate* themselves (in other words, live holy lives) irrespective of what others may say. He's interested in developing saints of honor and holiness — not merely successful businessmen, athletes, or public personalities who "just happen" to be Christians.

We've strayed a long way from the standards set by Jesus Christ in the New Testament. The manifestation of His glory and His power to live Godly are tragically lacking in evangelical Christianity today.

Why is this? I'll be perfectly frank with you — modern Christianity makes light of the things of God. We look instead for the *easy* way. We look to our prepackaged, instant society — and that has become the type of spiritual growth we expect. Unfortunately, God isn't the author of instant growth; you've got to go to the popular ad-agency-type franchises for that kind of effortless (and worthless) nutrition.

The problem lies with the world's view of grace. Grace is *not* without its price. Salvation was provided at tremendous expense. It cost Jesus Christ His very *life*! And because He gave His life for us, we have the *privilege* of serving Him. It's a perverted theology that gives the impression that *we* accept Him. There's something terribly wrong in the widespread impression that there is something noble and commendable in agreeing to follow Jesus. The truth is that we are infinitely privileged in that He who was and is perfect and without sin would stoop down to accept *us* — who have absolutely nothing to recommend us. We owe Jesus Christ our respect, our love, our service, our *everything*! Without Him we are but poor, pitiful beggars. We are unworthy, but *He* is worthy — of our praise, our honor, and our fidelity.

But we don't honor God with lofty expressions, eloquent displays, or showy services. This is not what pleases Him. We truly honor God when we desire to be conformed to His likeness. We honor Him when we come before Him in praise and thanksgiving, with unstained spirits seeking only that He will reveal our shortcomings to us.

Mahatma Gandhi once said that natural man wants:

> *Business without morality,*
> *Pleasure without conscience,*
> *Politics without principles,*
> *Science without humanity,*
> *Wealth without work, and*
> *Worship without sacrifice.*

How true this is! Natural man's ways are enmity to the ways of God. Unfortunately, this describes only too well the outlook of all too many in the church today. It's a deception spawned in hell. True, vibrant Christian living involves paradoxes contrary to man's thinking. If we want to live, we must first die. If we want honor, we must first experience debasement.

None of this is an instant or painless process. It takes time, tears, travail, and hardship. And only then is the end result a life lived in conformity to God's Word — one which brings Him glory and us the satisfaction of knowing we have, to a very small degree, inched up slightly toward *His* eminence.

THE NEW BREED OF DEMI-CHRISTIAN

Christianity used to involve *big* responsibilities. Women used to take axes and break up saloons. Men used to take bulldozers and smash down houses of ill repute. Today? We won't even turn off our television sets!

Whereas Christianity once demanded a life of rugged dedication, the new breed of demi-Christian makes such little impact on the world that it bothers no one. The relentless decay of our government and nation — more than anything else — should tell us that we're not doing our jobs; that we're not fulfilling our responsibility to take Christ to the people. Instead, the melding of the secular and the spiritual is now so complete that sinners "accept" our beliefs as just one more immature philosophy that competes in the vast market-basket of ideas vying for acceptance by men.

It would seem that this last great outpouring of God's Spirit — the Charismatic movement — would have made a tremendous impression on those around us, with many coming to Jesus. Of course, in some ways it has, but I believe it's not to be compared with what could still be if we would line up with God's Word, repent of our own sins, and then call a wicked nation to repentance.

Unfortunately, the Charismatic movement has shaken down to become little more than a "bless-me club." Like children with a new toy, immature Christians have played with one new experience after another; and many have fallen into the trap of "majoring in the minors" — having drifted away from Christ as their source of spiritual life.

Charismatics, enamored with lofty promises of prosperity, happiness, and power, have sought the easy way to spirituality and have jumped on a bandwagon promising deliverance, confession, discipleship, and faith as the total prescription for spiritual health. Now there's certainly nothing wrong with any of these in themselves, but it's the way in which they have been promoted (all out of proportion) that's in error.

You can stand in "deliverance lines" all day long, waiting for hands to be laid upon you; but no one can cast out the sinful, carnal desires of your own heart. Galatians 5:24 says, *"And they that are Christ's have crucified the flesh with the affections and lusts."* It is *you* who must determine in your heart that with God's help, and because of Jesus' death and resurrection, you will not serve sin. It is *you* who must:

> *"Neither yield ye your members as instruments of unrighteousness unto sin . . . But put ye on the Lord Jesus Christ, and make not provision for the flesh, to fulfill the lusts thereof"* (Romans 6:13; 13:14).

It is *you* who must *choose* the path in which you will walk. No one can "deliver" you to it, and no one can walk it for you.

THE CONFESSION PRINCIPLE

And then there's the "confession principle." By all means, we should confess Christ and the Word. We should even confess God's blessings when they are in accord with His will for us. But we get into trouble when we make a *doctrine* out of confession and attempt to use it like a magic wand to bring all our foolish or selfish desires into existence.

I marvel at God's patience with His children. Some chafe at *His* discipline, and then run after ordinary men who set themselves up as "shepherds" to the flock. They refuse to take up their crosses and follow Jesus, but they'll eagerly allow any earthly "shepherd" to direct their affairs — sometimes down to such matters as the kind of car to buy, or the most intimate of questions pertaining to marriage, ministry, or personal direction.

It's interesting how new "fads" sweep the Christian community. Why can't man be satisfied with God's plan just as it is? Why must he continually attempt to add to or take away from God's Word? It's a grievous thing, but it's because man's sinful nature will continue to strive for recognition and selfish gain if it is not kept in subjection to God's Word. Perhaps the "faith ministry" — more than any other recent religious trend — becomes a real snare, even to the sincere and dedicated.

Now when we use the term "faith ministry," we mean a ministry which overemphasizes one isolated aspect in the man-God relationship. We must all have faith; faith is the great rocklike foundation of God's plan for the ages. But whenever we take one aspect of God's Word and blow it up all out of proportion, we emphasize that one element beyond its true perspective.

People inevitably fall into error when they stray away from the balance set forth by the Holy Spirit. In this case, the principal emphasis centers on healings, miracles, riches, hundredfold return, faith, money, knowledge, and so on. But what about the salvation of souls? Isn't that the very *core* of Christian faith?

Balance is, of course, the key. You see, we talk about the Bible as *the* Holy Book, but we tend to disassociate the price from the product. The Bible was blood-bought. It's more than just a promise-box. Designed to release life in us, we must confess the Word until it penetrates our very spirits and produces *immovable* faith!

Unfortunately, our priorities are distorted. The truth is, we need faith in order to move mountains of evil and subdue kingdoms of darkness — not to obtain Cadillacs and houses and other material things. The world is dying and going to hell; and when we ignore this fact and ask for material possessions, *we're just dead wrong!*

We do need faith, but we will be judged by how we use our faith. Are we challenging hell, or are we believing for prosperity and success? God wants us to have power — power to be overcomers, power to drive back the forces of Satan, power to win souls, power to be witnesses.

Imagine a church like this one:

> *Members sue each other. Others attend social banquets honoring strange gods. One lives in open immorality and the church tolerates it. Others think it would be better for Christian couples to separate so they could be more holy!*
>
> *The worship services are shocking, and certainly not edifying. Speakers in tongues know no restraints. People come drunk to the Lord's Supper. Visitors get the impression that they are mad.*
>
> *Some doubt the Resurrection. Many have reneged on their financial pledges.*

Was there ever such a church? Yes. What's more, its founder and pastor for a year and a half was the Apostle Paul!

The church at Corinth could very well be one of our churches today. Located in one of the major cities of Greece, famous for wealth and the arts, this church was no stranger to pride, greed, luxury, and lust. And once insinuated into the body, these brought (as they always do) grievous error.

The Corinthians, although possessing spiritual gifts, were carnal, immature believers. In effect, they had the gifts of the Holy Spirit, but the Holy Spirit didn't have *them*. Despite high spiritual involvement, there was disturbing evidence of low moral standards. Because of their immaturity, they were not able to receive from Paul the higher secrets of the Spirit — secrets which are available only to the spiritually aware and mature. This is true of many of our Charismatic bodies today.

Wrong priorities and immature appetites seriously hamper spiritual growth. They must be put away. Believers must once again focus on the cross of Calvary and behold the Lamb of God afresh. We must see the nail prints in His hands, the bloodstained path of His lonely march to Calvary, the agony in the Garden. Unless we do, we will never push an inch beyond where we are standing today. And again, failure to move *ahead* spiritually means a sliding *backward*.

God destroyed Sodom and Gomorrah, and our sins surpass theirs. Sodom had no Bibles and no preachers. We have an abundance of both.

Israel was God's chosen nation, but God was nevertheless obligated to wrath because of their rebellion. Just because our nation was founded upon faith in God doesn't mean He can overlook our rebellion and wickedness.

If we were to study the fall of the Roman Empire, we'd be alarmed to see the similarities in our nation today. It's also shocking to realize that it took Rome some 2,000 years to deteriorate, while it's taken us only 150. We should shudder and be ashamed of our complacency. *We* are responsible for this generation.

Remember, even though Rome considered herself very liberal, giving man freedom to believe as he wished (in most cases), she banned Christianity and persecuted Christians. They were burned and they were thrown to the lions.

There are some in America today who would wish to do the same to us, but we must press forward. The church in Rome did so, and by the third century Christianity had triumphed over pagan Rome. We must present such an influence for good in our nation today.

IN GOD WE TRUST

America is the richest nation on the face of the earth today, possessing the wealth of Egypt, but she is without question spiritually bankrupt. Although a worldwide poll shows that Americans are the most "religious" people on the face of the globe, real commitment levels remain relatively low.[7]

A survey conducted by pollster George Gallup, Jr., revealed that "America is becoming a nation of Godless people with an incredible lack of knowledge about the Bible." Gallup says, "It is indeed time to sound the alarm about the future of our religious education in America."[8]

Even though 8 out of 10 Americans consider themselves Christians, only 12 percent think of themselves as "highly spiritually committed," and many feel that churches are "spiritually dry."

Of the 95 percent of all United States citizens who believe there is a God, 84 percent believe in heaven while only 67 percent believe in a literal hell.

Although we have churches, Bibles, Bible schools, and Christian schools on every corner, Americans by and large "play church." Most people would deny that, but their behavior suggests that this is true. They profess to be Christians, but they continue to hang around with the devil's crowd and to place selfish desires and fleshly ambitions before the things of God. Should it then surprise us that those who watch such people see very little that's either inviting or compelling? Whether they admit it or not, they cheat those about them. As poor witnesses, they actually become a hindrance to the cause of Christ.

Jesus said:

> *"They be blind leaders of the blind. And if the blind lead the blind, both shall fall into the ditch. . . . For [they] are like unto whited sepulchres, which indeed appear beautiful outward, but are within full of dead men's bones, and of all uncleanness"* (Matthew 15:14; 23:27).

Death can't generate life. As a result, scores of Americans — spiritually hungry and searching for answers — bypass Christianity as having little substance and little hope. That is what's been *demonstrated* to them.

As an alternative, the American Astrological Association generates 160,000 personal horoscope sales each year. In 1983, 79,000 people paid $7.00 each for "The Buddha," a good-luck, money charm.[9] The results of a survey conducted by a direct marketing agency conclude that 7,961,712 Americans purchased occult books, magazines, charms, voodoo pendants, and other assorted occult paraphernalia. These figures represent a 204.8 percent increase over 1980.[10]

Obviously, there is a widespread mental, emotional, and spiritual drift in the world while Satan, our universal enemy, has *not* been drifting. The church has been caught off-guard and unprepared to deal with the problems facing America and its body of believers. Content to accept half-truths and to ignore issues clamoring for attention, our churches have lost their influence.

America will not stand long in this dark battle against the forces of evil, unless we understand and defend the ideals for which she traditionally stands. As Christians, we must be ready to fight and die for the cause of Christ in our land and in the world.

We must never forget that the church of the Living God is the one hope — the one restraining force — that can keep the world from slipping backward into a new Dark Age. We stand to lose everything we hold dear. Therefore, we *must* challenge the atheistic, Godless, amoral, destructive forces which are so intent on enslaving us.

America made her biggest mistake when she gave her thought-forming institutions over to international, socialist, liberal forces. Once this was accomplished, our defeat was insured. It didn't happen overnight, but piece by piece the foundation stones which made America great were chipped away. One of the earliest symptoms of this new wave was the cracking of our foundations under John Dewey and his progressive education.

What were the results? *"Righteousness exalteth a nation: but sin is a reproach to any people"* (Proverbs 14:34). That's why we have abortion-on-demand — another term for legalized murder! The conscience of our nation has been seared. We're in serious shape when a physician comments, "On a number of occasions with the needle, I have harpooned the fetus. I can feel the fetus move at the end of the needle just like a fish on a line."[11]

This physician admits that it does distress him, despite the abortion rhetoric and the huge profits his specialty generates. But he keeps performing abortions nevertheless.

American liberalism corrupts morality and threatens our survival. When man began to forsake the counsel of God and His Word to replace it with the counsel of Egypt (his own existence, his conscience, and those of others like him), he signed his own death warrant. Today, the stench of decay is all around us. It permeates every strata of society and even diffuses into the church. Only *Life* — the life that God gives through Jesus Christ — can drive it away.

WHAT MUST WE DO?

Arise! We must stem the tide of evil in the government, in the schools, and in our communities. It's not enough that we preach against sin and corruption; we must actively promote righteousness, as well.

Ours is a twofold task. We are to call men to repentance, thereby spreading Christianity throughout the world. However, we need to be sure that the kind of Christianity we spread is the pure, New Testament kind. If the church is worldly minded and unspiritual, so are its members. God holds us responsible to conform to Scripture both in word and in deed.

Harry Conn, in his book *Four Trojan Horses of Humanism*, says, "One of the most thrilling truths of Christianity is this: Whatever deficiencies we may have had in our heredity, environment and training, if we will choose to turn from our selfish ways, seek and find the Lord in true conversion, we will get a new Father who will help and love us. The Spirit of God will dwell in us (which is a welcome change in our inner environment) and teach us His ways. We then have the power to change our environment for good and become a part of the solution to the world's problems." [12]

We must not be silenced! Since our downfall began when we aligned ourselves with teaching against God, the only hope is a *return* to God. It's time to forsake the counsel of "Egypt" and seek God for His wisdom and strength. It's time to acknowledge Him as our only source.

There's no room for compromise — the church must be ruthlessly cleansed of worldliness, the god of self, and the doctrines of demons.

The lines must be drawn: with sin, the devil, and hell on one side and with God, righteousness, and heaven on the other. The battle rages and there's no neutral ground. Only a return to righteousness will do. No longer can Christians embrace situations that lead to sin, or wallow in situations conducive to sin.

In other words, we must choose sides. If *you've* been putting off that decision, there is no longer time for equivocation. There is no longer time for avoiding a commitment. Even those who *refuse* to take a stand are going to be trampled by the onrushing forces as the battle lines are drawn. How much better to die as a fighter for righteousness than as a disinterested bystander.

PREACHERS BEWARE!

According to Harry Conn, in *Four Trojan Horses of Humanism*, "We must have a supernatural visitation of the blessed Holy Spirit in the realm of theology that will have a profound effect upon the sociological, political, and psychological realms. If not, this nation of ours is doomed to a 'one-world' assimilation. This assimilation will be the death knell to the 'preaching of the gospel' and will usher in a 'one-world religion.' It will also usher in Matthew 24:9."[1]

The hour is late! God is about to wrap it all up, and we'd best be prepared. Though there are similarities, we are not Israel in the wilderness nor are we the apostles in the book of Acts. We are going to see things others have never seen. Therefore, we must be ready for whatever God is about to do in the world today.

Before God pours out His wrath, He always warns His people. And unless we repent, His wrath is certain. God cannot, and will not, tolerate sin. Because sin is rampant in our nation, hard days will come. I believe we are about to see revival — an outpouring of God's Spirit like man has never known before — but first the purging must come.

You see, we *say* we trust the Lord, but all the time we're leaning on an arm of flesh. We want to "enjoy" all the things of this world. We say that this is because God *wants* His children to have all the "good things." As a result, the church has become worldly and "sophisticated" and religion has become *big business*.

Preachers, beware! Our present preoccupation with the spoils of Egypt may well be a warning of bitter days to come. God will not allow us to have other gods before Him. He will break our homage to them — the hard way, if necessary.

But, praise God, His mighty hand *can* cause us to look up and acknowledge Him as our all-in-all. History reveals that suffering has always sobered God's people and encouraged them to look for and yearn after the Lord's return.

Better to have the tribulation than to have "Ichabod" written across the door of the church *("the glory has departed"* [I Samuel 4:21]). We desperately need the power of God to work in the lives of the men and women He has called to work in His harvest fields. Once you get to the place where you're comfortable with your Christianity — or think you've "arrived" — take warning, you've almost lost it. When we think we've become so knowledgeable or so spiritual that God has no place in our efforts, "Ichabod" will be written across the door and the glory will depart from our lives.

When the glory departs, it not only wrecks the nation and the church, it causes the *children* to be lost as well. They're being lost today at an unprecedented rate, and the only thing that's going to save them is the power of God.

I believe that the message of the hour is:

> *"Repent, make the crooked paths straight, prepare ye the way of the Lord"* (compare Luke 3:3-5).

But first a work must be done in the heart of the *preacher* — before it can reach the nation.

God is looking for a people to proclaim His message. He will raise up prophets in this day who will boldly and uncompromisingly cry out, *"Repent! Make the crooked paths straight. Prepare ye the way of the Lord!"* But this will take men and women of both backbone and commitment. No mealy-mouthed, passive, docile preacher is going to stand up with such a message. It goes against the grain, it angers the "religious" crowd, and it makes the sinner squirm. It's everything the world *hates*.

Preacher, if you're worth your salt, you'll start preparing yourself to preach and teach in this Church Age. Obedience and holiness are required. Travail in prayer and soul-searching are essential. Some outdated, cold, dry religiosity won't do. You need 1985 prayer and commitment for 1985 warfare. The battle rages for the souls of men. We can't stand passively by while men fall into the fiery abyss where they'll be doomed for eternity.

Today's preacher needs to be something of a revolutionary — and we might add, Jesus was a "revolutionary." He turned the world of His day upside down. Oh, He offended many. He tore down traditions and destroyed the kingdoms of both men and darkness — but He set the captive free, gave peace to the tormented, healed the lame, and brought salvation to all who would believe. God sent His Son — the *man* Jesus — that the war between God and Satan might be settled for once and for all.

In fact, from the beginning, everything God has done has begun with man. Today He's calling men and women to go forth in the power and anointing of the Lord — with fire in their souls, the burden of the Lord upon their hearts, and the Word of the Lord on their lips.

In Acts 18:10 we read, *"I have much people in this city."*

Those people in Corinth weren't saved yet or identified with the Lord, but God knew they *would* be as soon as His people went about proclaiming the good news of Jesus Christ. In our cities today, there are *"much people."* He says to us as well, *"Be not afraid, but speak . . . for I have much people in this city."*

SHEEP WITHOUT A SHEPHERD

Mark 6:34 says, *"And Jesus, when he came out, saw much people, and was moved with compassion toward them, because they were as sheep not having a shepherd: and he began to teach them many things."*

America's lost sheep are as those without a shepherd. Even within the many churches across our land, hungry sheep wait to be fed and to be led into the things of God. Unfortunately, *multitudes* are as sheep without a shepherd.

And, unfortunately, while there's a yearning for God in the *pew*, there appears to be a falling away in the *pulpit*. Much of the modern clergy is spiritually bankrupt, and you can be sure it's an abomination to God.

It's a tragedy when those ordained of God to *lead* His children fall into religious slumber. Isaiah, though speaking of Israel, could have been speaking about many of today's clergy when he said:

> *"His watchmen are blind: they are all ignorant, they are all dumb dogs, they cannot bark; sleeping, lying down, loving to slumber. Yea, they are greedy dogs which can never have enough, and they are shepherds that cannot understand: they all look to their own way, every one for his gain, from his quarter"* (Isaiah 56:10, 11).

Isaiah pointed out that their condition was the result of forsaking the Lord and forgetting His holy mountain (Isaiah 65:11). We have many such men today — self-centered, preoccupied with selfish ambition and gain, spiritually impoverished — because they forget (or refuse to return to) the secret place of God for strength, direction, and the refreshing of His presence.

When they are drawn away by their own lusts, compromise becomes the order of the day. Instead of seeking a true revelation of Jesus Christ, we wrestle with cross-cultural barriers, reaching minority groups, penetrating enclaves of ethnicity, inner-city problems, acquisition of property, lack of finances, and finding the key man. Ironically, we almost seem content with our activity, our quest for vocational success, and the acclaim of man. We can become so caught up in ourselves and in doing our own thing that we fail to realize that *His* presence has been withdrawn.

The course of the modern clergy is a tragic one. It strays far from the path which recognizes the import of the Holy Spirit through whom men are called and separated unto God to do the work for Him. Unfortunately, there's so much spiritual apathy in our churches that such men are seldom sought after.

Take this story, for example:

> *One of the toughest tasks a church faces is that of choosing a good minister. A member of a certain official board undergoing this painful process finally lost patience. He'd watched the*

Pastoral Relations Committee reject applicant after applicant for some fault — alleged or otherwise. It was time for a bit of soul-searching on the part of the committee. So he stood up and read a letter purporting to be from another applicant:
    "Gentlemen, I understand your pulpit is vacant and I should like to apply for the position. I have many qualifications. I've been a preacher with much success and also some success as a writer. Some say I'm a good organizer. I've been a leader most places I've been.
    "I'm over 50 years of age. I have never preached in one place for more than three years. In some places I have left town after my work has caused riots and disturbances. I must admit I have been in jail three or four times, but not because of any real wrongdoing. My health is not too good, though I still get a great deal done. The churches I have preached in have been small, though located in several large cities. I've not gotten along well with religious leaders in towns where I have preached. In fact, some have threatened me and even attacked me physically. I am not too good at keeping records. I have been known to forget whom I have baptized.
    "However, if you can use me, I shall do my best for you."
    The board member looked over the committee. "Well, what do you think? Shall we call him?"
    The good church folks were aghast. Call an unhealthy, old, trouble-making, absent-minded ex-jailbird? Was the board member crazy? Who signed that application anyway? Who had such colossal nerve?
    The board member eyed them all keenly before he answered. "It's signed, 'The Apostle Paul.'"[2]

Unless men like Paul can be found to fill America's pulpits and return to spiritual leadership, the church will continue to compromise its essential message and purpose for the world. In order for the church to fulfill her mission, she must bring the life-changing Gospel of Christ to individuals and to nations — without compromise.

When we compromise, we *accommodate* ourselves to the world's system. We may *speak out* against it, but our protestations have no power behind them. Instead, our task requires us to become "agents of change"

— messengers of the cross. The cross was never meant to patch up a tattered system. The cross destroys all that went before and brings forth a totally new system.

A. W. Tozer pointed out that unless those in spiritual leadership positions grasp this truth, "We may expect a progressive deterioration in the quality of popular Christianity year after year till we reach the point where the grieved Holy Spirit withdraws — like the Shekinah from the temple."[3]

This certainly seems to be the case in many churches today. They've become cold, empty tombs of death, and God must hold the preachers responsible. Because the liberal church has accommodated itself to the liberal world system — rather than challenging all that is enmity to the cross of Christ — we stand today on the brink of destruction.

The reason the early church saw such miracles was that she was more — much more — than an organization or a movement. She was herself a "walking incarnation of spiritual energy." When she moved, she moved in power as God moved with her. When she preached the Word, He confirmed it with signs following. When she cried "Repent," the reverberating sound shook her world. Things happened wherever she went.

The sad indictment of today's church is that she moves — but without power. She moves only under the power of man — dependent on man's intellect, energy, ingenuity, superficial gifts, and personality. God will never honor man's power. He recognizes only the power of His Spirit. Only that which is accomplished through *His* Spirit will last eternally. All else will perish, and the preacher will stand before God in bitter remorse and anguish — because of the deception that has beguiled him.

Imitation may be acceptable to carnal man but under the all-seeing eye of God it is judged for what it is. Zwingli said, "The business of the truth is not to be deserted even to the sacrifice of our lives, for we live not for this age of ours, nor for the princes, but for the Lord."[4]

The preacher must have God's anointing upon his life and ministry or he will have nothing but *"a form of godliness [that denies] the power thereof"* (compare II Timothy 3:5). And no man can *claim* God's anointing unless he is willing to forsake the world's measure of a man and religion executive style. He must come before God in earnest. Before God can move as He desires, it will require self-humiliation for the preacher and deglamorization within his church.

I tell our people (in our church in Baton Rouge) over and over again that we can't *exist* without the moving of God's Holy Spirit. Although the preaching, the music, the choir are all important, we will slip down into the miasma of "form" if we try to exist on the basis of these alone. Only God's touch will do. And for every preacher who doesn't have it in the pulpit, hundreds suffer in the pews.

Now let me unburden myself for a moment. I get so *sick* of "Jimmy Swaggart." And please accept this as it's being offered. I'm not trying to present a phony image of humility. Maybe I shouldn't even say it, but in all honesty I get sick of hearing my name, seeing myself on television, and hearing myself preach. Why? Because I know how little I have to offer. What little *I* can do is utterly insignificant.

I can't heal the hurts. I can't dry the tears. I can't pour oil on the wounds. Only Jesus can do these things. Unless His Spirit flows through me, I can do absolutely nothing of even a *temporal* nature.

If you don't climb to the mount of God's presence and stay there until the fire of *His* glory burns in your soul, men will sit down to an elaborately set table — but they will go away empty. There will be no food or water for their famished souls. Their cups may be held out — but the fact is, they will never be filled to the brim by mortal man.

Today we need men sent from God who will upset the religious status quo and challenge the evil of our day. John the Baptist was such a man.

"There was a man sent from God, whose name was John. The same came for a witness, to bear witness of the Light, that all men through him might believe. He was not that Light, but was sent to bear witness of that Light" (John 1:6-8).

Speaking of John, Jesus said:

"Among them that are born of women there hath not risen a greater than John the Baptist: notwithstanding he that is least in the kingdom of heaven is greater than he" (Matthew 11:11).

What made John great? In all ways John was unique. His incorruptible sincerity, his humility, his courage, even his tragic death mark him as one who completely stood out from the crowd. Sent of God, he came to Israel in the power and spirit of Elijah and marked the great chasm that separated the Jewish dispensation from the Christian. He came as the forerunner of the Messiah.

Even though John was a man of sterling character — who was reared in the fear and admonition of the Lord — his true greatness emanated from something outside himself. But before we examine this, let's look at several points that today's preachers may consider.

THE MISSION

John was a man with a mission. His mission, as forerunner of Christ, was to prepare a people for His coming. First, however, John himself needed preparation. As a young man he left the temple life provided by his father, Zechariah, and relinquished the accompanying security, honor, and riches to go off into the wilderness. Joining himself to the Essenes (a sect made up of individuals who had forsaken the world and its vanities), he boldly denounced sin and committed himself to an austere life of prayer, fasting, and study.

No doubt he was considered, even then, a strange, brooding fanatic. But John knew that he was a man with a mission. Subsisting on elemental foods and ruggedly dressed, he gave himself to spiritual considerations not visible to earthly eyes. He prepared himself for his task and *waited* for God's calling. He did not reject the world as a religious "grandstand play"; he stayed hidden to *prepare* himself for God's purpose.

And attuned as he was to the promptings of the Spirit, he left the wilderness at precisely the right moment. There was an unusual spiritual awakening going on throughout Israel and in the fullness of *His* time, God thrust John into the harvest field.

Preacher, *you* have a mission awaiting *you* today — a mission to prepare people for the Lord's second coming. There's *another* spiritual awakening in the offing as men tire of dead religion and meaningless ritual. Arise! Go forth! Today's world is ready to hear that the lame walk, the blind see, the deaf hear, and that the captives are set free! But just as John bore witness to the Light, we as true witnesses can only tell what we see and hear.

THE MESSAGE

John was a man with a message! *"Prepare ye the way of the Lord, make his paths straight."*

He came preaching his heart out, and the people saw a man consumed with fire. He drew overflow crowds. Full of power and conviction, he seared every man's heart who paused to listen. He spared no one. Fearless and dauntless, he compelled people to listen as he struck at the very heart of evil.

His message wasn't meant to tickle the ears of the hearer or to placate the religious. It was meant to strip away all pretense and to bare the issues of life and death.

God looks today for men and women who will preach His truth in uncompromising holiness and obedience. And believe it or not, people hunger for such preaching. People are sick of watered-down religion and carefully rehearsed entertainment masquerading as "revival." People want the real thing. Go ahead and *upset* the status quo — you'll only drag people out of their despair and despondency.

THE MASTER

John was a man who had seen the Master. He said, *"I am not worthy even to untie his shoes"* (compare Mark 1:7).

That was the lowest, most humble act a servant could render his Master, but John said, "I am not even worthy of that."

He had seen Jesus. He had a revelation of His presence, His glory, His power, and His holiness. Oh, that *we* might see Jesus in that way today! We can't behold the Lamb of God without loving Him. But only those who repent of all sin will so behold Him.

If John was unworthy, how much more so are we today? Jesus stands in our midst, but all too often we ignore Him while falling prey to all the siren songs that beckon us from the world today.

John had learned an important lesson. He realized that a man can receive nothing — except it come from God. Therefore his eyes were on the Master — his ears were attuned to His voice. He was swayed not by peer pressures or by his own talents, gifts, or intellect. His only desire was to please the Lord. What is *your* desire today?

THE MOTTO

John was a man with a motto. He said, *"He must increase, but I must decrease"* (John 3:30).

He could have exploited his worldly popularity. He could have built a mighty personal ministry if he had manipulated this attention to his advantage. Crowds flocked to the wilderness to hear him, wanting to know, *"Who art thou? Art thou the Christ, art thou Elias, art thou one of the prophets?"*

Emphatically and vehemently he declared, *"No, I am not Christ, nor any of the great Old Testament figures. I am a mere voice."* (Read John 1:19-28.)

John chose to identify himself with the humble role of being a spokesman for Someone greater. His humility (which is so rare in any day) stands out in direct contrast to the scores of present-day ministers who use their relationship with Christ as a means of enhancing their personal reputations.

John would not rob God of his due. His preaching was so powerful, so captivating. But what was the *real* secret of his greatness?

THE EMPHASIS OF HIS MESSAGE

John preached so effectively that people left *him* to follow Jesus! There's the true indication of John's greatness. When men hear you preach, do they then leave you to follow after Jesus? When men look upon you, do they *see* Jesus?

If you would be great in God's eyes, you must decrease that He might increase. It's tempting to accept the praises of men and to build a following around yourself. This temptation may be very compelling, but if yielded to, the results will be excruciatingly painful to you — as well as to any poor, misguided soul who chooses to follow you.

God wants to use you. But the more He does, the greater your responsibility to *decrease*. Can you give *all* to Him? your desires, ambitions, labors, and successes? Are you willing to be used — and then to be set aside? We are mere voices, mere vessels. If we can't be emptied of ourselves that His Spirit may pour *through* us, then we've lost our reason for being.

WEEPING FOR YOUR FLOCK

How long has it been since you've wept for your city? We need revival, but only God can bring it. All the evangelistic programs in the world won't bring it. We must be willing to set aside everything until God shows up. We need to take seriously to heart the instructions in Joel 2:12:

> *"Therefore also now, saith the Lord, turn ye even to me with all your heart, and with fasting, and with weeping, and with mourning."*

Revival requires *waiting*. We must be willing to totally relinquish all personal evidences of dominion. The kingdom we are trying to establish may be a compromise and a substitute — therefore we must be willing to wait on God to see how *He* wants it done. When we are obedient, He can then establish His kingdom *through* us.

Throughout history the greatest miracles happened when God's people *stood still!* Unless *we* are willing to stand still and to allow God to do something radical in our midst, we run the risk of deception. Standing and waiting is what is most desperately needed in the church today. Men and women need to shut themselves away in their closets until God speaks to their hearts, moves upon their souls, and stirs their lives.

But that's not popular today. We don't hear much about it. In fact, if it happened very much in most churches, it would tear them to pieces. Hallelujah! Some of them *need* to be torn to pieces. They need a rushing, mighty wind to tear through them until men and women cry out, "I have to see Your glory. God, I have to see You move. Lord, I have to see Your Spirit move in my heart." That kind of praying will accomplish more than any program engineered by man, and the results will last for eternity.

We *can* see revival. We *can* reap the harvest. Satan is pulling out all the stops and he has spared no effort in bringing destruction. *But he is a defeated foe!* I hear *"the sound of a going in the tops of the mulberry trees"* (II Samuel 5:24). *I hear the sound of an abundance of rain.* Glory! I believe that old-fashioned Holy Ghost revival is coming to our land.

I believe it! I sense it in my spirit! I believe that God has spoken to my heart concerning the hundreds of thousands of people who are coming to Jesus. Today many of these are already *church* members — but they do not know Jesus personally. They are religious, but they are not born again. But these are going to be coming home to Jesus by the *scores*!

And I believe a great many preachers are going to pray through until Jesus comes into their hearts and they are born-again. I believe that hundreds of thousands of Catholics are going to be saved by the blood of the Lamb and that those behind the Iron Curtain are coming to the King of kings and Lord of lords by the *thousands*! I believe revival, as the world has never before known it, is about to appear because:

> *"When the enemy shall come in like a flood, the spirit of*
> *the Lord shall lift up a standard against him"* (Isaiah 59:19).

God is moving. And, preachers, we need to "get with the program." We've actually been *delaying* revival — perhaps because we haven't been willing to cope with the *consequences* of revival. Thousands will be saved, and we must be willing to disciple them.

Real revival is a sudden intervention of God that shakes our very existence. When God comes in like a flood, He changes all this. Real revival means a lot of changes in the structure of the church and in our very lives. We must prepare ourselves and allow God to move as He desires and in the *way* He desires.

Do you want to see revival? Great revival always comes through prayer. It *must* be prefaced by unusual times of corporate prayer by the body of Christ.

The preacher who is always posing for pictures to fill his magazine or who flaunts his Brooks Brothers suits won't see revival until he's ready to sweat, to cry, to travail, and to anguish before God.

Prayer is hard work. Don't let anyone tell you differently. Prayer that accomplishes things for God's glory means wrestling with the powers of darkness. It means standing in the gap and making up the hedge for lost humanity. It means isolation and painful self-examination. But, praise God, it also means victory in Jesus Christ. It means spiritual power and riches. It means purity of mind and of the spirit.

Why do we *neglect* prayer — that which takes care of all our spiritual maladies and moves the heart of God? Because we slumber in Zion! The longer we are out of His presence, the farther we stray from God's will.

We need to be stirred. Our hearts need to be melted. And the only way is to set ourselves to the task of prayer. Prayer ushers in life. Prayer will usher in the greatest revival the world has ever known. Prayer will cure dead fundamentalism and will deal a deathblow to communism, Romanism, liberalism, humanism, and modernism!

THE BATTLE IS THE LORD'S

Preacher, you have been called to be God's spokesman. As an oracle of God you must first *wait* for God's Word and then proclaim it *boldly*. If you want to be patted on the back and praised for your delivery, you're in the wrong business. Those who commit themselves to speaking for God must fear neither devils nor men for those moving under God's anointing will raise the wrath of hell and the anger of sinners. And if the preacher disagrees with dull, staid, dead religion, he'd better be prepared to be attacked, persecuted, lampooned, and lambasted.

Nevertheless, he must pursue his appointed course. He dare not pussyfoot past hot issues or whitewash sin. Lives are at stake; indeed all of Western civilization is at stake. If the preacher is more concerned for his own hide than for the life of the sheep, he is no more than a hireling or a false prophet. He isn't fit to lead — or even to fight in the battle for men's souls.

We can't challenge hell without feeling the heat of the battle. We can't tear down the enemy's strongholds without a fight. We can't come against evil philosophies and false doctrines without stirring up the hatred of men. They hated Jesus. They rejected Him. They will hate and reject us.

Light and darkness will not mix any more than oil and water will mix. There can be no compromise between Christianity and the world. Can you imagine Elijah consorting with the prophets of Baal, or Jesus seeking unity with the Pharisees? We hear a great deal today about "unity among the brethren," but I tell you there can be no unity between those who accept the blood of Jesus and those who reject it. There can be no unity between those who know He is God and those who believe He was "just a good man."

The truth must be preached at any cost. I know it's not popular, but the oracle of God has *never* been popular. He must be willing to stand up against the crowd, however. When a man touched by the fire of God speaks out against sin and iniquity, apostasy and apathy, worldly appetites and laziness — and calls men to repentance, commitment, separation, and holiness — he'll be branded a heretic by the religious crowd. He'll be hounded. Why? Because carnal men don't *want* their comfortable nests disturbed.

You see, God doesn't destroy a civilization because of the wickedness of *unbelievers*. He pours out His wrath because of the disobedience, rebellion, and wickedness of those who *have known and believed*. For this reason, it is carnal Christians who ultimately plague a society. Because they claim to know God, yet live ungodly, weak lives, they *"[make] the cross of Christ . . . of none effect"* (I Corinthians 1:17).

On the other hand, Christians who are dedicated to God and completely surrendered to His will are a strong and restraining influence against evil. All the laws of our nation will not stem the tide of immorality. Granted, they are needed to punish immorality — but what is more important is born-again, blood-washed, sold-out-to-Jesus, Holy Spirit-baptized believers. These will exert an influence and power through righteous living on this sin-sick world.

We are the *"salt of the earth"* (Matthew 5:13). God holds us responsible. We can't blame sinners for the state of the nation. We must look to our own church. God's judgment on cities and nations is directly related to what Christians do — or *fail* to do.

We must pray. We must call a holy fast. The only way our nation will escape the wrath of God is for us to reestablish God's holy standards and to forsake the things of this world. If not, we'll continue to lose power and influence — until we make a mockery of God. But Scripture tells us:

> *"If my people, which are called by my name, shall humble themselves, and pray, and seek my face, and turn from their wicked ways; then will I hear from heaven, and will forgive their sin, and will heal their land"* (II Chronicles 7:14).

IS THERE STILL TIME?

Beasts have come to devour the land. At times the problems that plague us seem almost insurmountable. There appears to be no cure for our national sins. Man sinks deeper and deeper into the pits of degradation and despair. But we know there is hope. The answers do not lie in philosophy, politics, economics, theology, or any other man-made institution; they are found only in Christ Jesus. He is the *only* way. But because most of humanity refuses to come to Him, they have no life. Nevertheless, we must wholeheartedly commit ourselves to the task of presenting salvation through Jesus Christ to the world — both as a personal experience and as an objective and verifiable fact of history — and in the changed lives of believers.

We must get back to the basics in our preaching and in living our lives in imitation of Christ through the power of the Holy Spirit. The world will then see Jesus. We have the privilege and responsibility of introducing them to Him.

What are the basics? The Bible as the infallible Word of God, the cross, the blood, the deity of Christ, and on and on. God can't place His stamp of approval on any church that denies these basics. It may serve as an institution of "religion," offering man some measure of solace, but it's as dangerous as a coiled rattlesnake. Such deceives and leads *away* from Christ.

Any church, no matter how old, how rich, or how powerful — that doesn't anchor its teachings in the holy, infallible, unchanging, unalterable Word of God (the Holy Bible) — becomes a hindrance to the people. The Bible is not just any book; it *is* the very Word of God — it doesn't just *contain* the Word of God.

Satan has used his hammers of atheism, agnosticism, materialism, and secular humanism to beat upon the anvil of the Word of God for centuries. The hammers break, but the anvil stands unmarred.

Civilizations that have damned this Book have come and gone while the Bible lives on. And it shall always remain — for Jesus said:

> *"Heaven and earth shall pass away, but my words shall not pass away"* (Matthew 24:35).

Base your life, your preaching, your future on the Word of God. It's the anchor and foundation to carry you through the pilgrimage of life. And when you cross the chilling tide of Jordan's death, it will still carry you through. No other book can do this. Any church or group that would dare to place the writings of any mere man — poor, pitiful, flawed man — beside the Bible is foolish indeed.

Second, Jesus Christ is divine; that is, He is God. Some modernists would have us believe that He was "just a good man," a superior teacher, or a mighty prophet. However, Jesus Himself said that He was the Son of God (John 5:17-18; 10:36; 11:4).

In addition, Jesus said:

> *"For the Father judgeth no man, but hath committed all judgment unto the Son: That all men should honour the Son, even as they honour the Father. He that honoureth not the Son honoureth not the Father which hath sent him"* (John 5:22-23).

That is about as clear-cut as you can make it. When you finally cross the bar, it's Him you'll have to reckon with — not the Virgin Mary, the prophets of old, the pope, or any preacher or evangelist. You're going to face Jesus, the Son of Almighty God, *"Immanuel [God with us]"* (Isaiah 7:14).

> *"And the government [of the world] shall be upon his shoulder: and his name shall be called Wonderful, Counsellor, The mighty God, The everlasting Father, The Prince of Peace. Of the increase of his government and peace there shall be no end"* (Isaiah 9:6, 7).
>
> *"He shall reign for ever and ever"* (Revelation 11:15).

I'm not ashamed to preach that. I want the world to know it. I want the devil, demons, the modernists, and the secular humanists to know it. Jesus is God!

Preacher, if you stumble and stagger over this, you'll be brought to shame. I tell people that if their church denies Jesus' divinity (or if their preacher does) they need to *flee* from such teachers and find a preacher who preaches the truth. Whether you accept it or not, Jesus *is* God and He alone can save you.

That is where I get into trouble. I have said unalterably, unequivocally, without stumbling or trembling that there is only one way — not five or even two — to God and that way is Jesus Christ. Jesus said:

> *"I am the way, the truth, and the life: no man cometh unto the Father, but by me"* (John 14:6).

I won't bend on this. I've been cursed, ridiculed, and lampooned. I've been smeared by the media and accused of destroying unity among the brethren and the "ecumenical movement." But I'm still going to proclaim that Jesus alone is the way. If this offends or upsets anyone's religious sensibilities, he has a problem; but I have no intention of suddenly starting to preach *lies* to gain the approval of men. I'm going to go right on preaching this:

> *"But we preach Christ crucified, unto the Jews a stumblingblock, and unto the Greeks foolishness; But unto*

them which are called, both Jews and Greeks, Christ the
power of God, and the wisdom of God. Because the
foolishness of God is wiser than men; and the weakness of
God is stronger than men" (I Corinthians 1:23-25).

Hallelujah! That makes me happy!

Third, there is no remission of sin without the shedding of blood (see Hebrews 9:22). Modernists recoil at this "bloody religion." One preacher has gone as far as to say that the blood of Jesus is no more than the blood of a dead dog. Mister, you can't get to heaven unless your sins are washed away — and this by *the blood of Jesus* — the blood of the one spotless, perfect Lamb of God. He came from heaven and died on the bloody cross of Golgotha's hill — but life is in the blood that He shed. If you make it through the portals of glory, it will only be because you've been covered by His blood.

Fourth, we must preach the cross that Jesus died upon. This is not a new cross that allows the old, carnal life of Adam to live on without interference. The cross that the second Adam died upon was the most revolutionary thing ever to appear among men. It brooks no compromise. It doesn't just bring an old life into a higher plane — it demands *death:* death of the old self and birth of the new. It doesn't just *redirect* our lives (as the cross of the modernists claims to do); it creates completely *new* lives, after a new birth.

Paul said:

"Brethren, be followers together of me, and mark
them which walk so as ye have us for an ensample. (For many
walk, of whom I have told you often, and now tell you even
weeping, that they are the enemies of the cross of Christ:
Whose end is destruction, whose God is their belly, and
whose glory is in their shame, who mind earthly things)"
(Philippians 3:17-19).

The reason so many Christians live weak and ineffective lives is that they have not submitted all of their lives to the cross. They are only partially delivered and in constant defeat and failure because they haven't allowed the cross to destroy the old life and build again in the power of the new.

THE PREACHER

It's an awesome thing to be called of God. We preachers bear a tremendous responsibility to dig out the Word of the Lord and then to *deliver* it to the people. In addition, we must live as examples of righteousness and holiness. You see, a man preaches more than a message; he preaches a *life*. Unless God's ways and will become an inseparable part of your life, your preaching will be empty and fruitless.

Preacher, you must *preach* to get results — the kind that truly last for eternity. For the most part, since the 1930s, Christian leadership has flowed *with* society rather than leading it against corrupt social practices, apostasy, and spiritual dissolution. It is time to become engaged in the battle for men's souls with a fervency that cannot be cooled.

By and large we've been losing the battle because we have not wielded the sword of the Spirit (the Word of God) under the power and anointing of the Holy Ghost. God's Word is the ultimate authority whereby all else must be judged. How long will the preachers of today refuse to assert biblical authority on American culture and society? How long will we passively stand by and allow Godless men to fill the vacuum with philosophies that deceive and damn?

Are you *confessing* Christ as a witness to Him in this world or are you merely *professing* Him? Remember, it's carnal Christians who ultimately bring down society — and carnal *preachers* most of all. There are strongholds to be pulled down and battles to be won, but they won't be won in our own strength, wisdom, intellect, talents, or personal charm. Spiritual battles are won with spiritual weapons:

> *"For though we walk in the flesh, we do not war after the flesh: (For the weapons of our warfare are not carnal, but mighty through God to the pulling down of strong holds;) Casting down imaginations, and every high thing that exalteth itself against the knowledge of God, and bringing into captivity every thought to the obedience of Christ"* (II Corinthians 10:3-6).

FOOTNOTES

Chapter 1 — CHILDHOOD LOST

1. John Dewey, "Man, Nature, and Society," *The Moral Writings of John Dewey: A Selection*, ed. James Gouinlock (New York: Hafner Press, 1976), pp. 23-54.

2. Leonard Peikoff, *The Ominous Parallels* (New York: New American Library/ Mentor, 1982), p. 130.

3. *Ibid.*

4. Samuel X. Radbill, "Children in a World of Violence: A History of Child Abuse," *The Battered Child*, ed. C. Henry Kempe and Ray E. Helfer (Chicago: University of Chicago Press, 1980), p. 3.

5. *Ibid.*, p. 6.

6. *Ibid.*

7. *Ibid.*, p. 3.

8. *Ibid.*, p. 8.

9. *Ibid.*, p. 9.

10. *Ibid.*

11. *Ibid.*, pp. 7, 10, 11.

12. W. G. Sumner, *Folkways* (Boston: Ginn, 1906), pp. 309-311.

13. Radbill, *op. cit.*, pp. 6 8.

14. *Ibid.*, p. 11.

15. Alvin Toffler, *The Third Wave* (New York: Bantam Books, 1980), p. 213.

16. *Ibid.*

17. *Ibid.*, p. 383.

18. Peggy Charren and Martin W. Sandler, *Changing Channels: Living (Sensibly) With Television* (Reading, MA: Addison-Wesley, 1983), p. 202.

19. John W. Whitehead, *The Stealing of America* (Westchester, IL: Crossway Books, 1983), p. 71.

20. Radbill, *op. cit.*, p. 12.

21. "Education for Human Sexuality," a course developed by the California State Department of Education, 1980.

22. *Ibid.*

23. *Ibid.*

24. Burton Yale Pines, *Back to Basics* (New York: William Morrow, 1982), p. 140.

25. *Ibid.*, p. 138.

26. John Holt, *Escape From Childhood* (New York: E. P. Dutton, 1974), pp. 18, 19.

27. Clifford L. Linedecker, *Children in Chains* (New York: Everest House, 1981), p. 115.

Chapter 2 — NO REGARD FOR LIFE

1. William Brennan, *The Abortion Holocaust* (St. Louis, MO: Landmark Press, 1983), p. 137.
2. Ronald Reagan, "Abortion and the Conscience of the Nation," *The Human Life Review*, Spring, 1983, p. 9.
3. Jesse Helms, "Foreword," *The Right to Live, the Right to Die*, by C. Everett Koop (Wheaton, IL: Tyndale House, 1980), p. 10.
4. L. Alexander, M.D., "Medical Science Under Dictatorship," *New England Journal of Medicine*, July 14, 1949.
5. Mark Gladstone, "Evidence Sought in Deaths of Fetuses," *Los Angeles Times*, February 7, 1982.
6. *Los Angeles Times*, February 6, 1982.
7. *Los Angeles Times*, May 26, 1982.
8. Dr. and Mrs. J. C. Willke, *Handbook on Abortion* (Cincinnati, OH: Hayes, 1979), p. 175, citing Marshall McLuhan.
9. *Victoria Daily Colonist*, April 5, 1972, cited in pamphlet *What Is a Baby Worth?* (Winnepeg, Manitoba, Canada: Winnepeg League for Life).
10. Willke, *op. cit.*, p. 131.
11. John A. Morris, *et al*, "Measurement of Fetoplacental Blood Volume in the Human Previable Fetus," *American Journal of Obstetrics and Gynecology*, April 1, 1974, p. 927.
12. Brennan, *op. cit.*, p. 77.
13. John Lofton, "Let Drugged Dogs Lie, Unborn Humans Live," *Washington Times*, August 3, 1983.
14. Brennan, *op. cit.*, p. 140.
15. *Ibid.*, p. 191.
16. William L. Shirer, *The Rise and Fall of the Third Reich: A History of Nazi Germany* (New York: Simon and Schuster, 1960), p. 979.
17. Alvin Toffler, *The Third Wave* (New York: Bantam Books, 1980), p. 147.
18. Lane P. Lester and James C. Hefley, *Cloning: Miracle or Menace?* (Wheaton, IL: Tyndale House, 1980), p. 135.
19. *Ibid.*, p. 35.
20. Paul Bagne, "High-Tech Breeding," *Mother Jones*, August, 1983, p. 23.
21. Robert A. Freitas, Jr., "Fetal Adoption: A Technological Solution to the Problem of Abortion Ethics," *The Humanist*, May-June, 1980.
22. James D. Watson, "Children From the Laboratory," *Prism*, May, 1973, p. 13.
23. C. Everett Koop, *op. cit.*, p. 114.
24. C. Everett Koop, cited in *Death in the Nursery*, a documentary film by Carleton Sherwood, Kennedy Foundation.
25. Sherwood, *Death in the Nursery, op. cit.*
26. R. S. Duff and A. G. M. Campbell, "Moral and Ethical Dilemmas in the Special Care Nursery," *New England Journal of Medicine*, Vol. 289, p. 890.
27. Stephen Chapman, "From Abortion to Infanticide," *Chicago Tribune*, April 22, 1982.

28. John W. Whitehead, *The Stealing of America* (Westchester, IL: Crossway Books, 1983), p. 43.
29. Sherwood, *Death in the Nursery, op. cit.*
30. *Ibid.*
31. *Ibid.*
32. *Ibid.*
33. *Ibid.*
34. *Ibid.*
35. *Ibid.*
36. Whitehead, *op. cit.,* p. 10.
37. James J. Diamond, "Humanizing the Abortion Debate," *America,* July 19, 1969, p. 36.

Chapter 3 — THE VANISHING FAMILY

1. "When Family Will Have a New Definition," *U. S. News & World Report,* May 9, 1983, pp. A-3, A-4.
2. *Ibid.*
3. "Death of the Family?" *Newsweek,* January 17, 1983, pp. 26-28
4. Alvin Toffler, *The Third Wave* (New York: Bantam Books, 1980), pp. 211, 212.
5. "When Family Will Have a New Definition," *op. cit.*
6. Charles Cooper, "Senate to Look at Family Problems," *Spotlight,* August, 1983.
7. Sheila Caudle, "Poverty Haunts USA's Children," *USA Today,* March 17, 1983.
8. "Death of the Family?" *op. cit.*
9. Caudle, *op. cit.*
10. "Death of the Family?" *op. cit.*
11. *Ibid.*
12. *Ibid.*
13. "When Family Will Have a New Definition," *op. cit.*
14. Toffler, *op. cit.,* p. 374.
15. *World Almanac and Book of Facts* (New York: Newspaper Enterprise Association, 1981), p. 273.
16. "College Credit," *Time,* July 25, 1983, p. 25.
17. David Wilkerson, *Parents on Trial* (New York: Hawthorn Books, 1967), pp. 47, 48.
18. John W. Whitehead, *The Stealing of America* (Westchester, IL: Crossway Books, 1983), p. 71.
19. "When Family Will Have a New Definition," *op. cit.*
20. *Ibid.*
21. Warren M. and Patricia Becker, "Mourning the Loss of a Son," *Newsweek,* May 30, 1983, p. 17.
22. "No Right to Spank," *Sword of the Lord,* July 15, 1983.

23. Tim LaHaye, *What Everyone Should Know About Homosexuality* (Wheaton, IL: Tyndale House, 1978), p. 75.

24. *Ibid.*

25. Lucy Komisar, *The New Feminism* (New York: Franklin Watts, 1971), p. 95.

Chapter 4 — A STRANGE GOD

1. Peggy Charren and Martin W. Sandler, *Changing Channels: Living (Sensibly) With Television* (Reading, MA: Addison-Wesley, 1983), pp. 3, 22, 170.

2. *NFD Informer* [National Federation for Decency], September, 1983, p. 7.

3. "Some Flaws in the Golden Age of Journalism," *The Reference Shelf*, Vol. 54, No. 5, p. 136.

4. Charren and Sandler, *op. cit.*, p. 38.

5. Tony Schwartz, *Media: The Second God* (Garden City, NY: Anchor Press/Doubleday, 1983), pp. 1-4.

6. *NFD Journal*, October, 1983.

7. Charren and Sandler, *op. cit.*, p. 55.

8. *Ibid.*, p. 52.

9. *Ibid.*, p. 61.

10. *Ibid.*, p. 69.

11. *Ibid.*, p. 40.

12. *Ibid.*

13. Thomas Radecki, Chairman NCTV [National Coalition on Television Violence], in an interview with *The Evangelist*.

14. Mavis Hetherington and Ross D. Parke, *Child Psychology: A Contemporary Viewpoint* (New York: McGraw-Hill, 1979), p. 628.

15. *Ibid.*, p. 190.

16. *Ibid.*

17. Charles S. Silberman, *Criminal Violence, Criminal Justice* (New York: Vintage Books, 1978), pp. 32, 33.

18. Charren and Sandler, *op. cit.*, p. 59

19. *Ibid.*, p. 170.

20. *Ibid.*

21. *Ibid.*, p. 41.

22. *Ibid.*

23. *Ibid.*, pp. 41-43.

24. "Teen-age Target," *Broadcasting*, August 15, 1983, p. 36.

25. *Ibid.*

26. Charren and Sandler, *op. cit.*, p. 180.

27. *Ibid.*, p. 173.

28. *Ibid.*

Chapter 5 — THEY BECAME FOOLS

1. Lawrence Brewer, "The Falling Away From Public Schools," *The Christian Citizen*, September, 1981, p. 32 f.

2. Samuel L. Blumenfeld, *Is Public Education Necessary?* (Old Greenwich, CT: Devin-Adair, 1981), p. 30.

3. *Ibid.*, p. 95, citing Orestes A. Brownson (1803-1876).

4. Leonard Peikoff, *The Ominous Parallels* (New York: New American Library/ Mentor, 1982), p. 130, citing John Dewey.

5. *Ibid.*

6. *Ibid.*, p. 132.

7. Jon Barton and John W. Whitehead, *Schools on Fire* (Wheaton, IL: Tyndale House, 1980), p. 65.

8. Lloyd L. Morain, "Humanist Manifesto II: A Time for Reconsideration," *The Humanist*, September-October, 1980, p. 5.

9. *Ibid.*

10. "Every Child Said Mentally Ill," *Christian Inquirer*, November 7, 1983, p. 11. (Taken from an address given at a childhood education seminar, 1973, by a Harvard University professor of educational psychiatry.)

11. John Dunphy, "A Religion for a New Age," *The Humanist*, January-February, 1983, p. 26.

12. Richard A. Baer, "Parents, Schools, and Values Clarification," *The Wall Street Journal*, April 12, 1982, p. 22.

13. *Ibid.*

14. Francis A. Schaeffer, *A Christian Manifesto* (Westchester, IL: Crossway Books, 1981), p. 29.

15. Lucien Saumur, *The Humanist Evangel* (Buffalo, NY: Prometheus Books, 1982), p. 38.

16. Kenneth Strike, *Educational Leadership*, November, 1977, p. 94.

17. *Ibid.*, p. 98.

18. Burton Yale Pines, *Back to Basics* (New York: William Morrow, 1982), p. 101.

19. "Forecast for the 70's," *Today's Education* [Washington, DC: National Education Association], January, 1969, pp. 52, 53.

20. "Those Dropping Test Scores — Experts Grope for the Reasons," *U. S. News & World Report*, November 24, 1975, pp. 33, 34.

21. *Ibid.*

22. Pines, *op. cit.*, citing Willard Wirtz, *et al*, *Report of the Advisory Panel on the Scholastic Aptitude Test Score Decline* (New York: College Entrance Examination Board, 1977), pp. 5, 37, 38.

23. Stanley N. Wellborn, *U. S. News & World Report*, May 17, 1982, p. 56.

24. Donald R. Tuttle, "Composition," in *The Case for Basic Education* (Boston: Little, Brown, and Co., 1959), p. 85.

25. "Johnny Can't Count — the Dangers for U. S.," *U. S. News & World Report*, February 15, 1982, p. 45.

26. Pines, *op. cit.*, p. 110.
27. *Ibid.*, p. 124.
28. Lynn Buzzard, *Schools: They Haven't Got a Prayer* (Elgin, IL: David C. Cook, 1982), p. 28.
29. Harry McKown, *Character Education* (New York: McGraw-Hill, 1935), p. 74.
30. *Baton Rouge Morning Advocate*, December 9, 1983.
31. Pines, *op. cit.*, p. 128, citing Neil Postman.
32. Jackson Toby, *The Public Interest*, Winter, 1980, pp. 31, 32.

Chapter 6 — SURVIVAL OF THE FITTEST

1. William A. Stacey and Anson Shupe, *The Family Secret* (Boston: Beacon Press, 1983), p. 3.
2. Mark Cannon, *The Reference Shelf: Representative American Speeches*, 1981-1982, p. 66, citing Alberta Siegel's speech "Crime and the Decline of Values," given June 4, 1981.
3. *Ibid.*, p. 68.
4. Kurt Andersen, "Private Violence," *Time*, September 5, 1983, p. 19.
5. *Ibid.*, p. 18.
6. Stacey and Shupe, *op. cit.*, p. 203.
7. Cannon, *op. cit.*, p. 69.
8. Nick Jordan, "The Ultimate On-Off Switch," *Psychology Today*, October, 1983, p. 14.
9. Andersen, *op. cit.*, p. 18.
10. Louise Armstrong, *The Home Front: Notes From the Family War Zone* (New York: McGraw-Hill, 1983), p. xii.
11. Murray A. Straus, Richard J. Gelles, and Suzanne Steinmetz, *Behind Closed Doors: Violence in the Family* (New York: Anchor Press, 1980), pp. 4, 62.
12. Armstrong, *op. cit.*
13. Andersen, *op. cit.*
14. *Ibid.*
15. Armstrong, *op. cit.*, p. 37.
16. *Ibid.*, citing Roberta Thyfault, "Childhood Sexual Abuse, Marital Rape, and Battered Women: Implications for Mental Health Workers," a paper for Colorado Mental Health Conference, Keystone, Colorado, October 24, 1980, p. 3.
17. Jane O'Reilly, "Wife Beating: The Silent Crime," *Time*, September 5, 1983, p. 23.
18. *Ibid.*
19. Lenore E. Walker, *The Battered Woman* (New York: Harper and Row, 1979), pp. 105, 106.
20. Stacey and Shupe, *op. cit.*, p. 31.
21. O'Reilly, *op. cit.*
22. Straus, Gelles, and Steinmetz, *op. cit.*, p. 109.
23. Armstrong, *op. cit.*, p. xiii, citing Anthony Storr, "Introduction," *Family Violence: An International and Interdisciplinary Study*, eds. John M. Eekelaar and Sanford N. Katz (Toronto, Ontario, Canada: Butterworths, 1978), p. 5.

24. O'Reilly, *op. cit.*, p. 24.
25. Stacey and Shupe, *op. cit.*, p. 89.
26. Kenneth W. Petersen, "Wife Abuse: The Silent Crime, The Silent Church," *Christianity Today*, November 25, 1983, p. 23.
27. Straus, Gelles, and Steinmetz, *op. cit.*, p. 31.
28. Petersen, *op. cit.*
29. *Ibid.*, p. 25.
30. Andersen, *op. cit.*, p. 19.
31. *Ibid.*
32. O'Reilly, *op. cit.*, p. 24.
33. *Ibid.*
34. *Ibid.*
35. *Ibid.*
36. Katherine Williams, "One Crime, Two Victims," *Cornerstone*, p. 13.
37. "The Family That Abuses or Neglects Their Children," an excerpt from *Training in Parenting Skills* by Phoenix South Community Health Center.
38. Shirley O'Brien, *Child Abuse: A Crying Shame* (Provo, UT: Brigham Young University Press, 1980), p. 10.
39. *Ibid.*
40. Henry C. Kempe, *et al*, "The Battered Child," *Journal of American Medical Association*, 1962, Vol. 181, p. 17.
41. O'Brien, *op. cit.*
42. *Ibid.*, p. 11.
43. Ed Magnuson, "Child Abuse: The Ultimate Betrayal," *Time*, September 5, 1983, p. 21.
44. Harold P. Martin and Martha Rodeheffer, "Effects of Parental Abuse and Neglect on Children," *Journal of Pediatric Psychology*, 1976, p. 12.
45. James Dobson, *Hide or Seek* (Old Tappan, NJ: Revell, 1979), p. 19.
46. Ralph S. Welsh, "Violence, Permissiveness and the Overpunished Child," *Journal of Pediatric Psychology*, 1976, Volume 1, p. 70.
47. Martin and Rodeheffer, *op. cit.*, p. 14.
48. Dagmar Lagerberg, Katarina Nilsson, and Claes Sundelin, "Lifestyle Patterns in Families With Neglected Children," *Child Abuse and Neglect*, 1979, Vol. 3, p. 487.
49. *Ibid.*, p. 488.
50. Rebecca Black and Joseph Mayer, "Parents With Special Problems: Alcoholism and Opiate Addiction," *Child Abuse and Neglect*, 1980, Vol. 4, pp. 45-54.
51. Hendrika Cantwell, "Sexual Abuse of Children in Denver, 1979: Reviewed With Implications for Pediatric Intervention and Possible Prevention," *Child Abuse and Neglect*, 1981, Vol. 5, p. 80.
52. Andersen, *op. cit.*, p. 18.
53. Cliff Yudell, "I'm Afraid of My Own Child," *Reader's Digest*, August, 1983, p. 78.

54. *Ibid.*, p. 79.

55. *Ibid.*, p. 80.

56. Andersen, *op. cit.*, p. 19.

57. Yudell, *op. cit.*, p. 79.

58. *Ibid.*

59. *Ibid.*

60. *Ibid.*, p. 80.

61. Charles E. Silberman, *Criminal Violence, Criminal Justice* (New York: Vintage Books, 1980), p. 83.

62. *Ibid.*

63. Margaret Mead and Elena Calas, "Child-Training Ideals in a Postrevolutionary Context: Soviet Russia," in *Childhood in Contemporary Culture,* eds. Margaret Mead and Martha Wolfenstein (Chicago: University of Chicago Press, 1955), p. 181.

64. Silberman, *op. cit.*, p. 4.

65. *Ibid.*, p. 53.

66. Arthur Stinchcombe, *Crime and Punishment: Changing Attitudes in America* (San Francisco: Jossey-Bass, 1980), p. 50.

67. Cannon, *op. cit.*, p. 64.

68. George Gallup, ed. *America Wants to Know: The Issues and the Answers of the Eighties* (New York: A & W Publishers, Inc., 1983), p. 66.

69. Gary D. Gottfredson, "What Can the Schools Do to Help in Reducing the Overall Program of Crime in America?" cited in Gallup, *op. cit.*, p. 81.

70. Silberman, *op. cit.*, p. 5.

71. *Ibid.*, p. 80, citing George D. Newton and Franklin E. Zimring, *Firearms and Violence in American Life* [A Staff Report to the National Commission on the Causes and Prevention of Violence], (Washington, DC: U. S. Government Printing Office, 1969), Vol. 7, Chapter 4.

72. Cannon, *op. cit.*, p. 70.

73. Ken Kelly, "How Can We Best Reduce Juvenile Crime? Adult Crime?" cited in Gallup, *op. cit.*, p. 75.

74. Cannon, *op. cit.*, p. 80.

75. Ralph Gardner, Jr., "The Prison Population Jumps to 369,725," *Corrections,* June, 1982, pp. 6-8.

76. Kenneth Harms, "Why Is Violence on the Increase in Populated, Industrial, and Urban Areas? What Can Be Done About It?" in Gallup, *op. cit.*, p. 69.

77. G. O. W. Mueller, "What Can Religious Institutions Do to Help in Reducing the Overall Problems of Crime in America?" in Gallup, *op. cit.*, p. 90.

78. George C. S. Benson and Thomas S. Engeman, *Amoral America* (Durham, NC: Carolina Academic Press, 1982).

79. Cannon, *op. cit.*, pp. 67, 68.

Chapter 7 — SODOM AND GOMORRAH REVISITED

1. Clifford L. Linedecker, *Children in Chains* (New York: Everest House, 1981), p. 22.
2. Jamie Cohen, "Child With Cerebral Palsy Is Taken From Hospital and Sexually Abused," *Los Angeles Herald Examiner,* November 12, 1983, p. A-22, Col. 3.
3. Linedecker, *op. cit.*, p. 121.
4. Morton A. Hill, "Pornography: The Desecration of Women," *Morality in Media,* November, 1983, p. 2.
5. *Ibid.*
6. Linedecker, *op. cit.*, p. 109.
7. Tim LaHaye, *What Everyone Should Know About Homosexuality* (Wheaton, IL: Tyndale House, 1978), p. 34.
8. "The Sexual Revolution of the Twentieth Century," *Christianity Today,* November 11, 1983, p. 29.
9. *Ibid.*
10. Linedecker, *op. cit.*, p. 25.
11. Michael Braun and George Alan Rekers, *The Christian in an Age of Sexual Eclipse,* pp. 130, 131.
12. *Ibid.*
13. James Robison, *Pornography: The Polluting of America* (Wheaton, IL: Tyndale House, 1982), p. 17.
14. Hill, *op. cit.*
15. Jon Trott, "Pornography," *Cornerstone,* Vol. 11, No. 61, p. 19; citing Andrea Devorkin, *Pornography: Men Processing Women* (New York: G. P. Putnam's Sons, 1981), p. 18.
16. Robison, *op. cit.*, pp. 25-27.
17. Lois H. Dick, "A Victimless Crime," *Live,* July 10, 1983.
18. *Ibid.*
19. *NFD Journal* [National Federation for Decency], October, 1983.
20. Maureen Dowd, "Rape: The Sexual Weapon," *Time,* September 5, 1983, p. 27.
21. *Ibid.*
22. Robison, *op. cit.*, p. 35.
23. Shirley O'Brien, *Child Pornography* (Dubuque, IA: Kendall/Hunt, 1983), p. 5.
24. William Marden, "Sex Abuse May Affect 33% of Nation," *Florida Times-Union,* December 9, 1983.
25. Linedecker, *op. cit.*, p. 90.
26. Robin Lloyd, *For Money or Love: Boy Prostitution in America* (New York: Vanguard Press, 1976).
27. *Morality in Media,* November, 1983, p. 1.
28. Linedecker, *op. cit.*, pp. 28, 29.
29. Dick, *op. cit.*
30. O'Brien, *op. cit.*, p. 37.

31. *Ibid.*, pp. 40, 41.
32. *Ibid.*, p. 37.
33. *Ibid.*, p. 36.
34. *Ibid.*, p. 8.
35. *Ibid.*, p. 68.
36. *Ibid.*, p. 67.
37. *Ibid.*
38. *Ibid.*, pp. xi, xii.
39. Linedecker, *op. cit.*, p. 285.
40. John Leo, "A New Furor Over Pedophilia," *Time*, January 17, 1983, p. 47.
41. "Medicine: Battling a Deadly New Epidemic," *Time*, March 28, 1983, p. 53.
42. "The Real Epidemic: Fear and Despair," *Time*, July 4, 1983, p. 56.
43. Jean Seligmann, "New Theories About AIDS," *Newsweek*, January 30, 1984, p. 51.
44. Tom Morganthau, "Gay America in Transition," *Newsweek*, August 8, 1983, p. 36.
45. Vincent Coppola, "The Change in Gay Life-style," *Newsweek*, April 18, 1983, p. 80.
46. LaHaye, *op. cit.*, p. 178.
47. Vincent Coppola with Marsha Zabarsky, "Coming Out of the Closet," *Newsweek*, August 8, 1983, p. 34.
48. LaHaye, *op. cit.*, p. 44.
49. *Newsweek*, August 8, 1983, p. 33.
50. LaHaye, *op. cit.*, p. 35.
51. Tom Morganthau, *op. cit.*, p. 30.
52. "Your Tax Dollars Finance the Homosexual Movement," a special report prepared by *Christian Voice*, Pacific Grove, California.
53. *NFD Journal, op. cit.*
54. David Wood, "Special Report: Homosexuals Lose Michigan," *Moral Majority Report*, January, 1984.
55. *The Review of the News*, August 17, 1983.
56. *Ibid.*

Chapter 8 — TOO MUCH, TOO SOON

1. Bernard Rubin, *Media, Politics, and Democracy* (New York: Oxford University Press, 1977), p. 33.
2. Jon Barton and John W. Whitehead, *Schools on Fire* (Wheaton, IL: Tyndale House, 1980), pp. 9, 10.
3. Alvin P. Sanoff with Jeannye Thornton, "Our Neglected Kids," *U. S. News & World Report*, August 9, 1982, p. 58.
4. *Ibid.*, p. 54.
5. *Ibid.*, p. 55.

6. *Ibid.*
7. *Ibid.*
8. Interview with Joseph Procaccini, "Parent Burnout: Latest Sign of Today's Stresses," *U. S. News & World Report*, March 7, 1983, p. 76.
9. *Ibid.*
10. *Ibid.*, p. 77.
11. Sanoff, *op. cit.*, p. 54.
12. *Ibid.*
13. Jeannye Thornton, "Behind a Surge in Suicides of Young People," *U. S. News & World Report*, June 20, 1983, p. 66.
14. *Ibid.*
15. *Ibid.*
16. Chris Ramsey and Deana Pavlac, "The Suicide Fantasy," *Cornerstone*, Vol. 11, No. 62, p. 4.
17. Thornton, *op. cit.*
18. Mary Ann O'Roark, "The Alarming Rise in Teenage Suicide," *McCall's*, January, 1982, p. 14.
19. Thornton, *op. cit.*
20. Sanoff, *op. cit.*, p. 57.
21. Ramsey and Pavlac, *op. cit.*, p. 6.
22. *Ibid.*
23. J. D. Teicher, "Children and Adolescents Who Attempt Suicide," *Pediatric Clinician of North America*, August, 1970, pp. 687-696.
24. John Langone, "Too Weary to Go On," *Discover*, November, 1981, p. 74.
25. O'Roark, *op. cit.*
26. *Christian Inquirer*, December, 1983.
27. *Ibid.*
28. *Ibid.*
29. Ramsey and Pavlac, *op. cit.*
30. K. Barrett and J. Fincher, "Teenage Runaways," *Ladies Home Journal*, August, 1982, p. 81.
31. *Ibid.*, p. 128.
32. *Ibid.*
33. *Ibid.*, p. 129.
34. *Ibid.*
35. *Ibid.*, p. 130.
36. Shirley O'Brien, *Child Pornography* (Dubuque, IA: Kendall/Hunt, 1983), p. 22, citing Dotson Rader.
37. *Ibid.*
38. *Ibid.*

39. James Mann, "An Endless Parade of Runaway Kids," *U. S. News & World Report*, January 17, 1983, p. 64.

40. *Ibid.*

41. Clifford L. Linedecker, *Children in Chains* (New York: Everest House, 1981), p. 175.

42. Mann, *op. cit.*

43. Barrett and Fincher, *op. cit.*, p. 128.

44. *Ibid.*

45. *Ibid.*, p. 131.

46. Mann, *op. cit.*

47. Citing Gaylord Shaw, "Children in Jail," *The Humanist*, September-October, 1980, p. 59.

48. Pamela Abramson, "Cops and Kids in Boise," *Newsweek*, June 21, 1982, p. 42.

49. *Ibid.*

50. Mann, *op. cit.*

Chapter 9 — A SEDATED SOCIETY

1. John G. Fuller, *Are the Kids All Right?* (New York: Times Book, 1981), p. 3.

2. Gene Busnar, *It's Rock 'n Roll* (New York: Wanderer Books, 1979), p. 24.

3. R. Serge Denisoff and Richard A. Peterson, *The Sounds of Social Change* (Chicago: Rand McNally, 1972), p. 122.

4. *Ibid.*, p. 154.

5. *Ibid.*, p. 138.

6. Tony Palmer, *All You Need Is Love* (New York: Grossman, 1976), p. 231.

7. Denisoff and Peterson, *op. cit.*, p. 20.

8. *Ibid.*

9. *Ibid.*, p. 160.

10. *Ibid.*

11. *Ibid.*, p. 145.

12. *Ibid.*, p. 162.

13. *Ibid.*

14. *Ibid.*, p. 192.

15. *Ibid.*, p. 14.

16. *Ibid.*, p. 152.

17. *Ibid.*, p. 159.

18. *Ibid.*, p. 166.

19. *Ibid.*

20. *Ibid.*, p. 159.

21. Alvin Toffler, *The Third Wave* (New York: Bantam Books, 1980), p. 365.

22. "High Times," an excerpt from Larry Sloman, "Reefer Madness: The History of Marijuana in America" (New York: Grove Press, 1983).
23. Kenneth P. Norwick, ed. *Lobbying for Freedom in the 1980s* (New York: G. P. Putnam's Sons, 1983), p. 171.
24. George L. Farnham, "Marijuana and Other Drug Laws," in Norwick, *op. cit.*, pp. 164, 172.
25. J. Hopkins, "Cocaine: A Flash in the Pan, a Pain in the Nose," *Rolling Stone*, April 29, 1971, p. 6.
26. *Review of the News*, October 26, 1983.
27. Thomas Radecki, Chairman NCTV [National Coalition on Television Violence] in an interview with *The Evangelist*.
28. *Ibid.*
29. "Teenage Drinking: A National Epidemic," *Behold*, November, 1983.
30. Kathleen Whalen Fitzgerald, "Living With Jellinek's Disease," *Newsweek*, October 17, 1983, p. 22.
31. *Ibid.*
32. *Behold, op. cit.*
33. Fitzgerald, *op. cit.*
34. *Behold, op. cit.*
35. *Ibid.*
36. *Ibid.*
37. "Check Points to Catch Drunk Drivers?" *U. S. News & World Report*, July 4, 1983, p. 65.
38. *Ibid.*
39. *Behold, op. cit.*
40. Chris Ramsey, "Getting Away With Murder," *Cornerstone*, Vol. 12, No. 66.
41. *Ibid.*
42. *Ibid.*
43. Don Wilkerson, *Shocking New Facts About Marijuana* (Old Tappan, NJ: Revell), p. 97.
44. George Gallup, ed. *America Wants to Know: The Issues and the Answers of the Eighties* (New York: A & W Publishers, Inc., 1983), p. 119.

Chapter 10 — AMERICA: ON THE EVE OF DESTRUCTION

1. J. Edgar Hoover, *Masters of Deceit* (New York: Pocket Books, 1958), p. 8.
2. Reuben Maury, "Communism: A Plan for World Conquest" (America's Future, 1980), p. 3.
3. *Ibid.*
4. Moshe Decter, *The Profile of Communism* (New York: Collier, 1961), p. 11.
5. Hoover, *op. cit.*, p. 3.
6. Cleon W. Skousen, *The Naked Communist* (Salt Lake City, UT: Ensign, 1961), p. 357.
7. *Ibid.*

8. Agnes Murphy, *An Evil Tree: The Story of Communism* (Milwaukee: Bruce, 1962), p. 7.
9. Harry and Bonaro Overstreet, *What We Must Know About Communism* (New York: W. W. Norton, 1958), p. 48.
10. Murphy, *op. cit.*, p. 60.
11. *Ibid.*, p. 64.
12. *Ibid.*, p. 71.
13. Malcolm Muggeridge, *The End of Christendom* (Grand Rapids, MI: Eerdmans, 1980).
14. Murphy, *op. cit.*, p. 117.
15. Harry Conn, *Four Trojan Horses of Humanism* (Milford, MI: Mott Media, 1982), p. 9.
16. Skousen, *op. cit.*, p. 350.
17. *Ibid.*
18. *Ibid.*, p. 349.
19. Murphy, *op. cit.*, p. 94.
20. *Ibid.*, p. 98.
21. Conn, *op. cit.*, p. 11.
22. Hoover, *op. cit.*, p. 213.
23. *Ibid.*
24. John W. Whitehead, *The Stealing of America* (Westchester, IL: Crossway Books, 1983), p. 3.
25. "Humanist Manifesto II," *The Humanist*, September-October, 1973.
26. Conn, *op. cit.*, p. 24.
27. *Ibid.*, p. 26.
28. J. P. van Praag, *Foundations of Humanism* (Buffalo, NY: Prometheus Books, 1982), p. 139.
29. *Ibid.*, p. 36.
30. Conn, *op. cit.*, p. 34.
31. Lucien Saumur, *The Humanist Evangel* (Buffalo, NY: Prometheus Books, 1982), p. 9.
32. *Ibid.*

Chapter 11 — A PLEA FOR SANITY

1. Richard Viguerie, *Conservative Digest*, August, 1983, p. 48.
2. *Ibid.*
3. Aleksandr Solzhenitsyn, "Men Have Forgotten God" [Templeton Award Address], in *The Presbyterian Layman*, September-October, 1983, p. 10.
4. *Ibid.*
5. Robert E. Webber, *Secular Humanism: Threat and Challenge* (Grand Rapids, MI: Zondervan, 1982), p. 49.
6. Cited by David Wilkerson in "The Corn on the Top of the Mountain," *The Evangelist*, March, 1984, p. 19.
7. "Godless Americans," *Weekly World News*, October 11, 1983.

8. *Ibid.*

9. *Christian Contender,* October, 1983.

10. *Ibid.*

11. Carl Horn, "How Freedom of Thought Is Smothered in America," *Christianity Today,* April 6, 1984, p. 16.

12. Harry Conn, *Four Trojan Horses of Humanism* (Milford, MI: Mott Media, 1982), p. 55.

Chapter 12 — PREACHERS BEWARE!

1. Harry Conn, *Four Trojan Horses of Humanism* (Milford, MI: Mott Media, 1982), p. 74.

2. Told by the Reverend C. W. Kirkpatrick, Union Church of Christ, Ludlow, Massachusetts.

3. Leonard Ravenhill, *Why Revival Tarries* (Zachary, LA: Fires of Revival, 1959), p. 74.

4. *Ibid.*, p. 75.

SELECTED
BIBLIOGRAPHY

Armstrong, Louise. *The Home Front: Notes From the Family War Zone*. New York: McGraw-Hill, 1983.

Benson, George C. S., and Thomas S. Engeman. *Amoral America*. Durham, NC: Carolina Academic Press, 1982.

Blumenfeld, Samuel L. *Is Public Education Necessary?* Old Greenwich, CT: Devin-Adair, 1981.

Brennan, William. *The Abortion Holocaust*. St. Louis, MO: Landmark Press, 1983.

Busnar, Gene. *It's Rock 'n Roll*. New York: Wanderer Books, 1979.

Buzzard, Lynn. *Schools: They Haven't Got a Prayer*. Elgin, IL: David C. Cook, 1982.

Charren, Peggy, and Martin W. Sandler. *Changing Channels: Living (Sensibly) With Television*. Reading, MA: Addison-Wesley, 1983.

Conn, Harry. *Four Trojan Horses of Humanism*. Milford, MI: Mott Media, 1982.

Decter, Moshe. *The Profile of Communism*. New York: Collier, 1961.

Denisoff, R. Serge, and Richard A. Peterson. *The Sounds of Social Change*. Chicago: Rand McNally, 1972.

Devorkin, Andrea. *Pornography: Men Processing Women*. New York: G. P. Putnam's Sons, 1981.

Dobson, James. *Hide or Seek*. Old Tappan, NJ: Revell, 1979.

Eekelaar, John M., and Sanford N. Katz, eds. *Family Violence: An International and Interdisciplinary Study*. Toronto, Ontario, Canada: Butterworths, 1978.

Fuller, John G. *Are the Kids All Right?* New York: Times Books, 1981.

Gallup, George, ed. *America Wants to Know: The Issues and the Answers of the Eighties*. New York: A & W Publishers, 1983.

Gouinlock, James, ed. *The Moral Writings of John Dewey*. New York: Hafner Press, 1976.

Hetherington, Mavis, and Ross D. Parke. *Child Psychology: A Contemporary Viewpoint*. New York: McGraw-Hill, 1979.

Holt, John. *Escape From Childhood*. New York: E. P. Dutton, 1974.

Hoover, J. Edgar. *Masters of Deceit*. New York: Pocket Books, 1958.

Kempe, C. Henry, and Ray E. Helfer, eds. *The Battered Child*. Chicago: University of Chicago Press, 1980.

Komisar, Lucy. *The New Feminism*. New York: Franklin Watts, 1971.

Koop, C. Everett. *The Right to Live, the Right to Die*. Wheaton, IL: Tyndale House, 1980.

LaHaye, Tim. *What Everyone Should Know About Homosexuality*. Wheaton, IL: Tyndale House, 1978.

Lester, Lane P., and James C. Hefley. *Cloning: Miracle or Menace?* Wheaton, IL: Tyndale House, 1980.

Linedecker, Clifford L. *Children in Chains*. New York: Everest House, 1981.

Lloyd, Robin. *For Money or Love: Boy Prostitution in America*. New York: Vanguard Press, 1976.

McKown, Harry. *Character Education*. New York: McGraw-Hill, 1935.

Mead, Margaret, and Martha Wolfenstein, eds. *Childhood in Contemporary Culture*. Chicago: University of Chicago Press, 1955.

Muggeridge, Malcolm. *The End of Christendom*. Grand Rapids, MI: Eerdmans, 1980.

Murphy, Agnes. *An Evil Tree: The Story of Communism*. Milwaukee: Bruce, 1962.

Norwick, Kenneth P., ed. *Lobbying for Freedom in the 1980s*. New York: G. P. Putnam's Sons, 1983.

O'Brien, Shirley. *Child Abuse: A Crying Shame*. Provo, UT: Brigham Young University Press, 1980.

_____. *Child Pornography*. Dubuque, IA: Kendall/Hunt, 1983.

Overstreet, Harry and Bonaro. *What We Must Know About Communism*. New York: W. W. Norton, 1958.

Palmer, Tony. *All You Need Is Love*. New York: Grossman, 1976.

Peikoff, Leonard. *The Ominous Parallels*. New York: New American Library/Mentor, 1982.

Pines, Burton Yale. *Back to Basics*. New York: William Morrow, 1982.

Ravenhill, Leonard. *Why Revival Tarries*. Zachary, LA: Fires of Revival, 1959.

Reagan, Ronald. "Abortion and the Conscience of the Nation." *The Human Life Review*. Spring, 1983.

Robison, James. *Pornography: The Polluting of America*. Wheaton, IL: Tyndale House, 1982.

Rubin, Bernard. *Media, Politics, and Democracy*. New York: Oxford University Press, 1977.

Saumur, Lucien. *The Humanist Evangel*. Buffalo, NY: Prometheus Books, 1982.

Schaeffer, Francis A. *A Christian Manifesto*. Westchester, IL: Crossway Books, 1981.

Schaeffer, Franky. *A Time for Anger: The Myth of Neutrality*. Westchester, IL: Crossway Books, 1982.

Schwartz, Tony. *Media: The Second God*. Garden City, NY: Anchor Press/Doubleday, 1983.

Sherwood, Carleton. *Death in the Nursery*. Kennedy Foundation Films.

Shirer, William L. *The Rise and Fall of the Third Reich: A History of Nazi Germany*. New York: Simon and Schuster, 1960.

Silberman, Charles S. *Criminal Violence, Criminal Justice*. New York: Vintage Books, 1978.

Skousen, Cleon W. *The Naked Communist*. Salt Lake City, UT: Ensign, 1961.

Stacey, William A., and Anson Shupe. *The Family Secret*. Boston, MA: Beacon Press, 1983.

Stinchcombe, Arthur. *Crime and Punishment: Changing Attitudes in America*. San Francisco: Jossey-Bass, 1980.

Straus, Murray A., Richard J. Gelles, and Suzanne Steinmetz. *Behind Closed Doors: Violence in the Family.* New York: Anchor Press, 1980.

Sumner, W. G. *Folkways.* Boston: Ginn, 1906.

Toffler, Alvin. *The Third Wave.* New York: Bantam Books, 1980.

Van Praag, J. P. *Foundations of Humanism.* Buffalo, NY: Prometheus Books, 1982.

Walker, Lenore E. *The Battered Woman.* New York: Harper and Row, 1979.

Webber, Robert E. *Secular Humanism: Threat and Challenge.* Grand Rapids, MI: Zondervan, 1982.

Whitehead, John W. *The Stealing of America.* Westchester, IL: Crossway Books, 1983.

Whitehead, John W., and Jon Barton. *Schools on Fire.* Wheaton, IL: Tyndale House, 1980.

Wilkerson, David. *Parents on Trial.* New York: Hawthorn Books, 1967.

Wilkerson, Don. *Shocking New Facts About Marijuana.* Old Tappan, NJ: Revell.

Willke, Dr. and Mrs. J. C. *Handbook on Abortion.* Cincinnati, OH: Hayes, 1979.

World Almanac and Book of Facts. New York: Newspaper Enterprise Association, 1981.